Mergers and Acquisitions

Mergers and Acquisitions

Second Edition

A Step-by-Step Legal and Practical Guide

EDWIN L. MILLER JR.
LEWIS N. SEGALL

WILEY

Published by John Wiley & Sons, Inc., Hoboken, New Jersey.
The first edition of Mergers and Acquisitions was published by John Wiley & Sons, Inc.
in 2008.
Published simultaneously in Canada.

For general information on our other products and services or for technical support, please
contact our Customer Care Department within the United States at (800) 762-2974, outside
the United States at (317) 572-3993 or fax (317) 572-4002.

Wiley publishes in a variety of print and electronic formats and by print-on-demand. Some
material included with standard print versions of this book may not be included in e-books or
in print-on-demand. If this book refers to media such as a CD or DVD that is not included in
the version you purchased, you may download this material at http://booksupport.wiley.com.
For more information about Wiley products, visit www.wiley.com.

Library of Congress Cataloging-in-Publication Data:

Names: Miller, Edwin L., author. | Segall, Lewis N., 1970– author.
Title: Mergers and acquisitions : a step-by-step legal and practical guide
    +website / Edwin L. Miller, Jr., Lewis N. Segall.
Description: Second edition. | Hoboken, New Jersey : Wiley, 2017. |
    Series: Wiley finance | Includes index.
Identifiers: LCCN 2016051178 (print) | LCCN 2016051981 (ebook) |
    ISBN 9781119265412 (hardback) | ISBN 9781119276753 (pdf) |
    ISBN 9781119276777 (epub)
Subjects: LCSH: Consolidation and merger of corporations—Law and
    legislation—United States. | BISAC: LAW / Mergers & Acquisitions. |
    BUSINESS & ECONOMICS / Mergers & Acquisitions.
Classification: LCC KF1477 .M55 2017 (print) | LCC KF1477 (ebook) |
    DDC 346.73/06626—dc23
LC record available at https://lccn.loc.gov/2016051178

Cover Design: Wiley
Cover Images: (top) © fztommy/Shutterstock;
(bottom) © zffoto/Shutterstock;
© Dmitri Mikitenko/Shutterstock

Printed in the United States of America
10 9 8 7 6 5 4 3 2 1

From Ed:

I dedicate this book to my family—my extraordinarily tolerant and supportive wife, Barbara; my son, Russ, who beat me at chess at age 5; and my daughter, Lindsay, who was one of 150 admitted to her medical school out of 11,000 applicants.

From Lew:

I also dedicate this book to my family, who could be an excellent law firm in their own right one day—my wife, Christian, the best nonpracticing lawyer I know; Garnett (8), the advocate; Sawyer Jane (12), the negotiator; and Harper (13), the mediator. And Birdie, our Cavalier King Charles, who keeps us all on our toes.

Contents

Preface

This book attempts to convey a working knowledge of the principal business terms, customary contractual provisions, legal background, and how-tos applicable to business acquisitions. It is not meant to be either a traditional law text or a purely business book, but combines elements of both.

Entrepreneurs and other business professionals should have a working knowledge of the legal basics of their deals. The best business lawyers counsel their clients not only on the legal framework of a transaction but also on the interplay between legal concepts and business terms. In a sense, there is no distinction between them.

Our hope is that reading these materials will benefit business owners and managers who want to understand more deeply the acquisition process and the major corporate, tax, securities law, and other legal parameters of business acquisitions; lawyers who would like to know, or need a refresher on, what they should be discussing with clients who are either buying or selling a business; and law or business school students who want to learn the legal and business fundamentals of acquisitions, and who also want to get a jump on real-world acquisition practice. Each chapter consists of commentary on what's really going on in typical situations at each stage, and an in-depth discussion on the particular subject. The appendixes include model or sample documents for a number of common transactions, as well as additional materials. (Appendixes can be found on the Web. See "About the Website.")

More specifically, this book attempts to do three things. The first is to survey and explain the principal legal factors that affect the feasibility and economic consequences of acquisitions. Almost all transactions are feasible in the sense that it is legally possible to do them. One rare exception would be blockage by the antitrust authorities. It is also true that acquisitions usually can be structured and implemented in a number of different ways. Different structures have different economic consequences to the parties that might not be initially apparent. The business lawyer and other deal professionals (investment bankers as well as business development and other personnel) must devise different structures and implementation schemes and analyze the economic consequences of each. Along with factors that are purely economic, like whether a transaction is taxable, the risks involved in various approaches also must be analyzed and explained.

Given a particular structure, the economic consequences and risks of a particular transaction are affected by what is called the *private ordering* of the transaction. That means that the business and legal terms of a transaction can be incorporated into applicable legal documents (e.g., a merger agreement) in a wide variety of ways. The experienced deal professional will know the alternatives and, as negotiator, will have the task of getting the other side to agree to as many provisions as possible that are favorable to the client.

Lastly, we discuss some of the policy implications of various rules and cases, along with some of the academic theory behind them. This information is not of great practical value, and not much time is spent on it. Most academic textbooks and the press spend a hugely disproportionate amount of time on the blockbuster deals of the day. Legal practitioners spend huge amounts of time trying to make sense out of the latest Delaware takeover case (to the extent that is possible). That is all interesting and important to know, but these cutting-edge tactics and theories have little application to the large majority of merger and acquisition (M&A) transactions. Public and private deals differ in many respects. Also, in many ways, the business and legal terms in these large public transactions tend to be less variable—there is no time for the deal professionals to fiddle around, and the incremental value of an improvement in terms may be miniscule compared to the value of the deal. We do not ignore these issues, but our larger intent is to prepare the reader in greater depth for the acquisitions that make up the large majority of transactions.

So, going back to regulatory and other legal factors, what is the basic mental legal checklist that a deal professional should run through when presented with a particular transaction? The principal structuring parameters are:

- Tax law (definitely first)
- Corporate law
- Securities law
- Antitrust law
- Bankruptcy and insolvency law
- Accounting

We explore each of these factors in detail.

Different types of acquisition transactions have very different legal parameters. The basic types of acquisition transactions are:

- Publicly traded company acquires another public company for stock.
- Publicly traded company acquires another public company for cash.

- Publicly traded company acquires a private company (i.e., not publicly traded) for stock or cash.
- Private company acquires a public company for cash (leveraged buyout, or LBO).
- Private company acquires another private company for stock or cash.
- Acquisition of a product line versus an entire business, generally for cash.

We will discuss the sequence of the various steps in acquisition transactions and the seller and buyer's perspectives and interests at each step. For each step, we will also analyze in detail the various documents that are used to effect the transaction.

We will call the company that is being acquired the *Target* because it may not be the actual seller—in a stock acquisition, it is the Target's shareholders who are selling their stock to the acquirer, or the *Buyer*. In acquisitions, Buyers often use subsidiaries as the acquisition vehicle. We will not generally make that distinction unless it is relevant, and it is often relevant for tax purposes. We also assume for simplicity that, unless otherwise noted, the Buyer and the Target are both Delaware business corporations.

Comments and questions are welcome. If you have any comments or questions, feel free to contact us at *edwinlmiller@gmail.com or lewsegall@gmail.com.*

Acknowledgments

A number of our colleagues at Sullivan & Worcester contributed to this book.

In particular, Chapter 4 on tax was substantially rewritten from Ed's original draft by Jonathan Dubitsky; and the sections in Chapter 7 on fraudulent conveyances and bankruptcy were written by Pat Dinardo and Pam Holleman. Rick Mastrocola and Kathy Rizzo of Tonneson & Co. provided valuable feedback on the accounting sections in Chapter 3.

Other colleagues who were kind enough to review parts of the book were Jay Abbott, Zach Altman, Shy Baranov, Harvey Bines, Sam Bombaugh, Bob Buchanan, Chuck Charpentier, Bill Curry, Paul Decker, Lee Dunham, Steve Eichel, Adam Gopin, David Guadagnoli, Will Hanson, Vivian Hunter, Andrea Matos, Neil McLaughlin, Chris McWhinney, Laura Miller, Tricia Wall Mundy, Adriana Rojas, Ryan Rosenblatt, George Selmont, Amy Sheridan, Walt Van Buskirk, Carol Wolff, Chelsea Wood, and Amy Zuccarello.

Nevertheless, the views expressed herein are our own and do not necessarily reflect the views of others at our firm. We are solely responsible for the contents of this book.

Mergers and Acquisitions

CHAPTER 1

Structuring Fundamentals

BASIC CORPORATE FINANCE CONCEPTS

We will violate our initial promise of practicality by starting with a few pages on the corporate finance concepts underlying acquisitions and then a short section on the reasons for acquisitions.

Valuation Theory

At its simplest, there is really only one reason for a Buyer to do an acquisition: to make more money for its shareholders. A fancier way of expressing this is to *create shareholder value,* but that is not very precise or helpful. Creating shareholder value simply means making the acquirer's business more valuable. In an academic sense, how is the value of a business or asset theoretically determined?

At the most theoretical level, the value of a business (or an asset) is the economic present value of the future net cash generated by that business. *Inflows* are roughly equivalent to the operating cash flow component of the company's net income. *Net income* means the revenues of the business minus the expenses to run it determined on the accrual basis as described in the paragraphs that follow. There are other cash inflows and outflows that are not components of net income (e.g., cash investments in the business that are used to finance it). Also, a business's valuation is partially dependent on its balance sheet, which lists the company's assets and liabilities as of a point in time. In a purely theoretical sense, however, the balance sheet is relevant only for the net cash inflows and outflows that ultimately will result from the assets and liabilities shown. In other words, a balance sheet is a component of future net cash flow in the sense that the assets ultimately will be sold or otherwise realized, and the liabilities will take cash out of the business when they are paid.

An income statement looks pretty simple: Money in, money out over a period of time, not as of a particular point in time. But in order to truly understand an income statement, one must understand accrual basis accounting.

Cash flows are uneven and do not necessarily reflect the health of the business on a period-to-period basis. Accounting attempts to rectify this problem by employing the accrual method that puts cash flows in the period when the actual service or transaction occurs, not when cash is exchanged. A simple example is where you buy a widget-making machine for $100 in year one and that machine generates $20 in cash each year for 10 years, at which point it can no longer be used. In evaluating the health of the business in year one, you would not look at it as the business losing $80 in that year ($20 minus the $100 cost of the machine) because you will not have to spend money to buy a new machine for another 9 years. So accrual accounting depreciates the machine by $10 per year for 10 years. Thus, the real income of the business is $10 in each year in our example ($20 of generated cash minus the $10 depreciation on the machine).

Ultimately, the *intrinsic value* of the business is, as already stated, the present value of all future net cash flows generated by the business. Because stock market analysts and others in part try to evaluate the ultimate value of the business, they would like to know what cash the business is generating in each accounting period. The reconciliation of the income statement to cash flow is contained in the statement of cash flows, which is one of the financial statements that are required to be presented to comply with generally accepted accounting principles (GAAP).

In valuing a business, you also have to consider the element of risk that is involved in generating the future cash flows that are to be discounted to present value. More precisely, the value of the business is the sum of each of the possible outcomes of net cash generated to infinity *multiplied by* the probability of achieving each one, then *discounted* to present value.

Take the example of a ski resort. The cash flows from the business looking out indefinitely are dependent on whether or not there is global warming. If there is no global warming, cash flows will be one thing; if there is, cash flows will be less. So, in valuing that business, we need to take an educated guess as to the likelihood of there being global warming. More generally, in valuing a business, you have to estimate the range of possible outcomes and their probabilities. This is what stock market analysts do for a living. Because it is not practical to value cash flows to infinity, analysts typically will look at projected cash flows over a period of five years, for example, and then add to that value the expected terminal value of the business at the end of the five years using another valuation method.

Comparing Investments

Another problem faced by an investor or an acquisitive Buyer is to analyze the desirability of one acquisition versus another by using common measures of return on investment. In reality, investments will be made, to the extent of available funds, in the opportunities that are better than the others, *provided that* the rate of return on those investments meets minimum standards.

So take our widget-making machine example. The so-called internal rate of return or *yield* on that investment of $100 in year one is computed algebraically by solving the following equation:

$$100 = 20/(1 + r) + 20/(1 + r)2 \ldots 20/(1 + r)10$$

where r is the rate that discounts the stream of future cash flows to equal the initial outlay of 100 at time 0.

Another method is the *net present value* method where the cash inflows and outflows are discounted to present value. If you use a risk-free interest rate as the discount rate, that tells you how much more your dollar of investment is worth, ignoring risk, than putting it in a government bond for the same period of time.

Element of Risk

Adding in the concept of risk makes things even more complicated. The term *risk* as used by financial analysts is a different concept from the probabilities that are used to produce the expected present value of the business. Risk is essentially the separate set of probabilities that the actual return will deviate from the expected return (i.e., the variability of the investment return).

In the economic sense, being *risk averse* does not mean that an investor is not willing to take risks. Whether the investor wants to or not, there are risks in everything. The first cut at an investment analysis is to take all of the possible negative and positive outcomes and then sum them, weighting each outcome by its probability. For most investors, that is not sufficient, however. The reason is that investors are *loss averse,* meaning that the value of a negative outcome of x multiplied by its probability of y is not the exact opposite of a positive outcome of x multiplied by its probability of y. As an example, if you were offered the opportunity to toss a coin—tails you lose your house and heads you are paid the value of your house—you would probably not take this bet because your fear of losing your house would outweigh the possible dollar payout—you would be loss averse.

Risk and Portfolio Theory

These risk concepts are applied to the construction of a portfolio of securities. The concept of *diversification* is commonly misunderstood. Using the term with reference to the foregoing discussion, you attempt to reduce the risk of a severely negative outcome by placing more bets that have independent outcomes, or diversifying. You equally reduce the chance of spectacular gains. Taking the example of the coin toss/bet the value of your house, if you were to agree to do 10 bets in a row, betting 10 percent of the value of your house each time, the odds of your losing the entire value of your house are infinitesimal since you would have to lose ten 50/50 bets in a row. On the other hand, the odds of your doubling the value of your house are infinitesimal as well.

In the case of the stock market, you can never reduce your risk to zero because the market itself has a base level of risk that results from risks that affect all stocks. If you want an essentially risk-free investment, you have to invest only in U.S. Treasuries.

The term *beta* is simply a measure of the extent to which a particular stock's risk profile differs from the market generally. In theory, if you held all available stocks, you would have diversified away all of the risks of each of the stocks in your portfolio other than those that affect all stocks. You cannot completely eliminate them, but in economic terms, the stock-specific risks with any particular stock should, if the worst happens, have a minuscule effect on the overall portfolio. Put another way, if one of your stocks experiences a loss or gain from its specific risk, it changes the risk profile and return of your portfolio close to nothing because you hold thousands of stocks. The implicit assumption here is that it is unlikely that your portfolio would experience many bad outcomes from individual stock-specific risks.

Portfolio Theory as Applied to Acquisitions

What do these risk concepts and portfolio theory have to do with acquisitions? Simply, an acquisition is an investment by the Buyer. What a Buyer will rationally pay for a business or asset in an efficient market is a combination of the expected return from that asset, the riskiness of the investment, and the Buyer's appetite for risk.

An interesting way to look at portfolio construction is by using what are known as *indifference curves*. The curves in Exhibit 1.1 show that for a hypothetical investor (and everyone is different), if that investor were happy with the risk/reward profile for an investment represented by a particular point on the grid (risk on one axis, return on the other), then you could construct a curve of the points on the grid where the investor would be equally happy (i.e., the investor presumably would be happy with an investment that offered greater returns as risk increased). Everyone's curves would be different, but it is thought that the curves would look something like those in Exhibit 1.1. The other thing depicted here is that each higher curve (in the direction of the arrow) represents a better set of investments for the particular individual investor than any curve in the opposite direction, because for

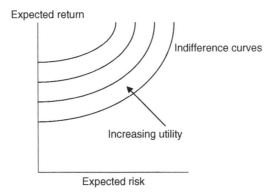

Expected return

Indifference curves

Increasing utility

Expected risk

EXHIBIT 1.1 Indifference Curves

any given amount of risk, the higher curve offers more return. That is what the words *increasing utility* mean in this diagram.

So far, we are dealing with theoretical sets of risks and returns that may have no relation to what is actually available in the market.

So, for an exclusively stock portfolio, one can plot sets of actual stock portfolios. Each actual stock portfolio has a different risk/reward combination. In Exhibit 1.2, the shaded area represents all of the possible combinations of stocks that are actually available in the market. If, within this area, you choose any particular point, the point immediately higher than it or immediately to the left of it would represent a better set of stocks—either it would have the same risk but a higher reward or it would have the same reward but a lower risk. So, in portfolio theory, the optimal stock portfolio for the particular investor is obviously the one that achieves the optimum risk/reward ratio. In terms of this diagram, you keep moving straight up in the shaded area to get a better return for the same amount of risk, or you move straight left in the box to achieve the same return at lower risk. The *efficiency frontier* essentially represents the results of that exercise.

Combining this concept with the preceding concept of indifference curves, the optimal portfolio is the tangent where the efficiency frontier touches the highest indifference curve.

Another interesting element of portfolio theory is what happens when you add risk-free assets to the portfolio (i.e., U.S. government bonds or U.S. Treasuries). Assume that the risk-free return is represented where the dotted line touches the y-axis in Exhibit 1.2. The dotted line is drawn between this totally risk-free investment on the y-axis to the tangent where the efficiency frontier curve meets the highest indifference curve; it represents a varying mix of increasing amounts of that risk-free investment combined with the

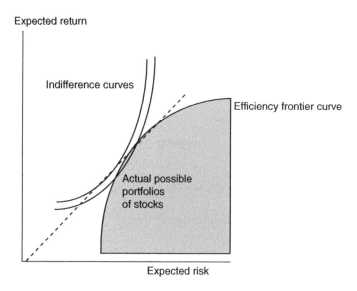

EXHIBIT 1.2 Optimal Stock Portfolio

risky stock portfolio. Interestingly, assuming the curves are shaped as they are in the exhibit, there is a point in that portfolio that is at a higher indifference curve than the one that contains the tangential point for the all-stock portfolio. That higher point represents the optimal portfolio for that particular investor.

There is another derivative of this theoretical exercise called the *capital asset pricing model* (CAPM), which simply says that in an efficient market, expected return is directly and linearly proportional to risk.

Of course, all of this is a worthwhile game and not purely academic *if* these curves can actually be derived and *if* there is any credibility to the risks and returns assigned to the actual portfolio. However, taking a typical personal portfolio as an example, this is purely academic. It seems that in reality, the broker's stock analysts do not simply take each possible investment, determine each possible cash flow result, and assign an appropriate probability to it, calculate the expected outcome, add it into the actual possible portfolio, and see where the efficiency frontier meets the highest indifference curve. This appears to be more easily said than done.

Efficient Market Hypothesis

There are a few more buzzwords here, most importantly, the *efficient capital market hypothesis* in its various forms. One variant of this hypothesis is that market prices at any given time will reflect an unbiased forecast of future cash flows that fully reflect all publicly available information.

There is a corollary of this hypothesis that is relevant to acquisition pricing: If a Buyer is paying above market for a publicly traded company, then the combination of the two businesses will increase cash flows or create a better risk profile, or the Buyer has information that the market does not have—or, a third possibility, the Buyer does not know what it is doing or got outfoxed by the Target.

There is continuing debate as to whether, or to what extent, the efficient market hypothesis is actually true. There are also other hypotheses to explain market behavior. One theory is that uninformed investors irrationally chase market trends and/or that too much weight is put on new information. It certainly seems to be the case that the market overreacts to bad news. How many times have we seen that if a company misses expected earnings per share (EPS) by a penny, its stock gets clobbered?

Another reason that markets may not be entirely rational is that money managers may base their decisions on what is best for them instead of their clients, based on their own risk/reward profile. For example, some money managers get paid on a straight percentage of assets under management. Other investment vehicles such as hedge funds pay managers a portion of profits made but do not require the managers to pay out equivalent losses. This skewing of values affects decisions. If you are playing with other people's money (OPM), you might as well make investments that have the potential for abnormally large gains and losses. In effect, you have a lot more to gain than you have to lose, given that you have no personal funds at risk.

Decisions are also skewed in other ways. Holders of debt would like a company to make different decisions than shareholders would, because they get none of the upside from risky decisions. Shareholders and management with stock options have different incentives because managers can never lose money on stock options. So, in theory, managers may be more prone to taking risks. But managers are not as well diversified as shareholders because they tend to have a disproportionate amount of their net worth in their company's stock, so they may in theory be *more* loss averse than shareholders because they have not diversified away the specific risk inherent in their company's stock.

Bottom line, nobody really knows how all of this works.

REASONS FOR ACQUISITIONS

If any of the preceding corporate finance concepts are valid, they should bear directly on acquisition practice. In the most theoretical sense, a Buyer would acquire a Target because the future cash flows of the combined business, discounted for risk, would ultimately net the Buyer's *existing* shareholders more money. What are the ways that can happen in an efficient market?

Intrinsic value can be created, in a theoretical sense, if the combined businesses would generate an increase in aggregate cash flow. That should always be the case.

In addition to a simple additive increase in value, an increase in intrinsic value can be achieved in other ways by such things as *financial engineering,* economies of scale, better management of the combined business, or changes in the capital structure that should increase cash flows to shareholders, perhaps with an attendant increase in risk. A leveraged buyout (LBO) is an example of financial engineering: A business is purchased partly with borrowed funds; the Buyer believes that it will make money from the deal because the present value of the cash flows from the leveraged business will exceed the price paid by the Buyer with its own funds, often because the Buyer thinks that the business does not have enough leverage.

Acquisitions should all be additive in the sense that the combined business is worth more than the separate businesses. The real question is how the addition to value is allocated between the Target's shareholders and the Buyer. The Buyer's goal is that the portion of the increased value allocated to the Buyer is worth more than what the Buyer paid. In a deal where the Buyer pays only in cash, *all* of the increase in value is allocated to the Buyer, and the question comes down to whether the increase in value exceeds the purchase price. In a deal where stock is used as currency, the question is whether the increase in value allocated to the Buyer (i.e., the percentage of the combined company that the Buyer's shareholders will own) is greater before or after the deal. So the allocation occurs via the acquisition price, with the better negotiator taking a bigger slice of the pie.

Other than by simple addition, how is value created? What are some of the synergies in acquisitions?

Enhancing financial performance—that is, increasing earnings per share (EPS)—can sometimes be accomplished by financial engineering. EPS is the net income of the business divided by the number of shares outstanding. One business may acquire another for purely financial reasons, particularly where the Buyer has a higher price-to-earnings ratio (P/E ratio) than the Target. P/E is the ratio of a company's stock price to its earnings per share. If the acquisition is for cash, then the costs of the new business have to be measured against the loss of the income from the cash spent in order to determine whether EPS goes up. Where stock is involved, the measurement is the addition to net profits from acquiring the business against the number of additional shares issued to pay for the acquisition.

This deserves a bit of background. After all is said and done on the various academic theories of value, the stock market and company managers are largely focused on a company's EPS and its P/E ratio. The company's P/E ratio multiplied by its EPS multiplied by the number of shares outstanding equals the company's market capitalization or market cap. Public companies are valued (traded) in significant part as a multiple of EPS or expected future EPS. So, all things being equal, the price per share goes up (and managers get richer) if EPS goes up. The P/E ratio is the market's shortcut way of expressing its view of the company's future value—it is a measure of how much the market perceives that EPS and cash flow will grow over time. So-called growth companies have higher P/E ratios.

Managing EPS is the reason companies introduce debt into their capital structures. Basic modern corporate finance strategy seeks to maximize EPS within acceptable risk parameters. Earnings per share can be increased with the prudent use of debt in the right circumstances, which are that the company can, with the cash proceeds of the debt, generate incremental earnings that are greater than the interest paid on the debt. No shares of capital stock are issued with straight (nonconvertible) debt, so EPS goes up.

If sold at the right price, sales of additional equity can increase EPS as well. The company expects, either in the short or long term, to be able to grow its business and earnings from the cash generated by the sale of additional shares of capital stock so that after the growth occurs, EPS will go up even though more shares are outstanding.

In the M&A context, if buying a business will increase *pro forma* EPS—that is, what is expected to happen to EPS if the deal happens—then that is an important reason for doing the deal. In one sense, it is often just a substitute for the so-called real reasons for acquisitions, such as economies of scale, discussed shortly—but not always.

Stock acquisitions can be done for pure financial engineering reasons. Take the following example. Two companies each have a million dollars in annual earnings and one million shares outstanding. If the Buyer has a P/E ratio of twice that of the Target, in order to acquire the Target for a price that merely equals the current market price of the Target, it must only issue half a million shares. So it doubles its income but only has 50 percent more shares outstanding. Its EPS, therefore, goes up. Surprisingly, the stock market frequently maintains the old P/E ratio of the Buyer or something close to it, so that the Buyer's stock price rises as a result of the acquisition. This also gives the Target company some negotiating leverage; because the deal is *accretive* to the Buyer's EPS, there is room to keep the deal accretive, but less favorably to the Buyer, by forcing the Buyer to pay a premium to the market as the acquisition price. A deal that prospectively raises EPS is called a *nondilutive* or *accretive* deal, even though there may be more shares outstanding (and thus dilution in another sense) in a stock deal.

Of course, acquisitions are done other than for pure short-term financial considerations, as previously mentioned. Even though a deal may not be initially accretive, the Buyer may still want to acquire the business for its future economic potential, believing that the acquisition will ultimately become accretive because of the growth of the acquired business or expected cost savings or other synergies over time. That type of transaction takes brave managers at the Buyer.

What, then, are some of the *real* reasons (synergies) why one business acquires another? In other words, how is value created other than by the mere additive combination of two businesses?

- *Economies of scale.* In an acquisition of one company and a competitor, economies of scale can be achieved where the acquisition results in lower average manufacturing costs or by elimination of redundancies in the organization. A good example of this is the consolidation in the banking industry. Banking competitors in different locations may combine and streamline their operating and marketing functions. Banking competitors in the same location may combine to increase their customer base but eliminate costs like redundant branch offices in the same location.
- *Time to market.* A variant on economies of scale is extending a product line, for example, where it is cheaper or faster (or both) for the Buyer to purchase the product line and its underlying technology rather than develop it independently, or where the Buyer cannot develop it independently because it is blocked by the prospective Target's patent portfolio. This logic also applies to enhancing a particular business function—for example, sales and marketing—where similar cost and speed considerations are present. One company in a particular business may have a great marketing team and poor technology, while its Target has the opposite. Another common rationale in the technology company arena is that the disincentives for potential customers to deal with a small and possibly unstable technology company will be eliminated if it is acquired by a larger company with market presence.
- *Combination of customer and supplier.* Here, a company buys a supplier, or a supplier acquires a customer. A company might do that in order to reduce the risk of dependence on an outside supplier. Bringing the supply function in-house also eliminates the risk of price gouging.
- *Product line diversification.* A business might also want to diversify into other areas to change its risk profile.

- *Defensive acquisitions.* Sometimes businesses are acquired because the acquirer may be facing a severe downturn in its business, and the acquisition will alleviate the cause of the severe downturn. An example is a drug company that has massive marketing power but is running out of patent protection on its key drugs. It may acquire a promising new drug and put it into its powerful marketing channel.
- *New and better management.* Managers may not act in the best interest of the shareholders for different reasons. They may be lousy managers, lazy, stupid, inexperienced, or a combination, or they divert for their own benefit certain assets of the business, like paying themselves too much. An acquirer might think it can enhance the value of an acquired business by replacing its management.
- *Acquisition of a control premium.* Some argue that the public trading markets always misprice publicly held stocks because the value of the stock in the market is that of the individual holder who is not in a control position. Bidders may bid for companies simply to capture the control premium inherent in the stock, which they then can cash out by selling the control premium to another purchaser.

Regardless of the motives for acquisitions, those involved must still have an understanding of the basic acquisition structures that are available to them and of the structural and other legal and business aspects that dictate the use of one structure over another.

THREE BASIC ACQUISITION STRUCTURES

There are three basic ways to structure an acquisition:

1. *Stock purchase,* where the outstanding stock of the Target is sold to the Buyer or a subsidiary of the Buyer by the shareholders of the Target.
2. *Merger,* where the Target is merged, pursuant to the applicable state merger statute(s), with the Buyer or merged with a subsidiary of the Buyer that has been formed for the purpose of effecting the merger. After the merger, either the Target or the Buyer (or its subsidiary) can be the corporation that survives the merger (called the surviving corporation).
3. *Asset purchase,* where all or a selected portion of the assets (e.g., inventory, accounts receivable, and intellectual property rights) of the Target are sold to the Buyer or a subsidiary of the Buyer. In an asset purchase, all or a selected portion or none of the liabilities and obligations of the Target are assumed by the Buyer.

In each of these cases, the purchase price may be paid in cash, stock, or other equity securities of the Buyer, promissory notes of the Buyer, or any combination. Sometimes a portion of the purchase price is paid on a deferred basis tied to the subsequent performance of the acquired business. This technique is called an *earnout*. Sometimes, as in a leveraged buyout, the Buyer buys only a majority of the stock of the Target and does not acquire all or part of the stock held by management or others who are to continue to be involved in the business.

Following is a brief additional explanation of these three forms of acquisition. We go into them in much greater detail later.

Stock Purchase

In a stock purchase, the Buyer (or a subsidiary—we will not keep making this distinction unless necessary) purchases the outstanding capital stock of the Target directly from the Target's shareholders. If the Target is a private company, this is effected by a stock purchase agreement signed by the Buyer, the Target's shareholders if they are relatively few in number, and sometimes the Target itself. In a public company, this is effected by a tender offer, in which the Buyer makes a formal public offer directly to the Target's shareholders because with a public company the Target's shareholders are always too numerous to deal with separately. Where the Buyer is offering to pay in stock, a tender offer is called an *exchange offer*.

A stock purchase (but not a tender offer) in many ways is the simplest form of acquisition. Assuming that all of the outstanding stock of the Target is acquired by the Buyer, the Target becomes a wholly owned subsidiary of the Buyer, and the Buyer effectively acquires control of all of the assets and, as a practical matter, assumes all of the liabilities of the Target. (Technically, the Buyer does not assume these liabilities itself and they remain at the Target level, but unless the Buyer wants to abandon its new wholly owned subsidiary, as a practical matter it normally would make sure those liabilities get paid.) No change is made in the assets or liabilities of the acquired business as a direct consequence of the acquisition of the Target's stock.

Merger

If a private company has so many shareholders that it is impractical to get everyone to sign the stock purchase agreement, or if there are dissidents, then the usual choice is a merger.

For Targets that are public companies, a merger is used because a public company has a large number of shareholders and it is not feasible for all of the shareholders to sign a stock purchase agreement. An alternative is a *two-step* acquisition where the Buyer first acquires through a stock purchase a majority of the Target's outstanding stock from the Target's shareholders in a tender or exchange offer, and then follows that up with a *squeeze-out merger* approved by Buyer as majority shareholder. In that case, the minority shareholders are forced to take the acquisition consideration in the *back-end merger* by virtue of the statutory merger provisions (unless they exercise their *appraisal rights,* which they rarely do).

Two-step acquisitions where the Buyer buys less than a majority of the outstanding Target stock are sometimes used in public transactions because such a purchase can be wrapped up quickly. In that case, depending on the percentage of the Target's outstanding stock that the Buyer purchases, the Buyer can make it more difficult for an interloper to come in and steal the deal from the Buyer. The interloper has that opportunity in public deals since compliance with the Securities and Exchange Commission (SEC) regulatory process is very time consuming. Those particular regulations generally do not apply to private acquisitions.

A merger is a transaction that is created by the relevant business corporation statutes in the states of incorporation of the parties. Statutes applicable to other types of entities, such as limited liability companies, govern mergers involving those entities. We assume throughout this book that both the Target and the Buyer are Delaware corporations. The majority of business corporations of any size are Delaware corporations. Other states' business corporation statutes (and the Model Business Corporation Act) differ in details from Delaware's, but in the acquisition arena, the common theme is that the merger provisions of a statute permit two corporations to merge one into the other so that all of the assets and liabilities of the disappearing corporation in the merger get added to the assets and liabilities of the surviving corporation by operation of law.

With minor exceptions, mergers require the approval of both the board of directors (at least in Delaware) and the shareholders of the merging corporations. The famous Delaware takeover cases involving rival bidders arose in situations where the Target's board of directors had approved the merger and a merger agreement had been signed by the Target and the Buyer, but the merger could not close immediately because of the need for shareholder approval and/or antitrust approval. Between the time of signing the merger agreement and shareholder approval, the rival bidder made its upset offer.

The relevant merger provisions of the state business corporation statutes specify the requisite shareholder vote, usually a majority. Sometimes the Target's corporate charter, as an anti-takeover device, specifies a super-majority vote or a separate vote by the different classes or series of stock outstanding.

Also by operation of law and as agreed in the merger agreement between the Buyer and the Target, the outstanding stock of the Target is automatically converted into cash, stock, notes, or a combination thereof (or other property) of the Buyer or its corporate parent. This technique, therefore, is the vehicle for the Buyer to acquire 100 percent ownership of the Target, which is generally imperative for reasons we discuss later. In either a one-step merger or a two-step merger involving a stock purchase followed by a squeeze-out merger, all of the stock held by each shareholder of the acquired corporation gets converted into the merger consideration, whether a particular shareholder voted for the merger or not.

The one exception is so-called appraisal rights created by the statutory merger provisions. Under certain circumstances, the Target's shareholders can object to the merger terms and seek an appraisal of their shares in a court proceeding. This rarely occurs because of the expense involved versus the dollars that may or may not be gained, but it is a threat that must be considered in structuring the transaction.

Asset Purchase

In an asset purchase, the Buyer acquires all or selected assets of the Target and assumes all, a portion, or none of the liabilities of the Target pursuant to an asset purchase agreement. Most state statutes require shareholder approval of a sale of "all or substantially all" of the assets of the Target. As we will see, there are a number of reasons why a deal may be structured as an asset purchase, principally tax. In some cases, such as where the Buyer is acquiring only a division or a product line from an established business with multiple divisions and product lines that are not separately incorporated, an asset purchase is the only practical way to accomplish this objective.

STRUCTURING CONSIDERATIONS: OVERVIEW

We now discuss the principal structuring parameters that determine whether a stock purchase, merger, or asset purchase is the appropriate acquisition structure. In most cases, tax considerations are the starting point, and so it is important for business lawyers to understand the basic tax aspects of acquisitions. Tax considerations are discussed at length in Chapter 4. Non-tax-structuring considerations are discussed in Chapter 3. This section provides an overview.

Tax

Acquisitions can be done on a tax-free (meaning tax-deferred) or taxable basis. Ordinarily, a shareholder recognizes taxable gain or loss upon the sale of the shareholder's stock, whether the consideration paid is cash, a note, other property, or some combination thereof. Congress acknowledged that, under certain circumstances, where a shareholder continues the investment through equity in another corporation, imposing a tax on the sale of a corporation or a merger of corporations could inhibit otherwise economically beneficial transactions.

For example, shareholders owning corporation A might be willing to sell their shares to corporation B for cash in a taxable transaction, but not for B shares if a tax were due. Corporation B has insufficient cash. The A shareholders might not have sufficient cash to pay a tax if their only proceeds were illiquid B shares. Also, if corporation B continues the business previously operated by corporation A, it might be said that the A shareholders have simply continued their investment in another form and so should not be subject to tax.

A series of tax code sections permit the deferral (not elimination) of the tax realized by shareholders when corporations combine in transactions that meet certain requirements. These so-called reorganization (or tax-free reorg) provisions contain specific technical statutory requirements that are amplified by judicially imposed requirements designed to implement the Congressional intent that tax be deferred only when a shareholder's investment and business continue in a new form.

In the most fundamental terms, in order to qualify as a tax-free reorganization, a significant portion of the acquisition consideration must be voting stock of the Buyer. The required percentage ranges up to 100 percent for certain reorganization structures. The percentage is lowest for an "A" reorg, which relates to nonsubsidiary mergers and *forward* subsidiary mergers (explained later), and substantially higher for reverse subsidiary mergers, stock-for-assets deals, and stock-for-stock exchanges. The portion of the acquisition consideration that is not stock is called *boot* and its receipt is taxable. Therefore, most reorganizations are only partially tax-free.

Unfortunately, the reorganization provisions do not permit tax-deferred combinations between partnerships (or limited liability companies taxed as partnerships) and corporations. These entities can typically convert to corporations on a tax-deferred basis (under an unrelated set of tax code provisions), but they cannot convert to corporations on a tax-deferred basis as part of a plan to combine with a corporation under the reorganization rules. This means that a partnership or a limited liability company (LLC) taxed as a partnership must plan in advance for possible exit strategies, so that a conversion to a corporation, if desired, is done well before a plan to combine with a particular corporation is formulated.

Buyers and Targets have different and conflicting tax objectives with respect to acquisitions. From the *Target's* perspective, the shareholders of the Target want the acquisition to be tax-free to them if it is a stock transaction, which is a practical necessity where the shares are illiquid and cannot be sold to pay the tax. In a taxable transaction, the Target's shareholders want to get long-term capital gain treatment and not recognize ordinary income at higher rates. A tax-free deal allows the Target's shareholders to defer recognition of their gain until they sell the new shares. In the event of a shareholder's death, the cost basis of the assets of that shareholder can be stepped up to their then-fair market value, thus permanently avoiding income tax on that gain. In a taxable transaction, the taxable gain is measured by the value of the consideration received over the tax basis in the shares or assets being sold (cost less depreciation, if any).

The Target's shareholders most acutely want to avoid a deal that creates double tax—that is, taxation first at the corporate level and then at the shareholder level. In other words, a transaction is not tax efficient if the Target corporation pays tax on its gain and the shareholders of that corporation pay tax on the after-tax proceeds distributed to them. Double tax happens in an asset purchase, with certain exceptions—the Target pays a tax on its gain from a sale of its assets, and, when the proceeds are distributed to its shareholders, another tax is due from the shareholders on their gain. This potential for double tax is the reason that asset purchases are relatively rare. An asset purchase sometimes can be accomplished without double tax if there are sufficient tax loss carryforwards available to shelter the Target corporation's gains or if the acquired entity is a flow-through entity that doesn't itself pay tax, like a partnership or LLC.

From the *Buyer's* perspective, the principal tax concern relates to the tax basis that the Buyer receives in the Target's assets. The Buyer wants what is known as a *step-up* in basis, since a higher tax basis in depreciable/amortizable assets allows greater depreciation deductions that will shelter other income going forward or will reduce the amount of gain when the assets are sold. The opposite of a step-up in basis is *carryover basis,* which means that the assets have the same tax basis in the hands of the Buyer as they did in the hands of the Target. In a tax-free deal, there is carryover basis. In a taxable asset purchase, there is a step-up in basis, but unless the Target has loss carryforwards or is a flow-through entity, there is double tax. Taxable mergers can go either way, depending on the form of the merger. So you can see the points of contention between Buyer and Target developing already.

Let us approach it from another direction—the basic tax consequences of the three different structures. In a *stock purchase,* the Target's shareholders sell their stock directly to the Buyer. The Target itself is not selling anything, so the Target pays no tax and therefore double tax is avoided. You can accomplish a stock-for-stock tax-free deal, but the requirements are strict, as previously noted. Stock deals are tax adverse for the Buyer from the limited perspective that there is carryover basis, and not a step-up in basis, in the Target's assets. There are some esoteric exceptions here for stock purchases of a corporation out of a consolidated tax group and for Subchapter S corporations using a so-called Section 338 election. The election effectively treats the stock purchase as an asset purchase for tax purposes.

As for *mergers,* there are taxable and tax-free mergers. A taxable merger can be structured to resemble a stock purchase or an asset purchase. We will discuss different merger structures in Chapter 3 and their tax consequences in Chapter 4.

In a taxable *asset purchase,* if the Buyer acquires selected assets at a gain from the Target, the Target pays tax on the gain. If the proceeds are then distributed to the shareholders of the Target, then there is double tax if the transaction is followed by a liquidation (assuming that there is a gain on the liquidation of the stock). If the proceeds are distributed as a dividend and the corporation stays in business, a tax would be payable by the Target's shareholders on the dividend, assuming there are corporate earnings and profits. From the Buyer's tax perspective, taxable asset deals are good because there is a step-up in tax basis. (There are tax-free asset deals, but they are quite rare.)

Corporate Law

The corporate law parameters for an acquisition start with whether the Buyer wants to, or is forced to, acquire selected assets of the Target and whether the Buyer wants to avoid the assumption of certain or all liabilities of the Target.

Where the Buyer wants to acquire the entire business, asset purchase structures are generally not used if there is double tax. They are also more complex mechanically. As we said earlier, the next choice in this situation is a stock purchase. Buyers almost always want to acquire all of the outstanding stock of the Target in a stock acquisition, as opposed to a majority of the stock. That is because if there remain minority shareholders, any transactions between the Buyer and its new subsidiary that has minority stockholders are subject to attack for being unfair to the minority shareholders—a potential legal mess that Buyers generally (but not always) want to avoid. Also, funds flow is restricted from the subsidiary to the parent because if the subsidiary wants to pay a dividend to the parent, it must also pay it as well to the minority shareholders, which may not be desirable. For these reasons, Buyers will then choose to do a single-step merger or a partial stock purchase followed by a squeeze-out merger.

Another corporate law consideration in the choice of structure is the need to obtain consents from counterparties to contracts of the Target and/or from government entities. Commercial contracts generally prohibit the contract from being assigned by a party without the consent of the other party. In an asset purchase, what is required for the Buyer to get the benefits of the contract is an assignment to the Buyer of the contract rights of the Target under the particular contract. The need to obtain these consents creates the possibility of delays and also creates the possibility of a holdup by the other contracting party, which extracts some monetary or other concession as the price for its consent.

One way the need for consents can sometimes be avoided is by doing a stock purchase. In a stock purchase, because the contracting corporation remains in place and unchanged except for its ownership, it generally is not considered to be assigning its contract rights for purposes of requiring consents from counterparties. To avoid this loophole, some contracts require consent for an assignment and also give the counterparty termination or other rights in a *change in control* transaction—in other words, an acquisition by stock purchase or any form of merger.

Similar to a stock purchase in this regard is what is known as a *reverse triangular merger* where a subsidiary of the Buyer merges into the Target, with the Target being the surviving corporation. Just as in a stock purchase, a reverse triangular merger is not generally considered an assignment of the Target's contracts since the Target remains in place unchanged except for its ownership.

Securities Laws

The impact of the securities laws on acquisitions is discussed in detail in Chapter 3. In short, the issuance by the Buyer of its stock or other securities (or a vote by the Target's shareholders to approve a deal where they are to receive stock or securities of the Buyer) is considered a purchase and sale of securities requiring either registration with the SEC or an exemption from registration. State securities (or blue sky) laws may also be applicable.

Antitrust and Other Regulatory Considerations

One issue that has to be analyzed at the outset is what, if any, regulatory approvals are required for the acquisition. The need for regulatory approvals affects the timing, certainty of completion, covenants, and closing conditions of the deal.

The need for regulatory approval can arise for two reasons. First, one or both of the parties are in a regulated industry where acquisitions are scrutinized for compliance with applicable legal requirements, such as the acquisition of broadcasting assets. Second, the size of the parties and the size of the transaction may trigger filing requirements under the antitrust laws. Although all deals are subject, in theory, to being overturned because of antitrust concerns, the principal antitrust hurdle in the acquisition arena is the Hart-Scott-Rodino Antitrust Improvements Act (HSR, or Hart-Scott).

In acquisitions of a specified size (approximately $80 million or greater) and where the parties themselves exceed specified size hurdles (approximately $160 million or more in sales or assets for one, and approximately $16 million or more for the other), a filing with, and clearance by, the federal government is required. Some large deals get scrapped or modified because of antitrust review, but for most smaller deals, an HSR filing requirement is merely an expensive nuisance and unwelcome delay.

Acquisition Accounting

In the not-too-distant past, accounting considerations were frequently as important as tax considerations in structuring acquisitions. That is because there were two forms of accounting for acquisitions by the acquirer with drastically different consequences. In so-called *purchase accounting,* the acquirer reset the fair market value of the acquired assets and any related goodwill had to be depreciated, sometimes over a relatively short period. In the other form, a *pooling of interests,* there was no change in the book basis of the acquired assets and no amortization of goodwill. This was considered highly desirable, since it was difficult to do accretive acquisitions with goodwill amortization creating significant book expense going forward. The requirements for qualifying for a pooling were quite strict (e.g., the acquisition consideration had to be solely for voting stock). There were multiple other requirements as well.

This has all changed, and now there is only one form of accounting treatment for acquisitions. Post-acquisition assets have a new book basis tied to fair market value, and goodwill is not written off unless it is, or becomes, impaired. There is also something called *recapitalization accounting,* discussed in Chapter 3.

CHAPTER 2

The Acquisition Process

OVERVIEW

How does the mergers and acquisitions (M&A) process start? The process is more informatively looked at from the Target's point of view. The Target may decide to put itself up for sale because it needs to for financial reasons, because it thinks it has reached its peak value, or because one or more shareholders need or want liquidity; or it may have been approached by a potential Buyer (often a customer or supplier) who wants to talk about "items of mutual interest."

Before the Target puts itself up for sale, it is likely that its corporate and legal affairs will have to be cleaned up. The Target's lawyers may or may not have had close contact and involvement with their client during the course of their engagement. Companies vary widely in how highly they value their lawyer's input and the degree to which they pay attention to legal matters. The sale process is where the cracks in the concrete will show. Sometimes costly and unrectifiable mistakes have been made, and the sale price will reflect them. Even if significant mistakes have not been made, there will always be corporate housekeeping cleanup that will have to be done. Common problems include improperly documented customer arrangements; vague bonus arrangements for employees; nonexistent, inadequate, or unsigned customary employee arrangements (confidentiality agreements, covenants not to compete, etc.); or license agreements that terminate upon an acquisition. Additionally, there may not be good stock records as to who owns the business or other corporate records. The list of potential problems is extensive. It is far better to fix them at the outset. We discuss due diligence in more depth later in this chapter; in addition, we walk through a sample legal due diligence list with some suggestions as to where bombs may be buried.

If the Target wants to put itself up for sale, someone will need to sell it. Occasionally, management will try to handle the sale themselves, in which case they have fools for clients. Far more frequently, the Target will engage an investment banker to provide an initial valuation, analyze the market's appetite for acquisitions of companies like the Target, prepare marketing materials for the sale, and then identify potential Buyers, solicit them (hopefully creating a bidding war), and negotiate the sale.

Even though investment banking fees are high, even by lawyer standards, retention of an investment banker is likely to add significant value to the transaction (as with some but not all lawyers). Experienced investment bankers know how to market a company and have significant contacts within numerous potential Buyers. They are also skilled in playing the sale game to get the best price for the Target, by creating interest among multiple parties, or creating the impression that other parties are eager to participate. Where management will continue to work for the business after the deal, it is also prudent to get management out of the line of fire—negotiations can get tense, and bad feelings can result that may impair management's continuing relationships.

Once bankers are engaged (the engagement letter is discussed in detail later in this chapter), they will prepare estimates of possible value and identify potential Buyers. With the assistance of management, they will prepare a *book,* or marketing material, that is much like a prospectus, containing financial and business information about the Target. Unlike a prospectus, the marketing material will often contain a stronger sales pitch and will include projections.

The Target and the investment banker must decide on the approach they will take with prospective Buyers. They may approach one or a few companies that are the most likely Buyers, or approach a greater but still limited number of Buyers who are possibilities, or may cast a wider net and hope for surprise big fish to emerge. Usually, the process is the middle one. On the one hand, approaching only one or two potential Buyers may not create the proper leverage, and you never can be sure who is willing to spend how much; on the other hand, a broad-based auction is difficult to manage and disseminates a lot of confidential material about the Target, making it more likely that such information prematurely will reach customers and suppliers that the Target would prefer not possess the information.

Partly to minimize the quantity of confidential information disseminated, the first salvo of marketing material will be somewhat summary in nature, with the detailed financial and business information made available only to potential qualified Buyers who express serious interest. A request for recipients to execute confidentiality agreements at the outset of the process is standard. These agreements say, in essence, that the recipient of information about the Target will not use the information for any purpose other than to evaluate the Target as a possible acquisition, and will keep the information strictly confidential. (Confidentiality agreements are discussed in more detail later.)

A more limited group of finalists will be allowed to conduct a due diligence investigation, which includes an in-person presentation from management and the opportunity to dig deeper into the business, financial statements, and projections. Those who do not drop out are invited to make an offer. As we have noted, the banker's job at this point is to make it look like there is significant interest among multiple parties and to try to play interested parties off against each other.

One technique that is frequently very valuable is to ask the finalists to propose terms in enumerated business and legal areas. That is sometimes done by having the Target's counsel prepare a form of acquisition agreement and asking bidders and their counsel to comment on it. The actual value of a bid to the Target can be significantly affected by the higher-level business/legal aspects of the deal. It is not just about the price—or, put another way, these business/legal aspects affect and should be considered part of the price. Potential Buyers can be asked to address issues that are particularly sensitive to the Target's constituencies. For example, venture capital and other private equity investors are loath to have liability exposure beyond an escrowed amount that is set up at closing to fund indemnification claims by the Buyer for misrepresentations and the like. Under the investors' agreement with their own limited partners/investors, it is typically required that proceeds of disposition of investments be distributed to the investment fund's limited partners. If under the indemnification provisions of the acquisition agreement, the Target's shareholders, including the venture capital funds or other investors, ultimately have to give some of the previously distributed deal proceeds back to the Buyer, the mechanics of reclaiming the money from the funds' own investors may be quite awkward or unworkable.

Sometimes, instead of an orderly sale process initiated by the Target and conducted by investment bankers, the Target gets an unsolicited expression of interest from a potential acquirer. In that case, the process is somewhat simplified. Investment bankers may still be retained to help evaluate and negotiate the deal even though the potential Buyer has already been identified. In that case, the banker's fee is usually lower. Since these scenarios often go nowhere, the bankers can then conduct an orderly sale process if the Target wants to continue to try to effect a sale.

If the negotiations are successful and an agreement in principle is reached with a potential Buyer, the parties may or may not sign a nonbinding letter of intent that outlines the deal in summary terms. (Letters of intent are discussed in detail later in this chapter.) More intensive due diligence follows, and the preparation and negotiation of the definitive acquisition agreement and other documentation is often parallel-processed.

There are some subtleties to the foregoing process that are worth mentioning. From the Target's viewpoint, in order to ensure a smooth and efficient transaction, it should begin thinking about these steps well in advance. Due diligence will be done in advance of at least the final bidding, and continuing due diligence will be done after signing the letter of intent. It behooves the Target to make the due diligence process as smooth and easy as possible. One useful technique is to have the Target's counsel prepare a due diligence checklist as if it were representing the Buyer in the potential transaction. Most due diligence checklists are fundamentally alike and call for the same items to be produced. The Target and counsel together should annotate the due diligence list to show what items will be produced in response to each line item of the request and then assemble copies of these items.

As for practical considerations, the Target and its counsel will set up a data room where all of the responsive documents, as well as an index listing all of the documents, are made available to bidders. The documents are organized into folders corresponding to the line items on the list. An increasingly popular technique is to set up a *virtual data room,* which means simply that the documents and the index are uploaded to a password-protected website set up for the purpose. Where potential Buyers are, or are likely to be, widely scattered, this is a very efficient technique. It is particularly useful if the business is to be sold in a variant of the auction process. Potential bidders will want to do full or partial due diligence before making a bid, and the virtual data room ensures that their document inspection can be expedited.

Virtual data rooms can be set up by the Target's law firm using commercially available web-based document storage, and there are also many vendors, including the financial printers, that will handle the process for a fee. The vendor systems are more sophisticated and offer features like being able to track (and later prove) who saw what when and to permit limited access to certain bidders. The higher vendor cost must be weighed against the benefit to the transaction. However, it also must be considered whether the Target in fact wants to make the process easy for the Buyer, particularly where the Buyer has been identified. In that case, putting the Buyer and its lawyers into a crowded, overheated physical data room may dampen their enthusiasm for an in-depth investigation.

As previously noted, along with getting a head start on the due diligence process, the Target may want its lawyers to prepare the first draft of the acquisition documents before a Buyer is even identified. This is done for the same reasons. It is normally the Buyer's prerogative to draft the acquisition documents, but in an auction, or quasi-auction, preparation of the documents by the Target's counsel, with a request for comments as part of the bidding process, is quite common.

For the Target, the sale process is not without real costs and risks from the outset. These issues are particularly important to point out to unsophisticated Targets, who often injudiciously jump at the chance to talk to someone who has expressed an interest in acquiring them. Management and the Target's shareholders would love to hear from a bidder what their company is worth. But there are risks in doing so.

The sale process usually acquires a momentum of its own. Leaks are possible, and if word leaks out that the Target is up for sale, bad things can happen to it. There can be serious morale and retention issues for the Target's employees, significant concern among customers and suppliers about their future business relationship with the Target's potential new owner, and cutthroat business practices by the Target's competitors attempting to create or exploit this concern for their competitive advantage. For these reasons, the Target should be aware that there are dangers to responding to the casual inquiry where the principal motivation on the Target's part is to find out what the Target may actually be worth. Potential Buyers may be trying to find out more about the Target's business and customers without serious interest in buying the Target. This problem is particularly acute where the party expressing interest is a competitor, supplier, or customer.

Winning bidders in the process will always demand and get various deal-protection devices. These devices are discussed in Chapter 6 for public company acquisitions, but in essence they are provisions designed to prevent the Target from continuing to negotiate with, and furnish due diligence information to, other actual or prospective bidders. The Buyer wants the deal locked up. It does not want to spend a lot of time and money on a deal, only to lose it to another bidder.

Letters of intent contain binding exclusivity or "lock-up" provisions that preclude the Target from talking to other potential bidders. These clauses are useful to the Buyer even though they typically expire within a relatively short period of time. Unlike definitive agreements containing lock-ups, at the nonbinding letter of intent stage the Target can just sit around and wait for the lock-up to expire if it becomes dissatisfied with a deal. But there is a risk to the Target as well. Other bidders may lose interest in the interim, and the Target may be well advised to complete the transaction with the original bidder because, even though another party may have expressed interest at a higher price, that does not mean that the other deal will necessarily be completed after the lock-up expires.

Lock-up provisions are also contained in the definitive binding acquisition agreement to protect the Buyer in the period between signing and closing. Those provisions do not simply allow the Target to wait for the expiration of the lock-up as in a letter of intent. There is, however, a substantial body of case law, particularly in Delaware, invalidating lock-ups in definitive agreements under certain circumstances, which we discuss in detail later. In essence, these cases invalidate certain types of lock-ups because the board of directors of the Target was found to have breached its fiduciary duty in allowing itself to be constrained (i.e., locked-up) in its task to find the best deal for the shareholders. In these cases, under certain circumstances the board is obligated to *shop* the Target and even to hold an auction. The board of any company, public or private, has a duty to obtain the best deal for the shareholders. But, as a practical matter, the board of a private company is given a lot more leeway since there is usually significant alignment between the shareholders and the board; indeed, the board may largely consist of members designated by the major investors, who can hardly complain about their own nominee's decisions.

While the definitive acquisition agreement is being negotiated, the Target and its counsel are simultaneously preparing the disclosure schedule that accompanies the definitive agreement. The disclosure schedule, which is described in more detail in Chapter 5, is the vehicle for the Target to take exceptions to certain of the representations and warranties in the definitive agreement and to provide the extensive list of contracts and other data that definitive agreements usually call for. The preparation of the disclosure schedule is often left to the end of the process, which can be a mistake because its preparation can raise important issues. Some Targets, however, deliberately leave it to the last possible moment so that there is no time for the Buyer to review it closely, an approach that can backfire.

In private company transactions, frequently the definitive agreement is signed and the closing takes place simultaneously. That avoids awkward lock-up issues, and the acquisition agreement can be greatly simplified by not requiring conditions to closing and preclosing covenants (including the lock-up). If not done simultaneously, the period between signing and closing can be very awkward because of potential changes in the business that may give the Buyer a chance to back out of the deal.

There are a number of reasons why the closing may need to be deferred to a date after the signing of the definitive agreement. There may be regulatory approvals required, particularly antitrust clearance under the Hart-Scott-Rodino Act; consents from counterparties to key contracts or landlords may need to be obtained; and immediate shareholder approval by written consent may not be feasible, necessitating a shareholders meeting with the required notice period or continued solicitations of shareholder written consents. Where a public company is being acquired, a proxy statement, or proxy statement/prospectus where Buyer stock is being issued, is necessary. It is a very complex document, requiring a lengthy SEC approval process. There is also a time lag to schedule the shareholders meeting to approve the deal. The HSR filing and the request for contractual consents can be done between the letter of intent and the signing of the definitive agreement, but usually the Target is reluctant to do so because it wants to keep the process as confidential as possible until a definitive agreement is signed.

If there is a deferred closing, in the period after signing the parties go about the process of satisfying all of the closing conditions, including those just discussed. Because of the delay in closing, the agreement will contain extensive covenants on what the Target can and cannot do in the interim, such as requirements to operate in the ordinary course of business. There will also be closing conditions, meaning that the Buyer (or the Target) can get out of the deal if the closing conditions are not satisfied. One of the typical closing conditions is a so-called *bring-down* of the representations and warranties. That means that the Target and the Buyer must affirm the representations that they made in the definitive agreement at the time it was signed, stating that they remain true and correct, in order for the deal to close. Since one of the representations is virtually always that there has been no "material adverse change" in the Target's affairs since a certain date, if something adverse happens to the Target after the signing of the definitive agreement, like losing a key customer, then the Buyer may be able to back out of the deal. There are also a number of technical niceties that must be concluded, involving an exhaustive list of closing documents, including opinions of counsel and the like.

One of the closing conditions that must be artfully handled is the signing of noncompete and/or employment agreements with key managers, particularly where all or many of the key managers will continue to be involved in the business. For certain types of businesses where people are an important asset of the business, like technology companies, and for certain types of Buyers, like LBO funds, that do not get involved in day-to-day management, locking up key management is an integral part of the process.

There is a delicacy in dealing with these issues before the signing of the definitive agreement because it places the management in a conflict-of-interest situation. The managers may, consciously or inadvertently, trade off price concessions on the deal for sweetened terms for their own employment. Sometimes the process is left until after the signing because time does not permit tying down the employment details, or the parties do not appreciate the risk of not doing so.

The risk of not tying down management with employment agreements before signing the definitive agreement is that if that process is deferred until after the signing, it gives a great deal of leverage to the key managers to cut great deals for themselves with the Buyer. If their employment agreements are conditions to closing, they can potentially unilaterally blow up the closing by requiring deals that the Buyer will not agree to. If a deal on

employment terms is not struck, one of the conditions to the Buyer's obligation to close will have failed. In our view, the preferred course is to negotiate
all of these agreements *after* the basic points of the deal have been agreed
and *before* the signing of the definitive agreement, and have the signing of
the employment and noncompete agreements occur simultaneously with the
signing of the acquisition agreement, with the employee agreements to be
effective upon the closing under the acquisition agreement.

The definitive acquisition agreement is discussed in more detail in
Chapter 5.

VALUATION OF THE BUSINESS

We have discussed the role of the investment banker in M&A transactions.
One of the first things that an investment banker will do is to give the client
or prospective client an estimate of what the bank thinks the business will
be sold for. It is not a good idea for any of the participants to start down the
sale path if the Target's expectations bear no relation to reality.

One pitfall is that investment bankers use financial jargon that may create a misunderstanding with the client. For one, bankers use the concepts
of enterprise value and equity value. *Enterprise value* means what a Buyer
would effectively have to pay to own all of the claims on the business, including debt, or sometimes debt less cash on hand. Another way of looking at
this is that Buyers almost always pay off the Target's debt at closing, either
because the debt accelerates (becomes due) on a change of control or because
the Buyer has a different financing strategy. *Equity value* means the value of
the stock of the company. If a bank tells the client that it thinks the enterprise
value of the business is X dollars, make sure that the parties are speaking
the same language, particularly if the Target has significant indebtedness.

Ironically, bankers disregard much of the fancy valuation theory
explored in Chapter 1. For academic purposes, it is nice to throw around
concepts like the present value of all future cash flows of the business as
being its intrinsic value. But go try to calculate that.

Bankers take a much more practical and multifaceted approach. Because
there is a lot of subjectivity in all of the valuation methodologies, bankers
usually express value as a range, meaning that fair market value is some-
where between the minimum value a seller is willing to accept and the maximum value a buyer is willing to pay. Fair market value is the range in which
informed and willing buyers and sellers would buy/sell the business.

For private companies, the valuation process is more difficult. There
is no reference public market trading price. The business may or may not
have audited financial statements. In addition, private companies often get

creative for tax purposes. There may be excess compensation to reduce income and therefore avoid double tax; business expenses and personal expenses may not be properly differentiated; and the business generally may be run without net profit maximization as a primary goal. The bank, therefore, may have to *normalize* the financial prospects of the business to better reflect the performance that the Buyer should expect.

Normalization may include adjustments other than to correct for off-market compensation and expenses. Financial statements prepared in accordance with generally accepted accounting principles (GAAP) use rigorous principles to try to do their own normalization of period-to-period revenue and expense. For example, financial statements continue to reflect expenses associated with discontinued operations after they have been discontinued and are therefore of no interest to the Buyer. In addition, if the Target's and the Buyer's operations are to be consolidated, overlapping expenses must be eliminated. So-called nonrecurring *extraordinary items* may also be eliminated.

All valuation methodologies assume that the value of a company is based solely on the financial benefits it provides to its owners, either what they would receive on liquidation or what the going-concern value would be. *Going-concern value* is the value of the business, from a financial point of view, as an ongoing generator of cash.

The principal valuation methodologies used by bankers are:

- *Relative valuation.* The business is valued based on the observable market value of comparable properties—*comparable* meaning of similar size, having similar products and a similar risk profile. Financial measures are derived from the comparable properties, so relative value examines ratios like price-to-earnings or price-to-revenue of comparable businesses and applies those metrics to the Target's business.
- *Discounted cash flow valuation.* This methodology has its parentage in the theoretical measures discussed in Chapter 1, but cash flow is usually only projected out to five years or so since beyond that the numbers are usually speculative.

Relative Valuation

Relative valuation applies valuation metrics to comparable companies. A number of different valuation metrics are used in this type of analysis. Commonly used non-GAAP metrics include, in addition to net income, earnings before interest and taxes (EBIT) and earnings before interest, taxes, depreciation, and amortization (EBITDA). Both EBIT and EBITDA represent departures from GAAP that may better reflect what the Buyer will really look at in doing its own analysis, usually cash flow. Interest and taxes might be excluded because the Buyer may not need to use debt to capitalize the business and/or may have a different tax status than the Target. For example, the Buyer may have net operating loss carryforwards that will shelter future income. Depreciation and amortization might be excluded because they are noncash measures that the Buyer might think are not relevant at least to its short- or medium-term running of the business—the key capital equipment might not have to be replaced for many years.

Also, it should be noted generally, GAAP is based on the twin principles of conservatism and historical cost. Non-GAAP measures are used to extract out or modify items that are based on these principles where Buyers may think them to be irrelevant for their purposes. For example, a business's depreciation expense may not reflect the current purchase price of necessary assets.

In some cases, even these adjusted measures are irrelevant. An example is an Internet business that is just being started and has little or no revenue. Because the business likely will have no imminent earnings or EBIT, the Buyer will be expected to value the business for its revenue growth potential. Another example is the purchase of a product line rather than an entire business. In such cases, the closest metric is enterprise value to revenue.

Another metric that may be relevant is growth rate. Rapid growth may be predictive of future cash flow increases, and that must be factored into relative valuation analysis.

Valuation multiples are then derived once these base measures are calculated and then compared to those of comparable companies:

- Enterprise value to EBITDA
- Equity value to net income
- Enterprise value to EBIT
- Enterprise value to revenue
- Equity value to book value of equity

There are several discrete approaches in the relative valuation methodology. One is *comparable public company analysis,* where a peer group of publicly traded companies is examined. There is much available data on public companies from their SEC filings, but it may be difficult to find a comparable one given the limited universe of public companies. Conceptually, when public company comparables are used to value a private company, consideration must be given to a so-called private company discount, meaning that on an individual shareholder basis, privately held stock is inherently less valuable than publicly traded securities. At the same time, control is being sold when the entire business of the Target is sold, so a premiums analysis must be made that ratchets up the value of the company for what control would be sold for. Once the public company comparables are identified, the traditional financial ratios are compiled and compared to the company being sold. Some are considered more relevant than others depending on the nature of the business.

Another approach is *comparable transaction analysis,* where recent sales transactions for comparable companies are examined and financial metrics are compared.

Discounted Cash Flow Analysis

This resembles our theoretical intrinsic value analysis, with a couple of distinctions. The discount rate is usually the Target's cost of debt and equity capital, although it is hard to understand why the Target's cost of capital should be used rather than the cost of capital of the Buyer (particularly if the expected Buyer is a public company) or of a public company comparable to the Target, or an average cost of capital for public companies generally. The discounted cash flow analysis measures what the investment is meant to return, considering the cost to finance it—but, again, the cost to whom? The cost of equity capital is a somewhat ephemeral concept because of the wide variation in the so-called price of equity (e.g., venture capital is considered to be extremely expensive because of the risk involved in early stage investing).

Also, there is a lot of guesswork even in short-term projections, so that theoretical projections out to infinity make no sense. The solution is to use several years' worth of projections, often five, and to assign a terminal value to the business as of the end of the projection period based on relative valuation analysis. The projections are also discounted for risk.

In sum, all of the valuation methodologies have only limited usefulness because of the highly subjective nature of their elements. They provide a rough estimate of a valuation range, and the data accumulated are often used in the Buyer–Target price negotiation. What a business is worth comes down to what a Buyer is willing to pay for it. It is ultimately a matter of supply and demand, and so the process by which demand is generated is extremely important. That is where the investment banker fits in, as discussed earlier.

INVESTMENT BANK ENGAGEMENT LETTERS

Both Targets and Buyers frequently use the services of an investment bank in M&A transactions. Although Targets are reluctant to pay the related fees, most experienced Targets and their advisers believe that in transactions of any substantial size, an investment bank adds net value by locating potential Buyers, assisting in pricing the transaction, assisting in negotiating the agreements, and bringing the transaction to a successful conclusion. The principles of supply and demand would suggest that generating interest results in better pricing. For public companies involved in a transaction where the board is making a recommendation to the shareholders, receipt of a fairness opinion from an investment bank is almost universal practice as a protective measure for the board. These opinions are relatively rare in private acquisitions and are obtained only if the transaction is controversial.

Selecting the investment banker is the first consideration. The knee-jerk approach is that bigger or more famous is better. Although the large investment banks generally do a highly professional job in M&A engagements, the attention they devote to any particular smaller engagement varies. If the transaction is significant in size or prominence, or if they are not busy, the service is excellent. In the opposite case, the shepherding of the transaction may be delegated to more junior and inexperienced colleagues. Our personal experience is that the depth and quality of service at the midsize and regional banks is also extremely good. In all cases, the Target should explore the commitment of the investment bank and its senior staff to the transaction, as well as relevant industry expertise and contacts.

First on the list of matters to be negotiated in engaging the investment banker is the investment banker's fee, and the appropriateness and size of a retainer. Targets should ask the banker for a list of fees they have charged in comparable recent transactions; this request is normally acceded to in a public transaction, but not in a private one.

There are a number of widely known formulas for these fees. One example is the so-called Lehman Formula, which is 5 percent of the first million dollars in deal consideration, 4 percent on the next million, and so on, scaling down to 1 percent. This formula is commonly referenced but not frequently used any more. Another variation is the Modified Lehman Formula, or 2 percent, more or less, of the first $10 million and a lesser percentage of the balance. Many would argue that the most sensible formula is one where the percentage of the consideration increases the higher the selling price, thereby providing a better incentive to maximize price and not recommend the easy deal. The breakpoint might be the price that the investment bank has indicated is a likely result—in other words, hoist the bank on its own valuation petard.

Investment banks, particularly the larger ones, typically require a minimum fee for the engagement and always request a retainer. Retainers can frequently be eliminated or significantly reduced. If there is a retainer, the Target should always attempt to have it credited against the transaction (or *success*) fee and returned if the *banker* terminates the engagement.

Expense reimbursements, which are typical, should be limited to those that are reasonable and properly documented. An overall cap should be considered on expenses, as should preapproval by the Target of expenditures above a certain size.

The investment bank's engagement letter will also provide a definition of the consideration that is in the fee base. Obviously, there is no debate that cash paid for stock or cash merger consideration is in the base. So is stock, in a stock-for-stock deal or merger for stock, valued at the trading price if public securities are issued, or by some means to determine fair market value if not. Frequently, the Target will request, if the merger consideration is other than cash, that the bank take the same form of consideration, in whole or in part, in payment of its fee. A problem remains, however. For tax or accounting reasons, frequently a transaction is structured so that the real consideration is paid in part other than for the stock or assets of the Target. For example, payments for a noncompete may be paid to all or a select group of shareholders, and above-market employment contracts may be entered into with senior management. To protect themselves from those occurrences, investment banks typically broadly define the consideration base to include those and similar items.

Another thorny issue is how to define the consideration base so that each form of transaction results in the same payment to the banker. A stock purchase or a merger essentially equates to the purchase of all assets and the assumption of all liabilities. Investment banks will usually try to use the concept of enterprise value as the fee base, in which case debt actually or implicitly assumed is viewed as separate and additive consideration.

This concept is a little hard to get a handle on. One would think that the only measure that makes sense is one that says that the banker only gets a piece of what the shareholders actually receive when they actually receive it, regardless of the form of the transaction. At minimum, if the enterprise value concept is employed, debt in that context is or should be limited to funded debt, or debt for borrowed money, and not trade debt and the like. It also should be limited to debt less cash, or net debt. This approach potentially creates anomalies. For example, the fee may differ if a company drew down on its credit line immediately prior to closing and added the money to its cash balance (at least in the case where the measure is not net debt). These potential anomalies need to be carefully analyzed.

Arguing against using enterprise value as the base is a steep uphill climb since the banker will argue that in stating its requested percentage fee, it assumed that enterprise value would be the relevant measure.

Investment banks also usually seek to be paid at closing for the total deal value, even if a portion of the consideration is deferred by being paid with notes, or is put in escrow or is contingent (e.g., an earnout). Targets should argue, again to align interests, that the bank should only be paid when the company or its shareholders actually receive cash or marketable securities. If there is other consideration, the banker should be paid on a deferred basis as well. These arguments are usually persuasive, except in the case of escrows. In that case, the investment bank argues that it should not be penalized for company misrepresentations that are charged against the escrow.

Investment banks frequently seek to expand the nature of their engagement in the engagement letter. Their boilerplate typically provides that their engagement (i.e., the matters on which they get paid) includes not only a sale of the Target but also a private minority investment in the Target or a strategic relationship. The scope of the engagement should be limited to what the Target wants to use the bank for, but, in fairness, the investment bank needs to protect itself in a situation where the nature of the transaction changes during the course of an engagement—for example, the Target decides to accept a significant investment from a potential Buyer introduced by the banker. In that case, it is hard to argue that the banker is not entitled to a fee.

If a fairness opinion is to be required, it is best for legal reasons that there be no additional consideration payable for a favorable opinion. A specific payment for a fairness opinion is to be avoided because there are court decisions that look unfavorably upon opinions that are seemingly bought, because of the built-in incentive to render a favorable opinion in order to get the fee. The engagement letter may say the banker is paid the fee even if, after its analysis, it is unable to give a favorable fairness opinion. Somehow, however, since the banker is the one that lined up the deal, a favorable fairness opinion is usually produced. If separate consideration is to be paid, Targets should request that it be creditable against the transaction fee.

Next on the list of issues is whether there should be any exclusions from the fees. A related topic is exclusivity and *tails*. Targets should always consider whether to request that certain Buyer prospects be excluded from the fee, or that sales to those prospects carry a reduced fee. If the Target has already identified and commenced discussions with a potential Buyer, then a reduced fee may be in order. The banker will argue, however, that a reduced fee is not appropriate in that case since it has lent its name and its talent to the transaction.

Similarly, where an auction or limited solicitation is to take place and the company has itself identified certain prospects, a reduced fee may be in order.

First drafts of these letters from investment banks usually say that the engagement is to be exclusive, and sometimes that the Target itself is prohibited from discussing the transaction with potential Buyers. All leads are to be referred to the investment bank. This is negotiable. In fact, the Target should seek a different procedure where the bank first comes up with a list of potential Buyers and the Target may prohibit certain prospective Buyers from being contacted by the banker.

It certainly can be argued that exclusivity makes sense in order to ensure an orderly sale process. Nevertheless, exclusivity should always be largely neutered by a clause that says that the agreement is terminable by the Target at any time and with no consideration. The investment bank will rightly argue in that circumstance that it is unfair that it does not receive any compensation for a transaction that it has worked hard on that closes after it has been terminated; in an extreme case, the Target could fire the banker immediately prior to the closing. The standard compromise in this situation is the so-called tail clause. This clause says that if an M&A transaction is concluded by the client within a specified period of time (e.g., six months or a year or more), then the banker is nevertheless entitled to its full fee. The Target should object to this because of the possibility of paying two full fees, and therefore this clause is usually further compromised by providing that the banker is entitled to the full fee only if the client is acquired under the following circumstances: An acquisition is made by a potential Buyer identified by the banker, as opposed to by the Target (and set forth on the initial list of contacts, as amended); or the Target is acquired by a Buyer as to which the banker conducted substantive discussions or negotiations on behalf of the client prior to termination (or at least that the Buyer was contacted by the banker). Alternatively or in addition, the banker would be entitled to a reduced fee in specified circumstances. In no event should the Target agree to an exclusivity clause that limits its flexibility to terminate the engagement—the Target is put at great risk if the banker is not performing up to expectations and the Target cannot appoint a replacement.

Engagement letters also contain indemnification provisions protecting the banker from Target misrepresentations or securities fraud (Rule 10b-5) lawsuits. These provisions are rarely controversial. The parties should pay particular attention, however, to the mechanics of indemnification. For example, there should be one law firm for all indemnified parties that is reasonably acceptable to the parties; the indemnifying party should control the defense; and the indemnified party's consent should be required for settlements unless it is unconditionally released from liability. Occasionally, the Target will request reciprocal indemnification from the banker. Such requests are not kindly looked upon and are not worth pressing, given that the Target will have other remedies for banker misconduct.

An investment bank's typical first draft of an engagement letter, with the Target's suggested comments separately identified, is included in the appendixes.

CONFIDENTIALITY AGREEMENTS

Other than the investment bank engagement letter, if there is one, the confidentiality agreement between the Buyer and the Target is the first document typically signed in an acquisition transaction. In acquisitions of most companies, particularly technology companies, the issue of confidentiality is extremely important and delicate. First, in order to protect its intellectual property rights, the Target must always get anyone who is to have access to its confidential information, potential Buyer or not, to sign a confidentiality agreement before its confidential information is revealed. Second, the Target must realize that even the tightest confidentiality agreement is still just a piece of paper—if the agreement is violated by a potential Buyer in a failed acquisition, that fact may not ever become apparent, and even if it is suspected, it will likely be extremely difficult and expensive to prove. Furthermore, the potential Buyer may have far more resources than the Target.

For that reason, the management of the flow of confidential information from the Target to the potential Buyer is important, regardless of what is in the confidentiality agreement. The conundrum presented is that the Buyer will not be able to set a price for the business (or even decide to buy it) until the Buyer understands better the Target's trade secrets and their value. However, the Target will not want to disclose confidential information to a potential Buyer until the Target knows that it has a price and deal terms that are acceptable, at least in principle.

How are these conflicting interests managed? First, if at all possible, the Target must make a realistic assessment of what is truly sensitive information and what is not. After the confidentiality agreement is signed, in many circumstances the disclosure process should start with the disclosure of the less sensitive material. If there are truly deep secrets, they should not be disclosed until the last possible moment, in some cases not until the closing or even after the closing. That may not be feasible, for obvious reasons. The procedure that should be followed, in general terms, is that as the transaction progresses, an appropriate level of disclosure should be made for the stage of the transaction. For example, the Target may be able to disclose enough confidential information for the Buyer to make an offer, but the deep secrets may be disclosed only after the definitive binding acquisition agreement is ready for signature (or even immediately after). If the potential Buyer is a competitor of the Target, very strict limitations on the disclosure process are essential.

Confidentiality agreements themselves are (or should be) basically simple. Lawyers love to quibble over these agreements, but sometimes too much may be made of the details. A confidentiality agreement, in essence, says two things: (1) the recipient of the confidential information from the disclosing party agrees to keep the information confidential and agrees not to disclose it to anyone other than on a need-to-know basis and then only to those who themselves have signed written confidentiality agreements that cover the confidential information to be received from the disclosing party or are otherwise legally obligated to keep the information confidential; and (2) the recipient agrees not to use the confidential information for any purpose other than in connection with the proposed transaction. The description of what types of information are confidential is often gloriously long, but there are always exclusions from the definition of confidential information that are largely standard—the information is or becomes part of the public domain, other than by misconduct of the recipient; the recipient can prove that it already knew the confidential information before disclosure; or the recipient subsequently legitimately acquires the information from a third party or develops it independently without use of the Target's confidential information (and can prove it). Another exception is information received by the recipient after it notifies the disclosing party that it no longer wishes to receive confidential information.

The following discussion deals with some of the finer points. Confidential information may be defined to include only information that is in written form and is marked "confidential," or oral information that is subsequently reduced to writing memorializing its confidentiality. This definition is good for the recipient because it limits the scope of confidential information and may prevent a dispute later on as to what information is confidential, but it is not good for the disclosing party because the disclosing party may inadvertently fail to comply with the procedure. In our view, this approach is reasonable, but for technology companies we try to insert a clause that technical information (and/or information that is customarily understood to be confidential) should be considered confidential, whether or not the foregoing procedure is followed.

One very dangerous clause that should be strongly resisted by Targets is the so-called *residuals* clause, which basically states that information that stays in the heads of the recipient's personnel can be used for any purpose. Generally, only very large companies with a lot of leverage get away with including a residuals clause in a confidentiality agreement. They make two arguments: (1) that they are so big that it is simply impossible for them to identify and quarantine information that is not in tangible form (or people who receive it), and (2) that the lack of a residuals clause leaves them, as the deep pocket in the picture, vulnerable to meritless claims. In our view, those arguments are thin and dangerously vitiate the very purpose of the confidentiality agreement. If a residuals clause winds up in the confidentiality agreement, the disclosing party should take great pains never to disclose the truly deep secrets if at all possible.

Consideration should be given to including a nonsolicitation provision in the confidentiality agreement. In other words, potential acquirers who get to know the Target's management as part of the due diligence process are prohibited from soliciting them for employment if the deal doesn't go through with that potential Buyer.

Public company confidentiality agreements also typically contain a *stand-still* provision prohibiting the Buyer in a failed acquisition from accumulating Target stock in the market or commencing a hostile tender offer.

Another often-overlooked clause is the term of the agreement. Many, if not most, confidentiality agreements contain a clause to the effect that after a specified period of time (two to five years), the confidentiality obligations no longer apply. These clauses, although common and on their face sensible, should never be agreed to if the value of keeping the information confidential may extend beyond the period specified. In some cases, an effort is made to identify certain kinds of information that should remain confidential indefinitely.

A sample confidentiality agreement for an M&A transaction is included in the appendixes.

LETTERS OF INTENT

The use of letters of intent in acquisitions is not a universal practice. Some argue that they are a waste of time—the letter of intent, because of its brevity, can never raise all of the contentious issues that appear in the definitive agreement, so the parties might as well go straight to negotiating the definitive agreement.

Letters of intent are sometimes not used where either the Buyer or the Target is a public company, particularly the Target, because of the desire to avoid premature public disclosure under securities laws. There used to be a *bright-line* test for the necessity of disclosure under the securities laws. If the parties had agreed on price and structure, then the acquisition had to be disclosed if material. A letter of intent that memorialized agreement on price and terms created a paper trail for compliance purposes. Case law has eliminated the bright-line test and substituted what is essentially just a pure materiality test based on the probability and size of the acquisition. Under that test, the existence of a letter of intent to some degree makes it more difficult to assert that the deal was at an early stage and was still not probable and therefore not material.

Companies always press to avoid disclosure until the last possible moment, and the practice has developed not to use letters of intent in public company acquisitions—not because the lack of written documentation where there is, in fact, an actual deal necessarily permits nondisclosure, but because the practice at least avoids a paper trail as a practical matter. The practice is often to do a fairly comprehensive term sheet that is not signed by the parties and that has the price blank. The parties go straight to the definitive documents and then decide the price. Under that approach, lawyers can usually convince themselves (which they call *taking a position*) that the materiality stage has not been reached. There is also support for the idea that immediate disclosure is not legally required where it would damage the business or jeopardize the negotiations, but that is a murky area.

Most view the letter of intent as useful for both parties in private transactions. Before the parties spend a lot of time and money, and before the Target lets the Buyer in on its corporate secrets, the parties want to be sure there is at least a meeting of the minds on the big points of a deal. Buyers also sometimes insist on a letter of intent because it contains a binding *no-shop* agreement, or an agreement on the part of the Target that it and its representatives will not seek, and will not enter into, discussions with another bidder for a specified period of time. Depending on the length of the no-shop, this usually is not an unreasonable request on the part of the Buyer—all the Target has to do is not shop the company for 30 or 60 days. If the Target receives a better offer, or if it is convinced that it can get one, all it has to do is to wait until the expiration of the no-shop. Conversely, because the clause is so easily avoided, one can argue that the no-shop is not of great utility to the Buyer.

Targets often resist signing a letter of intent for another important reason: that it may increase the chance that the existence of the proposed transaction will leak out. Public disclosure of the deal before the parties are ready is often disastrous to Targets because it greatly complicates their lives in their dealings with employees, customers, and suppliers. As previously noted, employees may become extremely skittish and possibly even look for other jobs; customers and suppliers may be afraid of a change in their relationship with the Target; and competitors may use the instability of the situation to their competitive advantage.

While these are real problems, they may not really be problems with the letter of intent itself but, rather, with the process. With or without a letter of intent, the existence of the acquisition negotiations may leak out, to the detriment of the Target.

This leads to another issue. As already noted, the Buyer will need to investigate the full range of the Target's operations, including its relationship with customers and the appropriateness and strength of its intellectual property, product development, and the like. This process must be carefully managed not only from the viewpoint of protecting trade secrets but also from the viewpoint of avoiding disclosure of the existence of a possible transaction for as long as possible.

A critical point in dealing with letters of intent is how much should be in them, and in whose interest is more detail. In our view, Targets generally should try to get as much detail into the letter of intent as possible. By detail, we mean all of the key economic points, including legal points that have significant potential economic impact. Because of all of the potential pitfalls of the acquisition process for the Target, often the maximum point of leverage in the deal for Targets is at the outset. The definitive agreements contain provisions that are integral to the economics of the deal—for example, the scope of indemnification, escrows, and the like. Therefore, before the Target gets very far down the acquisition path, it is likely to be in its interest to raise all of the hard issues at the outset, unpleasant though it may be.

Detail can be in the Buyer's interest as well. Some Buyers may want to save the hard issues until the deal has more momentum, given the frequently increasing weakness of the Target's bargaining position. However, the Target may not be so weak in fact, and the Buyer, like the Target, does not want to spend a lot of time and effort on the deal only to find that the Target has taken a hard line on a number of key economic issues in the definitive agreement. Also, some Targets try to argue later that because a certain Buyer-favorable provision is not in the letter of intent, the Buyer is playing unfairly by including it in the definitive agreement.

To be more precise, if one accepts this point of view, that does not mean that a letter of intent has to be long. Some letters of intent mimic a short-form definitive agreement, with extensive predefinitive agreement covenants on how the business will be run and the like. This approach usually is not really necessary. What we mean by detail here, in addition to economic issues, are those issues that are *money issues* or are likely to be contentious in the negotiations. Experienced deal makers and acquisition lawyers know that the boilerplate issues can usually be worked out. The economic and quasi-economic issues are the ones on which deals falter. These would include price, obviously, but also detail on purchase-price adjustments and earnouts if those elements are in the deal. Employment arrangements with key employees should be agreed to in principle—you do not want key employees holding up the deal. Another example would be some detail on the indemnification and escrow provisions.

A sample letter of intent is included in the appendixes.

STAY BONUSES AND OTHER EMPLOYEE RETENTION ARRANGEMENTS

In acquisitions of private companies (and in particular, in acquisitions of technology companies, public and private), in significant measure what the Buyer is buying are the people who created the products and run the business. The acquisition process creates delicate employee-retention issues. First, there is the issue of disclosure. You do not want anyone, including employees, to find out about the pending acquisition if the acquisition subsequently fails. Businesses under those circumstances often acquire a taint. Word usually leaks out at some point, however. In a technology business where everyone shows up for work in a T-shirt, legions of stiff-looking lawyers and investment bankers visiting the company can tip off the employee base that something is up—either an initial public offering (IPO) or a sale of the company.

The danger in the process is that employees may want to leave before the acquisition is completed, thereby depriving the Buyer of one of the assets it is buying and putting the deal at risk. Employees may leave for many reasons: They enjoy working for a small company and do not want to work for a big company; they feel that they are expendable—as those in administration and finance usually are—and want to get a head start on their exit; or they just do not like living with uncertainty. From the Buyer's viewpoint, such an exodus may justify cancellation or renegotiation of the deal. In some deals, there may be a purchase price adjustment pre- or postclosing if a specified number of employees quit within a certain period.

It is therefore often prudent for boards of directors to implement in advance provisions that are designed to entice employees to stay with the Target. The employees to be covered are usually the more senior employees, who will know about the potential acquisition anyway. Inexperienced boards and counsel sometimes forget to deal with this important issue. Some boards will also sometimes take the shortsighted view that they do not want to give away any of the acquisition proceeds to employees—these bonuses are often a deduction from the purchase price.

As an aside, these issues should also be thought about in connection with the grant of equity interests to employees that vest. Vesting is discussed in detail later, but for now, recognize that employees often demand that a portion of their equity vest on an acquisition and the unvested portion be restructured so that it vests after a transition period following the acquisition. The latter is likely in the interest of both the employee and the employer as a built-in stay bonus for key employees.

Stay bonus programs can be quite simple, whether in the form of a plan or separate contracts. They provide that if the employee remains with the Target until the closing of the acquisition and/or through a specified transition period (frequently six months or a year), the employee will be entitled to a specified percentage of the acquisition proceeds as a bonus, or will be entitled to a specified dollar amount of bonus.

There is a distinction between these arrangements and severance arrangements. With a stay bonus, the employee is entitled to payment if he *stays* with the Target and the acquirer; a severance arrangement pays the employee a severance when he *leaves* the company.

So-called golden parachutes are really a combined form of the two arrangements. Generally, these agreements are entered into by public companies before an acquisition is on the horizon and provide that the employee becomes entitled to a payment if, after a change of control or acquisition of the public company, the employee is terminated. There is frequently a time period for how long the agreements remain in place, say two or three years after the change of control. There are also elaborate provisions to allow employees to receive severance arrangements if they are constructively terminated (or, as it is usually phrased, terminate their own employment for "good reason"). These change-of-control arrangements must be analyzed for the potential application of the Internal Revenue Code golden parachute tax provisions, which provide for severe penalties for "excess parachute payments."

When implementing a stay bonus plan, the planners must be mindful to deal with several different scenarios, such as the following:

- The employee is fired without cause before the acquisition or within a certain period before the acquisition.
- The employee is fired with cause before the acquisition.
- The employee is not offered employment by the acquirer.
- The employee is offered employment by the acquirer but at a reduced salary and/or benefits.
- The employee is hired but is subsequently terminated with or without cause.

Added to the foregoing can be a scenario where the employee quits "for good reason"—that is, the employee is constructively terminated by a reduction in salary, change in location, or the like.

The answers to these questions must be practical—the plan should be drafted to implement its retention purpose. So if the employee sees that he can be fired the day before the closing without cause and lose the benefits of the plan, the plan will have substantially diminished effectiveness.

Another issue that arises in connection with employee retention is whether the Buyer will attempt to utilize part of the purchase price to establish, or add to, these incentives. Most acute may be the sideways sales situation where the business is being sold for less than, or not much more than, the liquidation preference of the Target's preferred stock; the employees who have common equity will be disappointed in the result. In these cases, the Buyer will frequently attempt to take away part of the acquisition price from the shareholders, particularly the investors and/or preferred shareholders, and reallocate it among the employees for incentive purposes. Similarly, the preferred shareholders may be asked to share a portion of their proceeds with the common shareholders and other employees as a group. Paying money to the shareholders as shareholders, as opposed to continuing employees of the Buyer, is money down the drain from the Buyer's point of view. But if the acquirer can use that money to enhance morale and provide retention incentives to the Target's (and soon to be its own) employees, then the Buyer has used a part of the acquisition consideration to its advantage.

These arrangements can get complicated because of a number of potential anomalies, like whether a portion of the employee incentive pool is added to the funds set aside for an indemnity escrow. The shareholders' response will be that if the employees are getting the benefit of the payments, they should share in the burden of the escrow. The employees likely will feel that this is not fair since they did not participate in the drafting and disclosures under the acquisition agreement. But the shareholders may well argue the same.

If the employee does not already have a noncompetition agreement, the stay bonus contract can serve as consideration for a noncompete agreement. The same is true for confidentiality, assignment of inventions, and nonsolicitation clauses.

A sample stay bonus plan is included in the appendixes.

BUSINESS AND LEGAL DUE DILIGENCE

The phrase *due diligence* is actually a misnomer. It was originally used in connection with public underwritings. The principal liability section of the Securities Act, Section 11, establishes a defense in securities lawsuits for misleading prospectuses for certain persons, like underwriters, if they exercised due diligence in investigating the company before selling its securities.

The term is now more broadly used to mean the investigation that an investor or a Buyer undertakes of a prospective investee or Target. The due diligence process is extremely important as it affects the Buyer's decision whether to invest in or acquire the Target, on what terms, and for what price. Due diligence may also be done on the Buyer by the Target in a transaction in which the Target's shareholders are to receive private company (and sometimes even public company) stock of the Buyer as part of the Buyer's purchase price in acquiring the Target. In effect, the Target's shareholders are buying the Buyer's stock in the acquisition and need to better understand its value through the due diligence process.

There is both business and legal due diligence:

- *Business due diligence* is the process whereby the business development and financial personnel of the Buyer, and their investment banker, examine the Target to see if the acquisition makes sense from a financial and strategic perspective and to look for any business skeletons in the closet, like a tenuous relationship with a major customer or technology obsolescence. In addition to interviews of management of the Target and their own market research, the Buyer's personnel initiate this process by giving the Target a due diligence checklist. A sample business due diligence checklist is included in the appendixes. Larger Buyers have their own extensive business development staff that will conduct the business due diligence. Smaller Buyers will rely on their senior managers, personnel at their financial backers, or their investment banker. Some investment banks and consultants offer due diligence and transition services as a separate business line.
- *Legal due diligence* is the process whereby the Buyer's in-house counsel or outside law firm, or both, examines the legal affairs of the Target to uncover any legal skeletons in the closet. Lawyers usually initiate this process, often in connection with the business due diligence, by giving the Target a legal due diligence checklist. Sometimes, rather than furnishing a full-fledged legal due diligence checklist, the Buyer will wait for the preparation of the Target's disclosure schedule (discussed in Chapter 5) and then examine the documents underlying the disclosures made. This route is sometimes taken in smaller deals, particularly where the Buyer wants to defer any legal due diligence expense until a bit later in the process. A sample legal due diligence checklist is included in the appendixes. The sample is only a starting point, and all due diligence lists should be customized to reflect any concerns with respect to the Target already developed by the Buyer and any issues that may be peculiar to the Target or its industry. If preliminary due diligence is done by the Buyer's legal team prior to the preparation of the Target's disclosure schedule, it is critical to compare the results of this inquiry to the disclosure schedule ultimately furnished by the Target.

Problems discovered in due diligence are often used by the Buyer as bargaining chips for a reduction in the previously negotiated purchase price. It is common for a purchase price to be agreed upon in advance of in-depth due diligence in the letter of intent between the Buyer and the Target, but because the letter of intent is not binding, the Buyer can attempt to renegotiate the purchase price (as can the Target, theoretically). After a certain point, Targets are usually very reluctant to abandon a deal because of the momentum that the deal has taken on, the resources expended in working on the deal, and the taint that will come from a busted deal. Knowing this, Buyers sometimes use the due diligence process in an unscrupulous way, in effect making mountains out of molehills to set up a reduction in the purchase price. Some large companies and private equity firms are reputed to make a habit of it.

As one might expect from a review of the legal due diligence checklist, there are many potential legal skeletons in the closet for any Target, ranging from the Target not legally existing as a corporation or not actually owning its intellectual property to minor tax problems and other issues that nevertheless still have a quantifiable impact on value.

Legal due diligence, when undertaken by the Buyer's outside law firm, is usually left to the more junior members on the corporate team. To an extent, it is viewed as grunt work that does not justify high hourly rates. In a sense, this is backward. Thorough due diligence is critical to a successful deal, and it is often only relatively senior lawyers who have the knowledge and experience to identify the entire range of problems that may be present. It is therefore common for due diligence to be done, in part, by relatively senior legal specialists in certain areas like intellectual property, employment law/benefits, tax law, and environmental law. Outside financial specialists may also be asked to review the financial materials provided by the Target. Where there are unaudited financial statements, the Buyer may insist that they be audited. In foreign jurisdictions, CPAs (and lawyers) may be asked to issue due diligence "comfort letters" regarding the reliability of the Target's financial statements.

What are some of the items that the Buyer's lawyers should look for to avoid bombs in the areas covered by the standard legal due diligence checklist? The following expanded list repeats items from the sample due diligence checklist in the appendix and highlights some of the more common problem areas.

Corporate Records

1. Corporate charter, as amended to date, including pending amendments.

   Does the Target legally exist?

   Does the Target have enough authorized stock to cover what it has issued or promised to issue pursuant to options, warrants, and other convertible securities?

   What are the rights associated with each class of stock? Are there any veto rights held by certain classes of stock with respect to the acquisition, and are those shareholders in favor of the transaction?

   Are there any approval procedures that vary with the governing corporate law and the Target's corporate charter (e.g., does the Target need to obtain the approval of a supermajority of its shareholders in order to consummate the transaction)?

2. Bylaws or equivalent document, as amended to date, including pending amendments.

   Do the officers signing the transaction agreements actually have the authority to sign the documents?

   Do the bylaws contain any transaction approval procedures (such as shareholder meeting notice requirements) that the charter does not?

3. Minutes and other records of all proceedings of the board of directors (or equivalent body) and shareholders of the Target.

   Do the minutes contain any discussion of problems facing the business, such as threatened suits and the like, that have not already been disclosed?

   Have the directors and officers been elected in accordance with the charter and bylaws?

   Have the minutes been regularly kept in accordance with applicable corporate law, the charter, and the bylaws?

   Have stock issuances and major corporate transactions been approved in accordance with applicable corporate law, the charter, and the bylaws?

   Do the stock records tie to board authorization of the issuance of the stock (and stock options)?

4. List of jurisdictions in which the company does business, owns or leases real property, or otherwise operates, and all foreign qualification documents.

   Is the Target qualified to do business where it is supposed to be? If not, there may be back state income or sales taxes and penalties.

5. List of subsidiaries and other entities in which the company has an equity investment, if any.

   The list of subsidiaries is an important piece of information. If the company uses a complicated corporate structure for operational, financial, or tax reasons, you will need to understand the structure and conduct the same due diligence on each entity that is material to make sure there are no hidden bombs at the subsidiary level.

Stock Records/Documents

1. Stock record books.

   Does the Target have good stock records? Is there reasonable assurance that the list of shareholders supplied by the Target is correct? If not, there could be major issues after the closing if undisclosed shareholders come out of the woodwork looking for acquisition consideration.

Does the stock ledger match the number of outstanding shares indicated in the Target's financial statements?

2. Current shareholder list, with names and addresses.

If the deal is a private placement of the Buyer's securities, how many shareholders does the Target have, and can a private placement be properly structured under securities laws?

Has the Target complied with the securities laws in its sales of securities over the past several years? Do any Target shareholders have rescission rights, particularly where they are losing money in the deal, that might be asserted after the closing?

Have all outstanding shares of stock been paid for with valid consideration? Have any shares been paid for with debt, and will the Buyer allow such debt to survive the transaction or require it to be repaid before the closing?

3. Copies of all employee stock option plans or other equity incentive plans, related agreements, and a list of all outstanding stock options, including vesting schedules, exercise prices, and dates of grant.

How are outstanding restricted stock and stock options required to be treated in the acquisition under the Target's stock plans and stock option and restricted stock agreements? Is there any acceleration of vesting on an acquisition? Are the existing stock option grants sufficient retention incentives on a going-forward basis or will the Buyer have to supplement them? Is the Buyer required to assume all options? Did the shareholders approve a plan that allows for the issuance of incentive stock options (ISOs)? Do the minutes reflect a determination by the board as to the fair market value of the common stock that is equal to each stock option exercise price?

4. Copies of any agreements to which the company is a party, relating to:

   a. A commitment to issue or sell securities
   b. Loan agreements and other debt instruments
   c. A commitment or option to repurchase securities
   d. Past issuances or repurchases of securities (debt and equity)
   e. Rights of first refusal
   f. Preemptive rights
   g. Restrictions on transfer of stock

   Do any of the Target's equity financing documents require, as a matter of contract, the consent to the transaction of particular classes of investors? Are those investors in favor of the deal? Is the Buyer going to become a party to any of these agreements upon closing of the transaction? If so, are there any representations, warranties, or covenants that the Buyer would not make? Are these agreements assignable or must an assignment be consented to by the other party?

Are there any outstanding debt obligations that have not been properly accounted for? What debt is required to be paid at the closing pursuant to the operation of change-of-control provisions?

Is the Target in default on any of its obligations, or has the Target defaulted in the past, under any outstanding debt instruments?

5. Warrants or other rights to purchase securities.

May outstanding warrants be terminated or transferred, or does the Target need to obtain the consent of the holders of the warrants? What type of leverage do such investors have that could hold up the deal or make it more costly?

Have all outstanding warrants or other rights been properly authorized in accordance with the governing corporate laws and the Target's charter and bylaws?

6. Voting trusts or voting agreements to which the Target is a party or of which it is aware.

Are there any special voting requirements that need to be met to consummate the transaction? Can the Target obtain the requisite votes or approvals?

Financial Matters/Records

1. Audited financial statements for the past three fiscal years.

Is there anything interesting in the footnotes to the audited financial statements? Are there any agreements, arrangements, or transactions disclosed in the notes that have not been brought to the Buyer's attention?

Do the financial statements show any trends (e.g., declining earnings)?

2. Most recent internal business plan.

Is the plan reasonable? Has the Target achieved its business plan in the past, or does it continuously miss?

What do management's forecasts for the business show? Are the forecasts reasonable, and is the Target on track to meet such forecasts?

Has there been any significant investment into a new line of business that has not already been disclosed?

3. Reports, studies, or appraisals on the financial condition or business of the company.

What do third parties say about the value and strength of the Target and its assets?

4. Auditors' management letters with respect to the past three fiscal years.

   Does the Target have adequate internal controls so that its financial reporting can be quickly assimilated into the Buyer's (if a publicly traded company) Sarbanes-Oxley–compliant internal control systems?

5. Latest internal financial statements.

   Has there been any unusual activity since the audited financials were completed?

   Are the financials consistent with how the Target runs its business? Are all financial transactions properly represented in the financial statements?

6. Copies of all materials sent to all directors and/or shareholders within past 12 months relating to the Target.

   Have there been any communications with the board that are not reflected in the minutes?

   Have the shareholders received proper notice under applicable corporate law of all actions taken via written consent in lieu of a meeting?

7. Tax returns and other correspondence with taxing authorities for the preceding three years.

   Have all tax returns been properly filed and all taxes paid?

   Have there been any disputes with taxing authorities? Have there been, or are there any currently pending, investigations?

   Does the Target have loss carryforwards? What will be the effect of the transaction on the ability to use those losses?

Financing Matters

1. Credit agreements, loan agreements, and lease agreements.

   Does the Target have debt that will accelerate as a result of the acquisition? What liens are on the Target's assets?

   What is the extent of the Target's outstanding obligations, and is the Buyer assuming any of such obligations?

   Is the Target in default under any such agreements, and what are the other parties' remedies?

   What are the expiration dates of the Target's real property leases? What are the Target's rights to extend or terminate?

2. Security agreements, mortgages, and other liens.

   What liens are on the Target's assets?

3. Guarantees by the Target of third-party obligations.

   Has the Target guaranteed the debts of others? Have the Target's management or shareholders guaranteed the Target's debts? Will releases of the guarantees be required to be obtained before closing?

Material Contracts, Agreements, and Policies

1. All agreements between the Target and its directors, officers, key employees, subsidiaries, or affiliates (including information regarding unwritten commitments or understandings).

   To what extent are directors and officers entitled to any bonus, severance payment, or additional equity that will be triggered upon consummation of the transaction?

   Does the vesting of their options accelerate?

   Is management a party to noncompetition/nonsolicitation agreements with the Target?

   Are there any royalty obligations to any employees?

   Do any employees have any residual rights to the Target's intellectual property?

   Are there any outstanding debt obligations owed by an employee to the Target that need to be addressed in connection with the consummation of the transaction?

2. All (a) supply agreements, (b) value added reseller (VAR) agreements, (c) distributorship agreements, (d) marketing agreements, and (e) product development agreements.

   What are the Target's rights and obligations under these contracts? Are they consistent with the Buyer's policies?

   Are there any continuing obligations of the Target under such contracts that will be assumed by the Buyer?

   Did the Target give any unusual representations or warranties in such contracts for which the Buyer will be obligated?

   What is the duration of such contracts?

   Are such contracts assignable or terminable?

   Are there any restrictions contained therein that could be problematic to the transaction (e.g., rights of first refusal or rights of exclusivity)?

3. Documentation relating to (a) investments in other companies or entities; (b) acquisitions of companies or assets; and (c) the disposition of assets.

   See item 2 in this list. Also, did the Target agree to any noncompetition covenants in the particular transaction that will be problematic for the Buyer going forward? Do these agreements apply to the Target and its affiliates? Are there lingering indemnification obligations?

4. Joint venture, cooperative, franchise, or dealer agreements.

   See item 2 in this list.

5. List of principal or exclusive suppliers and vendors.

   You will need to review the contracts with all such suppliers and vendors for the same issues identified in item 2 in this list.

6. Any document restricting an issuance of the Target's securities.

   See item 2 in this list.

7. Any standard customer terms and conditions of sale or license.

   How is the business run? What are the Target's warranty, indemnity, and other obligations, and are they being assumed by the Buyer? Are they consistent with the Buyer's policies?

8. All other material contracts, agreements, and policies.

   See item 2 in this list.

Personnel Matters

1. Employment and consulting agreements.

   Have all employees and consultants signed confidentiality and assignment of inventions agreements? Which employees have signed noncompetition agreements?

   What are the terms, including any terms relating to stock options, loans, royalties, compensation, and noncompetition?

   What is the duration of such contracts?

   Are such contracts assignable or terminable?

2. Nondisclosure, development, assignment, and noncompetition agreements with any employee, consultant, or independent contractor, and a list of employees (including former employees) who are not parties to such agreements.

   Which employees have not signed confidentiality and assignment of invention agreements, and are any of them developers of the Target's technology?

   Are these agreements in such a form that they effectively protect the Target's confidential business information and intellectual property and assign ownership of any intellectual property developments to the Target?

3. Employee benefit plans, programs, or agreements (pension, health, deferred compensation, bonus, profit-sharing, and any other benefit plans).

   What are the relevant terms of each plan or agreement? It is a good idea to get Employee Retirement Income Security Act (ERISA)—that is, employee benefits—counsel involved early in the due diligence process to review these contracts.

   Are there any golden parachute tax issues?

   Does the Target have any deferred compensation plans that might trigger adverse tax consequences?

4. Loans and guarantees to or from directors, officers, or employees.

   What are the terms? If the Buyer does not want to assume any of these obligations, what is the process, if any, to terminate them?

5. Personnel policies, manuals, and handbooks.

   Are policies documented?

   Are there any unusual policies or rules that may have come about from past problems?

   Are all such policies compliant with the law? It is a good idea to get employment lawyers involved in the review of these materials.

   Has the Target ever deviated from its own policies, creating potential liabilities?

6. Résumés for all senior management of the Target (including all vice presidents).

   Does the Buyer want to hire any of these people?

   Is there an evident lack of experience that could indicate you should look more closely for problems?

7. List of all officers, directors, and key employees, including a schedule of all salaries, bonuses, fees, commissions, and other benefits paid to such persons (or accrued) for the latest fiscal year.

   If the Buyer does want to hire these people, will it be on the same or similar terms?

   Are there requirements in employment agreements that the Buyer must keep certain employees employed for a period of time after an acquisition on the same or similar terms and, if so, are these terms acceptable to the Buyer?

8. Agreements with unions, collective bargaining agreements, and other labor agreements.

   What are the relevant terms? It is a good idea to get employment or labor counsel involved early in the due diligence process to review these contracts.

9. List of independent contractors.

   Are these people properly classified as nonemployees for tax purposes?

Intellectual Property Matters

(Note that there is a more extensive intellectual property [IP] due diligence checklist included in the appendixes.)

1. Schedule of all trademark, copyright, and patent registrations or applications, and related filings.

   Does the Target actually own what it claims to own?

2. A catalog of each computer program used by the Target in the conduct of its business.

3. All records and documentation maintained by the Target documenting the development, authorship, or ownership of its intellectual property.

   Does the Target actually own what it claims to own?

4. List of all third-party software or other items or materials (including work under U.S. government contracts) incorporated in the Target's products.

   Is there any open-source code incorporated in the Target's software products and, if so, does the Target comply with the license terms?

5. List of all agreements or understandings with third parties, whether now in effect or terminated, for the design, development, programming, enhancement, or maintenance of the Target's technology and products.

   Was all intellectual property properly developed under valid "work for hire" arrangements or assigned to the Target?

   Are there any continuing obligations of the Target under such contracts?

6. List of agreements involving disclosure or escrow of any of the Target's source code.

   How many other persons know the Target's source code? Do these agreements contain adequate protection for further disclosure and use of the source code?

7. Description of the devices, programming, or documentation required to be used in combination with the Target's source code for the effective development, maintenance, and implementation of the Target's technology and products (e.g., compilers, so-called workbenches, tools, and higher-level or proprietary languages).

   Does the Target have the legal rights to use such devices, programming, or documentation?

8. List of agreements, options, or other commitments giving anyone any rights to acquire any right, title, or interest in the Target's intellectual property or technology.

   What are the relevant terms?

   Are such contracts assignable or terminable?

9. List of unregistered trademarks and service marks.

   Are there any significant marks that the Target uses that are not registered?

10. License and technology agreements.

    What are the relevant terms?
    Are such contracts assignable or terminable?

11. All documents, materials, and correspondence relating to any claims or disputes with respect to any IP rights of the company or any of its subsidiaries or any third party.

    Is the ownership or use of the Target's IP in jeopardy?

Real and Personal Property Matters

1. List of all offices and other facilities.

   Have relevant documents been provided with respect to each facility?
   Will the Buyer want to continue to operate each facility after the closing? Can it?

2. Leases or subleases of real property.

   What are the relevant terms?
   Are such contracts assignable or terminable? If the Buyer does not want to assume a lease, what are the costs associated with termination?

3. Deeds and mortgages.

   Are there any key encumbrances?

4. Purchase or lease agreements for material equipment or other personal property.

   What are the relevant terms?
   Are such contracts assignable or terminable? Who is the lessor?

Insurance Matters

1. Summary of insurance coverage (casualty, personal property, real property, title, general liability, business interruption, workers' compensation, product liability, key person, automobile, directors' and officers' liability, and self-insurance programs).

   What are the policy limits and deductibles?
   Are there any other parties listed as additional loss payees? Are the policies assignable?

2. List of any insurance claims (whether settled or not) in excess of a specified amount since a specified date.

   Are claims outstanding that may affect the value of the Target's property or business?

3. Indemnification agreements.

   What are the relevant terms?

Legal Matters

1. Threatened or pending litigation, claims, and proceedings.

   What is the nature of the litigation? How strong is the case? What are the potential damages?

2. Consent decrees, settlement agreements, and injunctions.

   Are there any continuing obligations? Were releases obtained?

3. All attorneys' *auditors' letters* to accountants since incorporation.

   Are there any litigation or other material matters disclosed in the letters?

4. Consents, decrees, judgments, orders, settlement agreements, or other agreements to which the Target is bound, requiring or prohibiting any activity.

   Are significant or necessary activities prohibited?
   Is the Target currently complying with such restrictions? Will the Buyer or its affiliates be bound by any such restrictions?

Compliance with Laws

1. Material government permits and consents.

   Have all necessary permits and consents been obtained by the Target?
   Are such permits and consents affected by new ownership of the Target or assignable?

2. Governmental proceedings or investigations threatened, pending, settled, or concluded.

   Similar issues as with pending and settled litigation matters.

3. Reports to and correspondence with government agencies.

   Have any government agencies raised compliance issues?

4. Regulatory filings since inception.

   Has the Target properly made all required regulatory filings?

5. All internal and external environmental audits.

   Have there been any? Do any need to be done now? Are there any issues involving hazardous waste or cleanup and liabilities associated therewith?

Business Information

1. Press releases, articles, or promotional materials published about the Target since a specified date that are in the Target's possession.

   Has the Target made claims that might be unsubstantiated or rise to the level of a violation of securities or other laws? Are there any significant transactions referenced in these documents for which other documentation has not been provided and should be requested?

2. Any external or internal analyses regarding the Target or its products or competitive companies or products.

   Has the Target identified any technical problems with its products that it needs to solve? Are there any barriers (such as blocking IP) to fixing such problems or making future improvements?

   What is the Target's analysis in terms of the competitive landscape? Does its own internal analysis indicate that its products are not as far ahead of the competition as management claims (in terms of the competition's time to market)?

3. Current backlog levels.

   Compare against historical numbers. Is there a significant decrease or increase and, if so, why?

4. Copies of advertising brochures and other materials currently used by the Target.

   What claims does the Target make with respect to its business or products?

5. Budgets or projections.

   Compare against the historical financials. Does the Target have enough cash on hand, or will the Buyer have to make a large infusion of cash?

   Are the projections realistic?

6. Product literature.

   These documents may be helpful in understanding exactly what the Target sells.

   Do the Target's products seem to match the descriptions in the product literature?

INTELLECTUAL PROPERTY DUE DILIGENCE

Components of Intellectual Property: Overview

Proper intellectual property (IP) due diligence[1] involves an understanding of the fundamentals of what intellectual property rights (IPRs) are and how they are properly perfected. The following discussion explains the difference

---

[1]This section is largely taken from Ed Miller's book, *The Lifecycle of a Technology Company: Step-by-Step Legal Background and Practical Guide from Startup to Sale*, also published by John Wiley & Sons (2008). The material in this section was originally written by Howard Zaharoff and Michael Cavaretta of Morse, Barnes-Brown & Pendleton, Waltham, Massachusetts.

between different forms of IP. For each form of IP, there is a list of procedures that should be used to protect it. If IP is not properly protected by the Target, that fact may diminish the value of the Target to a prospective Buyer or may even make the Target unsalable.[2]

Intellectual property is any intangible asset that consists of human knowledge and ideas, or a real-world representation of them. The forms of IP are patents; copyrights; trade secrets; and trademarks, service marks, and trade names.

Patents   A patent is a grant from the government conveying and securing for the owner of an invention the exclusive right to exclude others from making, using, selling, offering to sell, or importing the invention.

The *right to exclude others* is a significant phrase. Unlike other forms of IP, a patent does not give anyone a right to *do* something. Rather, it merely gives the owner of the invention the right to exclude others from practicing the invention. For example, if you invented and subsequently obtained a patent on rocking chairs, and another party held the patent on chairs (upon which your rocking chair is an improvement), you would not be able to make, use, or sell rocking chairs without a license to do so from the owner of the chair patent. You could, however, exclude others (including the owner of the chair patent) from making, using, or selling rocking chairs unless they obtained a license from you.

A patentable invention may consist of a process, machine, manufacture, or composition of matter, or any improvement thereof; an ornamental (nonfunctional) design for a manufactured article; a business method; or a distinct variety of an asexually reproduced plant or organism. Printed matter, algorithms, natural substances, and scientific principles are not patentable.

For a patent to be issued, the invention must be novel, useful, and non-obvious. With respect to novelty, the United States uses a "first inventor to file" approach; that is, the invention must not have been used by others or patented or described in a printed publication before the filing of the patent application, subject to certain exceptions. Outside the United States, many countries have even more restrictive rules regarding how early a patent application must be filed. With respect to usefulness, an invention must have a beneficial use. Finally, an invention must not be obvious to one skilled in

---

[2]Intellectual property law is complex and this section provides only a brief overview. Typically, intellectual property specialists are required for a proper due diligence effort.

the relevant technology. This is often the most difficult of the three tests for a layperson to predict. Often an inventor will assume that, since the invention was obvious to the inventor, it would be obvious to others skilled in the technology. However, nonobviousness is a legal determination, and an examining attorney from the U.S. Patent and Trademark Office (PTO) may have a different view of the obviousness of an invention than its inventor. Accordingly, it is advisable to obtain input from experienced patent counsel before disregarding the possibility of patenting an invention based on its presumed obviousness.

Another potential bar to patentability in the United States stems from recent court decisions finding some subject matter ineligible for patenting, for instance because an invention is too abstract. The test for subject matter eligibility continues to evolve, but as of this writing many computer-implemented patents have been recently invalidated essentially because they are alleged to be directed to abstract ideas.

A trap for the unwary can arise from early publicity or sales efforts related to innovation. Often this occurs when a company's marketing or business development departments are anxious to publicize a product in advance of its launch or when inventors describe the invention in academic publications or at trade shows. This publicity may prevent later obtaining patents.

A patent is issued to the inventor of the subject invention, unless the inventor has expressly assigned or is under an obligation to assign his rights in and to the invention (e.g., to an employer under an employment agreement) or if there is an implied assignment (e.g., where an employee was hired to invent). Where an assignment (express or implied) is not found, but the inventor utilized the employer's resources to develop an invention, the employer is given a *shop right*—a nonexclusive, nontransferable right to practice the invention. In such a case, the inventor retains ownership of the patent rights in the invention.

A U.S. patent, and thus the right to exclude others from practicing the subject invention, continues from patent grant until 20 years from the filing date of the patent application. This period may be extended by the PTO for delays in PTO processing and, if applicable, U.S. Food and Drug Administration (FDA) approval, for example. To protect their patents, businesses should consider at least the following. If the Target has not done them all, there are due diligence concerns:

- Require all employees and consultants to enter into invention assignment (and nondisclosure and noncompete) agreements.
- Educate staff using policies, handbooks, and training.

- Require all technical/inventive personnel to keep dated notebooks/logs of inventions.
  - Require that all entries in notebooks/logs be written in permanent ink, and prohibit tampering with or destroying notebooks/logs.
  - Require that all pages in the notebooks/logs be witnessed and dated by someone other than the inventor.
- Require invention disclosure forms.
- Conduct periodic legal and technical review of possible inventions.
- Involve experienced patent counsel at least three months before using, selling, offering to sell, or publicizing inventions.
- Apply to protect potentially valuable innovations.
- Use notices on products relevant to issued/applied-for patents: "Patent No." or "Patent Pending."

Copyrights Copyright protection subsists in original *works of authorship* fixed in any tangible medium of expression. Works of authorship may include literary, musical, dramatic, pictorial, graphic, and sculptural works; motion pictures and other audiovisual works; sound recordings; architectural works; and other works fixed in tangible form. This may include a company's software, as well as its documentation, technical drawings, website, advertising, marketing materials, white papers, research reports, and databases.

Copyright protection does not extend to any idea, procedure, process, system, method of operation, concept, principle, or discovery, regardless of the form in which it is described, explained, illustrated, or embodied in a work of authorship.

With respect to originality, a work is *original* if it owes its creation or origin to the author, which, in turn, means that the work must not be copied from another source. Thus, original creation is a defense against a claim of copyright infringement, even if the second work happens to be identical to or substantially similar to the first work.

The owner of a copyrighted work has the exclusive right to do, and to authorize others to do, any of the following with respect to the copyrighted work: reproduce, prepare derivative works, distribute, publicly perform, and publicly display.

A copyright is owned by the author of the work upon its creation, unless it is created in the scope of the author's employment or pursuant to a written work-made-for-hire agreement. Regarding the latter, because an independent contractor is not an employee, the contractor would own the creative work unless otherwise agreed to in writing. Accordingly, a company should enter into a written agreement with each party it engages to develop creative works that expressly assigns to the company all rights in and to such works. Since, technically, a work-made-for-hire agreement is effective only for the nine specific types of works delineated in the Copyright Act (none of which are of the type most likely to be created for most companies, including software), it is not sufficient for a development agreement to simply recite that the work is a work made for hire; rather, it must expressly state that all rights in and to the work are assigned to the company.

Copyright rights extend for the life of the author of the work plus 70 years. In the case of a work made for hire, copyright rights extend for the shorter of 95 years from the date of publication or 120 years from the date of creation.

Copyright registration is not required for copyright protection; rather, copyright protection is automatic. That is, as soon as an original work of authorship is fixed in a tangible medium of expression, the work is protected by copyright. However, in the United States, registration is a precondition to the filing of a copyright infringement action in federal court, and it also affords certain benefits to the owners of copyright registrations. Specifically, the owner of an infringed copyright work may be entitled to statutory damages plus attorneys' fees. Additionally, if it occurs within five years of publication of the work, registration acts as prima facie evidence of the validity of the stated facts (including the date of creation of the work). Copyright registration is inexpensive—registration fees are nominal and, as the copyright registration process is largely ministerial, attorneys' fees are nominal as well.

To protect their copyrights, businesses should consider taking the following steps. If the Target has not done them all, there are due diligence concerns.

- Use copyright ownership/assignment agreements with employees and (especially) contractors.
- Educate staff on the importance of the company's copyrights and other IP.
- Include copyright notices on all significant original works, including software, manuals, and advertisements.
- Similarly mark all Web-posted or publicly distributed works.
- Obtain copyright registration for valuable works, especially those likely to be infringed (e.g., consumer software or lyrics to a song).

Trade Secrets Trade secrets consist of valuable and confidential business information. One widely used definition of a trade secret is found in the *Restatement of Torts* published by the American Law Institute (ALI):

A trade secret may consist of any formula, pattern, device or compilation of information which is used in one's business, and which gives him an opportunity to obtain an advantage over competitors

who do not know or use it. It may be a formula for a chemical compound, a process of manufacturing, treating or preserving materials, a pattern for a machine or other device, or a list of customers.
(Restatement of Torts § 757, comment b)

Additionally, on May 11, 2016, President Barack Obama signed the Defend Trade Secrets Act (DTSA) into law, providing federal remedies for trade secret violations, among other things. Trade secrets may include any of the following, whether patentable or not: ideas, inventions, discoveries, developments, designs, improvements, formulae, compounds, syntheses, know-how, methods, processes, techniques, product specification and performance data, other data, computer programs, business plans, marketing and sales plans, research and development plans, manufacturing and production plans, pricing and other strategies, forecasts, products, financial statements, budgets, projections, licenses, prices, costs, customer and supplier lists, the terms of customer and supplier contracts, personnel information, and compilations of such information.

Ideas, in and of themselves, are neither patentable nor copyrightable, and to be afforded protection against their use by others, they must be protected as trade secrets or confidential information. Moreover, trade secret protection is in some ways superior to the protection afforded by copyright or patent because the subject remains—by definition—secret. To obtain a patent, an applicant must disclose the best way to practice the patent. Copyright prohibits copying of the copyright owner's work, but in itself does not provide for the confidentiality of the work.

Trade secret rights are neither conveyed by a grant from the government (like patent rights) nor do they arise as a result of the creation of a work (like copyright rights). Rather, trade secret rights arise as a result of the value of the information and the maintenance of its secrecy. Specifically, in most states, confidential business or technical information is protected as a trade secret if it is not generally known in the industry, it has value (i.e., it gives its owner a competitive advantage) in part because it is not generally known, and it has been the subject of reasonable measures to maintain its secrecy. Reasonable efforts to maintain secrecy are often cited as the most important element of a valid trade secret. The *Restatement of Torts* sets forth the following factors as those that must be considered in determining whether particular information is a trade secret:

- The extent to which the information is known outside the owner's business

- The extent to which it is known by employees and others involved in the owner's business
- The type of measures taken by the owner to guard the secrecy of the information
- The value of the information to the owner and to competitors
- The amount of effort or money expended by the owner in developing the information
- The ease or difficulty with which the information could be properly acquired or duplicated by others

Like patent protection, trade secret rights permit the owner to exclude others from using or maintaining control over the trade secret, if the secret is learned improperly. A trade secret is misappropriated if it is knowingly taken or used without authorization from the owner. Trade secret misappropriation remedies may include substantial damages and injunctive relief.

It is not misappropriation if a secret is discovered through independent creation and rightful discovery. Specifically, it is legally permissible to discover a trade secret by obtaining a product and reverse-engineering it. However, many products are obtained not by purchase but by license, and many licenses (including most software licenses) include provisions prohibiting the user from reverse engineering the product. Such prohibitions are generally enforceable under law except there is a carve-out for interoperability purposes in the software arena (but not necessarily elsewhere; for example, a European Union Directive ensures certain reverse-engineering rights that can't be waived by contract in EU member states).

Employers own the trade secrets developed by their employees (at least those paid to create information). As with patents, courts may also award shop rights.

Trade secret protection continues until the information is no longer secret. Thus, a trap for the unwary disclosing party is entering into a nondisclosure agreement of limited duration. Receiving parties often try to limit the duration of nondisclosure agreements to a finite period of time after disclosure, typically three to five years, for administrative as well as liability limitation purposes. Disclosing parties routinely enter into such agreements without much thought. However, once the nondisclosure covenant expires, it can be argued that the information disclosed is no longer protected as a trade secret vis-à-vis the receiving party or any other party.

Although the legal fees involved in the protection of trade secrets are generally low to moderate, the total cost to the client of maintaining its trade secrets could be quite high, given the proactive conduct required by the client, as recommended in the following list.

To protect their trade secrets, companies should consider doing at least the following. If the Target has not done them all, there are due diligence concerns.

- Perform predisclosure due diligence on prospective partners and employees.
- Use nondisclosure agreements and exit interviews with employees and contractors.
- Enter and enforce noncompetition agreements with key employees.
- Consider nonsolicitation (no employee poaching) agreements when contracting with competitors or others in closely related fields.
- Limit access to those who need to know.
- Respond to raids on employees by competitors.
- Destroy (shred) unnecessary media containing trade secrets.
- Control access to computers and networks.
- Screen potential business partners, vendors, and customers for legitimacy and reputation.

For highly sensitive materials:

- Keep under lock and key.
- Limit copying, number copies, and keep distribution and disclosure records.
- Where appropriate, require passwords.
- Mark all confidential materials as "Confidential" and use more elaborate notices where appropriate (e.g., for business plans).
- Avoid marking nonconfidential material as confidential.

Trademarks A trademark includes any word, name, symbol, or device, or any combination, used or intended to be used in business to identify and distinguish a company's products or services from products and services sold by others, and to indicate the source of the products and services. In short, a trademark is a brand name. For the purposes of this discussion, the terms *trademark, service mark,* and *mark* will encompass both trademarks and service marks. A trademark may be virtually any kind of symbol, including a word, letters, numbers, a tag line, a design, a shape, an object, a sound, a telephone number, a domain name, a color, or a smell.

Trademarks should not be confused with trade *names.* While a trademark designates the source or origin of a product or service, a trade name designates a company or entity. For example, the name Xerox, when used in the phrase "Xerox copiers," is a trademark, whereas when used in the phrase "Xerox makes the best copiers," it is a trade name.

Trademark law is founded on the right of the owner of a mark to protect and profit from the goodwill represented by the mark. Trademark law permits the owner of a trademark to exclude others from using the same or a confusingly similar mark in connection with identical goods or services, or goods and services that are so closely related to the owner's goods and services that confusion in the market is likely. Trademark rights are territorial; use in commerce gives rise to rights at common law in the geographic region where the mark is used, whereas federal registration affords national rights without respect to where the trademark owner actually used the mark.

Additionally, if the goods or services are not so closely related that confusion is likely, but the mark is famous, the owner may be entitled to exclude others from using the mark (or a similar mark) under the theory that the other party's use of the mark dilutes the strength of the mark—in other words, the other party's use blurs or tarnishes the mark.

The strength of a mark depends on whether it is generic, descriptive, suggestive, arbitrary, or coined. A generic mark is one that is the thing itself, such as the mark *water* for the product water. You can never obtain trademark protection for a word that is generic. A descriptive mark is one that conveys an immediate idea of the qualities or characteristics of a product or service, such as *Good Juice.* You cannot obtain trademark protection in a descriptive mark unless it has obtained *secondary meaning* (i.e., it has been used in such a way that, while its primary significance in the minds of prospective purchasers remains the quality or characteristic of the product or service, a secondary significance in the minds of prospective purchasers has developed that serves to identify the source of the product or service). A suggestive mark is one that requires thought, imagination, and perception to reach a conclusion as to the nature of the product or service, such as *Veryfine.* Suggestive marks are of moderate strength. Arbitrary or fanciful marks are ordinary words used in an unusual way, such as the mark *Apple* for computers. Arbitrary and fanciful marks are very strong. The strongest of marks are coined marks, which are original, made up, or fabricated words, such as *Xerox.*

Trademark rights arise under common law based on use in commerce, so federal or state registration is not required. However, registration does afford a mark owner certain valuable benefits. Federal registration provides prima facie evidence of the validity and ownership of the mark, and of the exclusive right to use the mark throughout the United States in connection with the goods or services identified in the certificate of registration. It also acts as constructive notice throughout the United States of the mark owner's claim, permits the owner to establish incontestability after five years of continuous and exclusive use, can serve as a basis for obtaining registration in foreign countries, and may be registered with the U.S. Customs Service to assist in preventing illegal importation of counterfeit goods. Federal trademark registration also permits owners to invoke the jurisdiction of the federal courts and may entitle owners to recover damages and costs from infringers' profits, including treble damages and (in exceptional cases) attorneys' fees.

For owners unable to obtain federal registration (e.g., if they are unable to satisfy the federal "use in interstate commerce" requirement), state registration may be beneficial. State registration is generally easier to obtain and provides some of the same benefits as federal registration (albeit only within the borders of the state) and can also act as a useful form of notice.

Trademark rights can be lost if the mark is abandoned or becomes generic. Abandonment can take place when the mark is no longer used, when an attempt is made to assign the mark without its attendant goodwill, or if a mark owner licenses the mark but fails to maintain adequate quality control over the goods or services in connection with which the mark is used. A mark can become generic when it starts to be used by the general public to describe the goods or services themselves, as opposed to their source or origin. For example, the *Aspirin, Cellophane,* and *Escalator* marks were once protected but have since become so widely used by the general public to identify not the source but the thing itself that the marks are no longer protected. Xerox Corporation spends a lot of time and energy educating the public that the term *xerox* is not a synonym for *copy* but is, rather, a brand—by, for example, publishing notices to this effect in newspapers.

Common law trademark rights are indefinite in duration; they last until the mark is abandoned or becomes generic. Federal registration initially lasts 10 years but can be renewed indefinitely.

The costs of obtaining and maintaining a federal trademark registration are moderate. As of May 31, 2016, the filing fee was $325 for electronic filing and $375 for paper filing per mark per class. Legal and third-party search fees for clearance, filing, and prosecution are typically on the order of $2,000 to $4,000.

To protect their trademarks, companies should consider doing at least the following. If the Target has not done them all, there are due diligence concerns.

- Perform a clearance search before adopting a mark—check marks, business names, domain names, and website content.

- If possible, federally register the mark based on use or intent to use.
- Provide trademark notices: ® for federally registered marks, ™ or ᔆᴹ otherwise.
  - Can use footnotes to identify trademarks.
  - Federally registered marks: "Registered in the U.S. Patent and Trademark Office" or "Reg. U.S. Pat. & Tm. Off."
  - Other marks: "X is a trademark of Acme Corp."
- Use the mark properly. Trademarks should always be used as proper adjectives. Specifically:
  - They should be capitalized or italicized or in some way stand out from the surrounding text.
  - They should be used as a proper adjective modifying a generic term—for example, "Pampers® disposable diapers" and "Xerox® photocopy machines."
- Adhere to proper licensing practices; in particular, no uncontrolled licenses.
- Squelch infringement.
- Online:
  - Monitor the Internet, domain names, paths, and metatags for infringement.
  - Consider reserving marks as domain names (and vice versa).
  - Consider reserving marks under other available top-level domains (e.g., *.org*, *.net*, and foreign national top-level domains).

IP Due Diligence

Intellectual property due diligence essentially consists of making sure that the Target has properly perfected its IPR, that it has followed the procedures suggested in the preceding text, and that there are no infringement issues. There are a few recurring items of note. An extensive IP due diligence checklist appears in the appendixes to this chapter.

Some general questions include the following:

- Have proper confidentiality and invention assignments been obtained from all employees and contractors?
- Has the Target been careful in structuring its cooperative development arrangements as to the ownership of IP arising from the arrangements?
- Are the Target's licenses assignable, and are there change-of-control provisions that might affect the surviving corporation's rights under those licenses?

Patent Due Diligence Well-advised companies usually have appropriate assignment-of-invention clauses in their standard employee documentation. What is often missed, however, is having those same assignment clauses in their contractor agreements and even in the agreements that the contractor uses with its subcontractors.

Inquiry should be made as to whether all of the inventors were named as such on the Target's patent applications. Failure to do so could result in unnamed co-inventors jointly owning the patent.

If the Target offered products incorporating the invention for sale or otherwise publicized them before filing a patent application, U.S. patent rights may have been jeopardized if the publication took place more than a year before filing. It would also jeopardize foreign rights if an application was not filed before any publication.

Inquiry should obviously be made to determine whether the Target's products might infringe third-party patents.

Copyright Due Diligence Have nonemployee authors assigned their rights to the Target? If not, the Target may not own that IP. Remember that copyright protection is the principal vehicle used to protect software code.

Regarding software, inquiry must be made as to whether any of the Target's software code incorporates so-called open source software. If so, the terms of the open source license applicable to that code will require, to varying degrees, that all related code developed by the Target be offered for free as open source code under the applicable open source license.

Trade Secret Due Diligence Have the Target's employees misappropriated trade secrets from prior employers?

Has the Target taken appropriate steps to preserve and protect the Target's trade secrets?

Trademark Due Diligence The Buyer's counsel should check the Target's website and marketing materials to make sure that the Target identifies its trademarks as such, and that they are not used generically.

FROM SIGNING TO CLOSING

As discussed earlier, there are multiple reasons why the parties cannot, or will not, sign and close the acquisition agreement at the same time. These reasons are principally the need for shareholder approval of the deal, third-party consents, and the need for regulatory clearances, particularly antitrust clearance under HSR.

So what do the parties do in the period between signing and closing of the acquisition? First, the parties and their respective counsel assign to someone the responsibility to make sure that they are prepared to satisfy the conditions to closing. The Target's shareholders will be solicited for their approval of the acquisition. Normally, as a matter of good corporate practice at a minimum and also as may be required under the securities laws, the Target's shareholders will be furnished with a formal or informal proxy statement soliciting their approval. In a public company, this is an elaborate process that requires complex filings with the SEC; these are discussed in Chapter 6. In a private company, as discussed in Chapter 3, in a stock deal if some of the solicited shareholders are not *accredited investors* under the securities laws, a detailed proxy statement must also be furnished. In a cash deal for a private company, the usual practice is to furnish a less elaborate proxy statement containing a description of the material terms of the deal.

During this period, if the deal and the parties are large enough, the parties must prepare their respective filings under HSR and/or foreign antitrust laws.

In addition to satisfying the shareholder and regulatory closing conditions, a plethora of other tasks are required to be performed either as a legal matter or as a matter of customary practice. Necessary third-party consents and bank payoff letters will be solicited. Closing documents, such as certificates of good standing from state authorities, officers' certificates, and legal opinions of the Buyer's counsel and the Target's counsel, will be prepared and agreed on.

To organize this process, the Buyer's lawyer will prepare a *closing agenda* that lists all of the tasks required in connection with the deal. A sample merger closing agenda is contained in the appendixes.

APPENDIXES

The following appendixes are located on the website that accompanies this book. For information on the website, see the "About the Website" section at the back of this book.

Appendix 2A, Investment Bank Engagement Letter with Target's Comments

Appendix 2B, Confidentiality Agreement

Appendix 2C, Letter of Intent

Appendix 2D, Stay Bonus Plan

Appendix 2E, Business Due Diligence Checklist

Appendix 2F, Legal Due Diligence Checklist

Appendix 2G, IP Due Diligence Checklist

Appendix 2H, Merger Closing Agenda

CHAPTER 3

Corporate (Nontax) Structuring Considerations

BUSINESS OBJECTIVES AND OTHER NONTAX STRUCTURING CONSIDERATIONS

Structuring acquisitions is like piecing together a puzzle or solving simultaneous equations. There are multiple structuring parameters, many of which conflict with one another. A solution that at least satisfies the deal breakers of both sides has to be found for the transaction to proceed, and if it is to proceed, then the solution must be optimized for the other parameters. The most important parameter is tax because the taxation of the parties has a substantial impact on the economics of the transaction. Tax considerations are discussed in detail in Chapter 4.

Before a deal is structured, detailed information about the Target and the Buyer, as well as basic deal economics, must be compiled for analysis. This information and the largely nontax reasons it is important address these questions:

- What is the form of the acquisition consideration—cash, Buyer stock, Buyer notes, earnout, or other? The Target's shareholders may want to cash out in whole or in part; the Target's shareholders may want or need to obtain tax-free treatment; and the Buyer may or may not have enough cash to do the deal.
- Does the Buyer want to acquire only selected assets? Does the Buyer have to acquire only selected assets because those assets are in a division of the Target and are not part of an entire business that is operated out of a separate legal entity? Are the Target's assets so numerous that a transfer of all assets is impractical because of the complexity and risk of delay?

- Does a transfer of the Target's assets trigger sales taxes that are prohibitive? Does the Buyer want to (or does the Target insist that the Buyer) assume all, none, or some of the Target's liabilities? Does the Target have such nasty actual or contingent liabilities that the Buyer will not do the deal unless it can escape responsibility for those liabilities?
- Are any of the Target's contracts so unfavorable as to make a deal impractical unless those contracts can be avoided or otherwise dealt with?
- Is there a need to accomplish the deal quickly for business reasons, like the Target is approaching insolvency, or because the Buyer fears an offer from a rival bidder?
- Are the parties public or private companies? Assuming they are private companies, what is the composition of the Target's shareholder base? Are there many shareholders? How many are sophisticated or accredited investors under the federal securities laws? That information is needed to determine whether a stock deal can be done in compliance with the federal securities laws; a large number of unsophisticated/unaccredited shareholders may make a stock deal impossible to structure as a private placement.
- What is the Target's corporate structure? Does it have subsidiaries? Is it a corporation and, if so, is it a Subchapter S corporation? Is it a limited liability company (LLC)? What kind of outstanding securities does the Target have? Do its outstanding classes of stock have class votes on an acquisition? Does anyone, like venture capital or private equity investors, have a veto over an acquisition? From a tax-planning viewpoint, what is the Target's basis in its assets? What is the fair market value of its assets? Does it have net operating loss carryforwards (NOLs)? Does it have corporate, individual, and/or tax-exempt shareholders? What is their tax holding period and basis in their Target stock?
- Are all of the Target's shareholders agreeable to the deal? Are there so many that it is impossible to tell at the preliminary stage? If all shareholders are supposedly agreeable, are there too many to make it practical for all of them to sign a stock purchase agreement? Are some opposed, such that a stock purchase structure will not get the Buyer 100 percent ownership of the Target (other than combined with a squeeze-out merger)? Does the Buyer insist on eliminating all of the Target's minority shareholders, or does the Buyer want certain shareholders, like Target management, to retain an equity interest?
- Does the structure create appraisal rights for the Target shareholders under applicable state law such that dissidents can initiate a court proceeding to appraise the value of their shares? Does the existence of this right create too much uncertainty for the Buyer, or jeopardize a

tax-free structure, because too much cash may be required to be paid at a later stage?

- Do the Target's material contracts prohibit assignment, such that an asset transfer/assumption of liabilities will trigger the need to obtain counterparty consents? Are those counterparties likely to hold up the deal in order to extract price or other commercial concessions in their contract? Will the Target's debt be accelerated as a result of the acquisition structure, either because of a change of control covenant or debt covenants that will be breached by the surviving corporation? Will stock options or other incentive equity interests in the Target be accelerated so that the Buyer will have to provide new ones that effectively increase the acquisition price?

Residual Minority Interest

One structuring parameter is that Buyers usually want to wind up with 100 percent of the outstanding shares of the Target. The reason is that they do not want to deal with the extensive body of law that has accumulated on the fiduciary duties of boards of directors and possibly majority shareholders to minority shareholders. If minority shareholders remain in place after the acquisition, the Buyer will have to pay more attention than it wants to in order to ensure that any loans or other intercompany transactions between itself and the Target it now owns are fair to the minority shareholders and are on arm's-length terms. That may sound like no big deal, but transactions between a parent and its subsidiary are rarely structured at arm's length—they are structured to be for the benefit of the collective enterprise. Also, funds flow is restricted from a subsidiary with minority shareholders to its parent because if the subsidiary wants to pay a dividend to the parent, it must also pay a proportional amount to the minority shareholders, which may not be desirable from a corporate finance viewpoint. If the Buyer is to acquire 100 percent of the outstanding equity in the Target, then it must get all shareholders (and maybe option holders, if the Target's stock option plan is poorly drafted) to sign a stock purchase agreement or use a merger structure to squeeze out the dissident shareholders, either as the first step in the acquisition or as a second step following a stock purchase from selected Target shareholders (preferably achieving a majority position to guarantee a favorable merger vote).

As previously noted, an asset purchase structure must be used if there is no corporation to buy—such as the purchase of a division of a larger company or the purchase of a product line. Asset purchases have become relatively rare, other than in connection with the purchase of a division or product line, because of the double tax problem discussed elsewhere.

Deferred Closings

An additional strategic consideration is that the agreed-upon deal may be upset by a rival bidder after the acquisition is announced. The only totally effective way to avoid this possibility is to sign and close the transaction simultaneously before the deal is announced—a simultaneous signing and closing. This is possible, as a practical matter, only for private companies, and even then it is not always feasible.

One way to effect a simultaneous signing and closing is to have all of the Target's shareholders sign the stock purchase agreement, with the closing to occur immediately after signing. That may not be possible, for a number of reasons:

- The transaction needs to be structured as a merger requiring a shareholder vote, and it is not feasible to obtain the shareholder vote immediately. Thus, a deferred closing is necessary where the acquisition agreement is signed and the closing is deferred until the requisite shareholder vote can be obtained.
- The transaction requires regulatory approval, and each party wants to sign an agreement to bind the other, with the closing deferred until regulatory approval can be obtained.
- The form of the transaction is a merger, and the Buyer does not want to close until it determines how many shareholders, if any, desire to exercise their appraisal rights. The exercise of appraisal rights throws a wrench into the deal because the Buyer, if it proceeds, will have to incur the expense of the appraisal proceedings and the ultimate cost of the payout ordered by the court (unless it has provided in the acquisition agreement that the Target's shareholders have to share some or all of this burden). The successful exercise of appraisal rights will require the Buyer to pay a portion of the acquisition consideration in cash, which it may not have or may not want to pay. In addition, the exercise of appraisal rights can destroy the tax-free nature of certain acquisition structures because no, or a limited amount of, cash can be paid in that form of a tax-free transaction.

In the acquisition of public companies, a deferred closing is necessary because, at minimum, shareholder approval must be obtained via the Securities and Exchange Commission (SEC) proxy statement process. The period between signing and closing in public deals creates a risk that a rival bidder will upset the deal between signing and closing. As is discussed in detail in Chapter 6, to deal with that problem merger agreements contain various deal-protection devices (like no-shops and voting agreements) to discourage rival bidders. The courts have set limits on what is permissible, such that it is essentially impossible now to totally lock up a deal, even where it may be theoretically in the interests of both parties.

One technique that has emerged because of these factors is a two-step acquisition, where stock is purchased, ideally a large block from the Buyer's point of view, and that step is followed by a *squeeze-out merger*. Alternatively, the acquisition agreement can be structured as a first-step tender offer followed by a squeeze-out merger. The reason for doing this instead of a traditional one-step merger is that tender offers can be launched and closed more quickly than mergers because mergers require SEC approval of the proxy statement that needs to be sent to the Target's shareholders, and a shareholders meeting with the requisite statutory notice must be held only after SEC approval of the proxy statement is obtained. Tender offers (or exchange offers where the consideration is stock rather than cash) can be launched immediately and closed relatively quickly, although the gap between the various techniques has been narrowed.

Need for Consents

Another structuring consideration is the need to obtain consents from counterparties to contracts of the Target or from government entities. Commercial contracts generally prohibit the contract from being assigned by one party without the consent of the other party. An asset purchase structure will require an assignment to the acquiring corporation of the contract rights of the Target under the particular contract. The need to obtain these consents creates the possibility of delays and also creates the possibility of a holdup by the other contracting party, who attempts to extract some monetary or other commercial concession as the price for its consent, or who even refuses to consent.

One way the need for consents can sometimes be avoided is by doing a stock purchase. In a stock purchase, because the party to the commercial contract in question (i.e., the Target) is not really a party to the acquisition transaction, it remains in place only with a change of ownership, and generally is not considered to be assigning its contract rights for purposes of requiring consents from counterparties. To avoid this loophole, some contracts require consent for an assignment and also give the counterparty termination or other rights in a change-of-control transaction—in other words, an acquisition by stock purchase or any form of merger.

Similar to a stock purchase in this regard is what is known as a *reverse triangular merger*, which sounds sophisticated but is really quite simple. Most mergers are structured as subsidiary mergers; that is, the Buyer forms a new corporate shell subsidiary that is the corporation that merges with the Target. One reason for this approach is that the Buyer may be able to avoid having to obtain approval of the merger from its shareholders. Literally, the merger statutes require approval by the shareholders of the two *merging* corporations. In a subsidiary merger, the shareholder approval relating to the Buyer can be that of the Buyer itself since it, not its shareholders, is the shareholder of the merging (subsidiary) corporation. (Note that there are also stricter stock exchange requirements for shareholder approval.)

In a subsidiary or triangular merger, if the acquisition subsidiary (or *acquisition sub*) merges into the Target, it is called a reverse triangular merger, and if the Target merges into the acquisition sub, it is called a *forward* triangular merger. Just as in a stock purchase, a reverse triangular merger is not generally considered as involving an assignment of the Target's contracts; in a forward triangular merger, an assignment is generally considered to occur since it is a new corporation that becomes a party to the contract. Forward mergers are sometimes required for tax reasons because the tax-free qualification requirements are less stringent than for reverse triangular mergers. In a cash deal, forward mergers are never used because they are taxed like an asset deal with double tax. Although reverse mergers are generally considered not to constitute assignments of contracts, there is some contrary case law, particularly in the area of patent rights.

Misrepresentations and Indemnification

Another significant structuring parameter is how Buyers can protect themselves from misrepresentations by the Target about its business. We will explore that topic in more depth in Chapter 5, but two basic techniques are used: indemnification and escrows.

Indemnification means that the Target's shareholders agree to pay the Buyer for any damages that the Buyer sustains that relate to a misrepresentation or contractual breach by the Target. An *escrow* means that a portion of the purchase price is set aside in a bank escrow account and is not payable immediately to the Target's shareholders. The escrow serves as a source of reimbursement of the Buyer's damages from a misrepresentation or breach.

If not all shareholders sign the stock purchase agreement, how do you get all shareholders to pay their fair share of any damages? This is important from both the Buyer's and the Target's shareholders' perspectives—the Buyer wants as many sources of reimbursement as it can get, and each of the Target's shareholders only wants to bear its proportionate share of any liability. One method by which recourse is obtained against all of the Target's shareholders is by a merger where a portion of the proceeds owing to each of the Target's shareholders is put into escrow as part of the terms of the merger agreement. So post-closing protection for the Buyer from all the Target's shareholders is another reason to do a merger over a stock purchase where all shareholders do not sign the stock purchase agreement. Indemnification and escrows are generally applicable only in private Target stock purchases and mergers.

In an asset purchase, the Target itself is the seller, and the selling corporation (which could be public or private) may thus be the only source of indemnification. If the Target is selling all or substantially all of its assets and plans to distribute the proceeds to its shareholders, what is left as a source of reimbursement to the Buyer for damages that the Buyer sustains as a result of the Target's misrepresentation or breach? In this situation, where the entire business is being sold and the proceeds are being distributed to the Target's shareholders, well-advised Buyers require the Target's shareholders to sign indemnification agreements as a source of indemnification or insist on an escrow. Even where the proceeds are not being distributed, Buyers may still want to obtain from the seller's shareholders guarantees of the seller's indemnification obligations.

Liability Avoidance

If the Buyer wants to avoid liabilities of the Target, it cannot merge with the Target. In a merger, the surviving corporation will inherit all of the Target's liabilities, actual and contingent, as a matter of law.

In a stock purchase or a triangular subsidiary merger, the Buyer does not become directly responsible for the liabilities of the Target; those liabilities remain in a subsidiary. As a practical matter, however, the Buyer indirectly inherits these liabilities since its consolidated assets are subject to the claims of the Target's creditors; in other words, the Buyer possibly could walk away from the business of the Target, but that would entail writing off its investment in the Target. Plus, if the Target's business, as conducted as a subsidiary of the Buyer, has become integrated into the Buyer's business, then the Buyer writing off its investment in the Target and letting it dissolve would entail significant business costs in addition to the cost of writing off its investment. Nevertheless, for the avoidance of direct responsibility by the Buyer of the liabilities of the Target, acquisitions are structured as subsidiary mergers or stock purchases, all else being equal. Of course, the Buyer may become directly responsible for the liabilities of its subsidiaries, including the Target, if corporate formalities are ignored and the doctrine of piercing the corporate veil applies.

One possible way to avoid the Buyer or its acquisition subsidiary becoming liable for the Target's debts is to purchase the Target's assets and assume no liabilities of the Target, or just specified liabilities. Although that works in theory, often it does not work in practice if any of the Target's creditors get shortchanged. For one, there are fraudulent conveyance and transfer laws, discussed in detail in Chapter 7, that may allow the Target's jilted creditors to sue the successor corporation. There are equivalent bankruptcy provisions. There are cases supporting successor liability and the *de facto merger* doctrine that are discussed in a subsequent section of this chapter. There are also *bulk sales* laws in some states that create a form of successor liability unless creditors are given notice of the sale; sending out bulk sales notices is an invitation for interference with the deal and is rarely done. In short, if an acquisition is done, and, as a result, some of the Target's creditors get shortchanged, a lawsuit becomes a distinct possibility, whether justified or not, including putting the Target into bankruptcy. These laws and supporting case law make such a lawsuit a real risk for the Buyer, in addition to the time and expense of the defense.

Certain liabilities of the Target are particularly daunting in the acquisition context. These risks are both potentially huge and also may not surface until many years after the acquisition and long after the indemnification provisions have expired:

- If the Target was part of a consolidated return group for tax purposes, the Target remains responsible for the taxes of its parent and the other corporations in the group.
- A similar situation exists in the Employment Retirement Income Security Act of 1974 (ERISA). The Target can remain liable for certain ERISA liabilities of its former ERISA group members. Other members in the new ERISA group of which the Target is now a part can be liable for the Target's ERISA liabilities (and vice versa).
- Environmental liabilities are potentially enormous, and the reach of environmental laws is broad, applying not only to owners of property or actual bad guys but also to subsequent operators of property who are not culpable. Consider the situation of the software company occupying a floor in a high rise that was built on a toxic waste dump. Technically, that company has a contingent environmental liability, even though that liability likely is remote. Because of the reach of the environmental laws, due diligence to find potential liabilities is very difficult. Such due diligence often includes an environmental assessment by outside environmental consulting firms.

Appraisal Rights

In mergers and sales of substantially all assets, state law allows shareholders who do not vote for the deal and who follow certain specified procedures to decline to receive the acquisition consideration and instead seek an appraisal of their shares requiring a cash payout in a state court proceeding. The exercise of appraisal rights, however, is relatively rare. Generally, the dissident who is a small shareholder does not want to spend the time and money to pursue the appraisal remedy, and all dissidents do not want to risk getting paid a *lower* price. In private company acquisitions, the big shareholders usually have contractual veto rights, and those deals generally do not get done if one or more major shareholders do not approve. If the exercise of appraisal rights is a concern, a condition to closing may be that no one, or a specified low percentage of shareholders, exercise their appraisal rights, with the closing deferred until that percentage is determined.

Sale of Control at a Premium

Generally speaking, shareholders can vote their shares or sell them as they see fit. There is some evolving law in the area of fiduciary duties of shareholders, but fiduciary duty issues generally are limited to the board of directors. There is a line of cases, however, that limits the ability of a controlling shareholder to sell its shares at a premium over market. Such a premium is available because, from a corporate finance point of view, shares with a controlling interest are worth more. It is still unclear, however, what, if any, restrictions apply to a controlling shareholder other than in the case where the controlling shareholder knows or has reason to believe that the Buyer will loot the corporation to the detriment of the remaining shareholders. In light of this uncertainty, sellers of a controlling interest are frequently advised to require a covenant pursuant to which the Buyer is obligated to offer the same deal for the stock of the minority.

Substantially All Assets

Most state corporation statutes require a shareholder vote for transactions involving a sale or transfer of all or substantially all of the corporation's assets. Under the leading case law, "substantially all" does not mean the obvious—all assets minus a few insignificant ones.

In the leading case in the area, *Gimbel v. Signal Companies,* the court considered four factors in making a determination as to whether the deal involved substantially all assets. The assets sold were analyzed against (1) percent of total assets sold; (2) percent of net worth; (3) percent of consolidated revenues; and (4) percent of consolidated earnings. Just before undertaking its analysis, the court summarized the rule as follows:

> *If the sale is of assets quantitatively vital to the operation of the corporation and is out of the ordinary and substantially affects the existence and purpose of the corporation, then it is beyond the power of the Board of Directors.*

The court effectively applied both a quantitative test and a qualitative test when analyzing whether assets transferred constituted "all or substantially all" of a company's assets. The qualitative analysis involves the courts asking such (vague) questions as: Does the sale make it impossible to run the business? Does the sale strike at its core assets or business, or represent the destruction of the means to accomplish the corporation's purposes or objectives? Are the assets sold "vital" to the corporation's operation? Is the sale out of the ordinary course, or does it substantially affect the existence and purpose of the corporation? If the answer to any of these questions is yes, a court might well require shareholder approval, and a corporation should consider carefully the risk of proceeding on a board vote alone.

As for the quantitative tests, a critical question in cases involving sales of assets is the correct valuation of the assets. Generally, under Delaware law, book value is not always a significant consideration; rather, the value of an asset may be determined by analyzing the asset's revenues and earnings potential, market value, and directors' estimates of value.

Whether shareholder approval in these circumstances is required is governed by the applicable state corporation statute and the cases interpreting it. The takeaway here is that substantially all does not simply mean substantially all in the common sense meaning of the words.

ACQUISITION STRUCTURE DIAGRAMS

As previously discussed, there are three basic ways to structure an acquisition: (1) stock purchase; (2) merger; and (3) asset purchase. There are also various kinds of merger consideration—cash, stock, and notes. Exhibits 3.1 through 3.12 depict a number of the possible variations on structure.

FORMS OF ACQUISITION CONSIDERATION

There are multiple possible forms of acquisition consideration. The type of consideration that is agreed to is based on the resources of the Buyer, the business objectives and necessities of the parties, and the tax consequences applicable to the different forms of consideration.

The Target's shareholders, particularly in a private company, may want liquidity for what may well be a significant portion of their net worth, but the Buyer may want the Target's shareholders, particularly management and employees, to have a continuing interest in the success of the business via holding Buyer stock. The Target's shareholders may want cash, but the Buyer may not have enough cash to do an all cash deal.

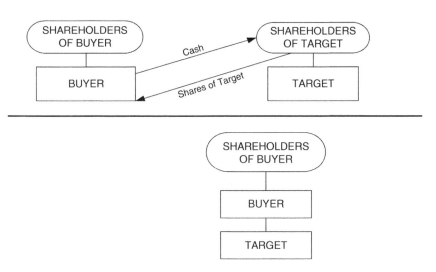

EXHIBIT 3.1 Stock Purchase of All Shares for Cash

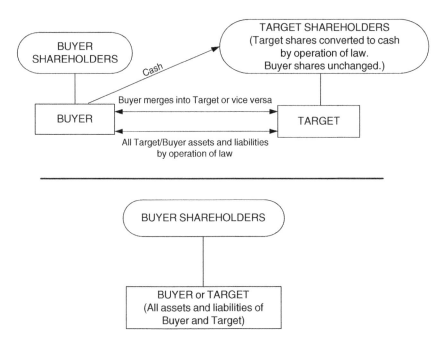

EXHIBIT 3.2 Direct Merger for Cash

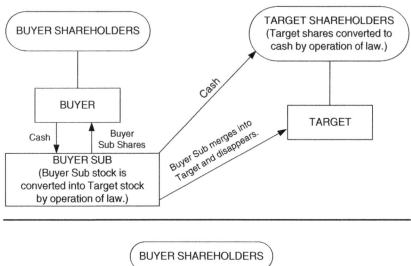

EXHIBIT 3.3   Reverse Triangular Merger for Cash

The Target's shareholders may want to defer recognition of gain for tax purposes and take the Buyer stock in a tax-free reorganization, either because some people have a deep aversion to paying taxes or because they are elderly and want to get a step-up in basis for their heirs without ever having to pay income taxes on their gains, but the Buyer may be a private company that does not want any additional shareholders. The Target's shareholders will want to receive all of the deal consideration at closing; in contrast, the Buyer of a private company usually requires that a portion of the deal proceeds be placed in escrow as a source of indemnification against misrepresentations or breaches by the Target or the Target's shareholders

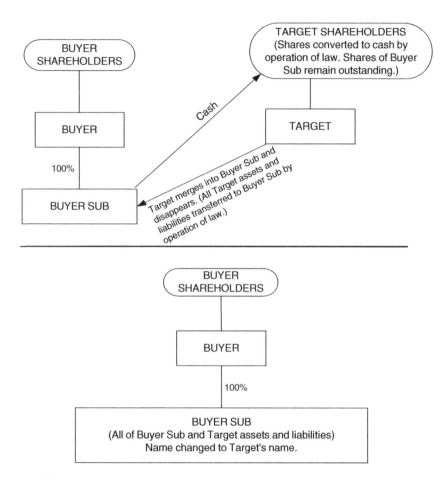

EXHIBIT 3.4 Forward Triangular Merger for Cash

in the acquisition agreement. (Indemnification and escrows are discussed in detail in Chapter 5.)

The Buyer and the Target may not be able to come to an agreement on price because the Buyer simply does not believe the Target's optimistic projections of the future financial performance of the business. To hoist the Target by its own petard of overly optimistic projections, the Buyer may suggest that a portion of the consideration be deferred in the form of an *earnout.* In an earnout, specified additional consideration is to be issued to the Target's shareholders after the closing, depending on whether the acquired business achieves specified performance objectives.

Possible forms of acquisition consideration include:

- Cash or other property paid by the Buyer, or paid by the Target in a redemption of a shareholder's stock or as a dividend.
- Debt, which can be senior or subordinated, secured or unsecured, have contingent payment features, have fixed or variable interest, be convertible into equity, and/or have varying payment schedules.
- Stock, which can be preferred or common, voting or nonvoting, participating or nonparticipating, redeemable, convertible, and/or exchangeable for another security.
- An earnout, whether payable in cash or stock, which is consideration paid after the closing based on the achievement by the Target of specified performance measures.

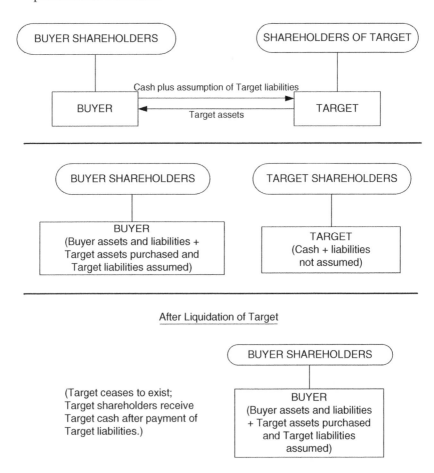

EXHIBIT 3.5   Asset Purchase/Assumption of Liabilities for Cash

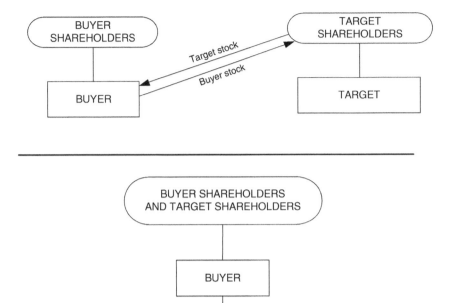

EXHIBIT 3.6 Stock-for-Stock Acquisition via Stock Exchange Offer

- Warrants to purchase Buyer stock at a fixed or variable price.
- Contingent value rights (CVRs), which provide a guarantee of the future value as of a point in time of one of the other forms of acquisition consideration, usually common stock of a public company.

We will begin a deeper exploration of these forms of consideration by looking at debt.

DEBT

Debt instruments are highly variable, and the variations produce widely different economic effects. The tax consequences to the Buyer and to the Target's shareholders are complex and are discussed in detail in Chapter 4. For example, there are a number of circumstances where the interest on debt issued in an acquisition is not deductible to the Buyer, and certain forms of debt may be subject to the original issue discount (OID) tax rules or may or may not qualify for installment sale treatment.

The debt can be issued by the Buyer, the Buyer's parent if the Buyer is an acquisition subsidiary, or by the Target. Payment can be a *balloon* payment, meaning payment of principal is not required until the debt matures. An alternative is for principal to be paid yearly or at other intervals, with interest on the outstanding principal being paid monthly, quarterly, or at other intervals. *Zero coupon debt* does not require the payment of principal or interest until maturity; because of the lack of stated interest, these instruments are issued at a discount, giving rise to OID. Payments can be structured like a home mortgage with level periodic payments to maturity; in this case, the portion of the payments attributable to interest decreases over the life of the debt. Interest can be paid in cash or other property.

One common technique is *payment-in-kind* (PIK) debt instruments where payment, at the issuer's option, is made in cash or added to the principal amount. The debt may or may not be prepayable before its stated maturity date (or perhaps prepayable with a premium or a prepayment penalty). Debt may be either straight debt or debt with equity features in

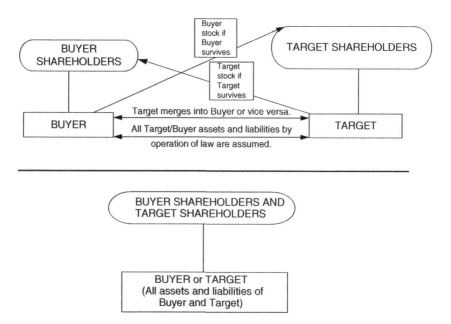

EXHIBIT 3.7   Direct Merger for Stock

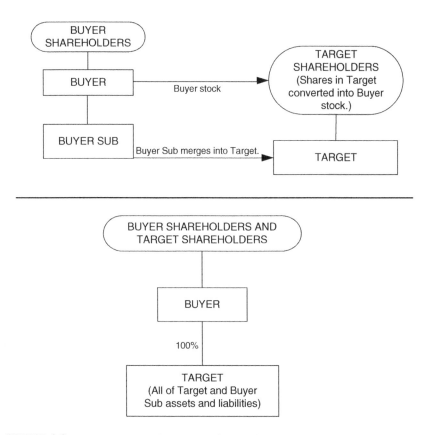

EXHIBIT 3.8   Reverse Triangular Merger for Stock

the form of being convertible into common stock or with accompanying warrants to buy capital stock.

Debt is used in acquisitions because it can enhance the return on the equity invested in the acquisition. Use of debt is a subset of the "other people's money" (OPM) game. If a portion of the purchase price comes from debt, the Buyer's return on equity (ROE)—that is, the return on its own equity investment—will increase if the value of the Target increases by more than the interest rate on the debt. If that were always the case, the best strategy would be to borrow as much of the purchase price as possible. But because of the fixed payments required by debt instruments, leverage increases risk. However, if the debt is *nonrecourse*, meaning the lender can only look to the assets or business financed and not to the other assets of the Buyer, then the lender will have borne a portion of the Buyer's loss in the

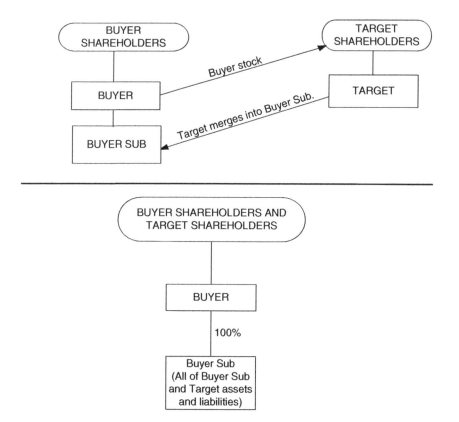

EXHIBIT 3.9   Forward Triangular Merger for Stock

sense that the Buyer would have borne all of the loss if the Buyer had used only its own money to fund the purchase price.

The loan can be made nonrecourse to the Buyer by limiting the remedy of the lender to foreclosing only on the assets of the Target, or by having a subsidiary of the Buyer incur the debt secured by the stock of the Target with no guarantee by the Buyer, or by having the Target incur the debt with an intermediate subsidiary guaranteeing the debt. Of course, there is no recourse to the assets of the investors in the Buyer/borrower unless the lender requires guarantees of the debt from them.

From the lender's point of view, lenders always want to lend to the assets, meaning that if the debt goes into default they have a direct security interest in the *assets* of the Target rather than an interest in the assets of the parent of the Target, particularly where the *parent* is a holding company with few or no assets other than the stock of the Target. In the case where the

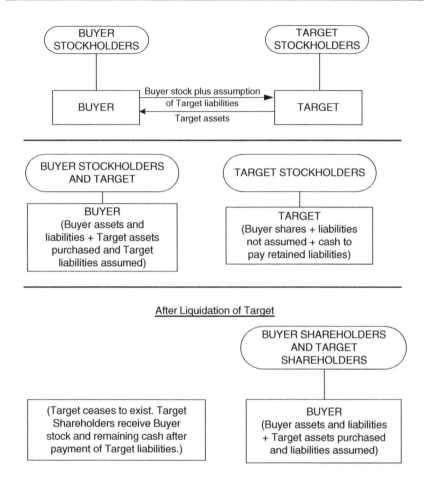

EXHIBIT 3.10   Asset Purchase/Assumption of Liabilities for Stock

Buyer/borrower is a holding company and the lender only has a security interest in the stock of the Target held by the holding company, the lender effectively can only access the assets of the Target if all of the Target's creditors have been paid. This is called *structural subordination*. Lenders also will try to get as much credit support as they can for the debt, including guarantees of the debt from other parties in the picture, such as investors, subsidiaries if the borrower is the parent, and the parent if the borrower is the subsidiary.

Use of leverage is not simply a matter of comparing the ultimate return on equity, but also a matter of carefully analyzing the expected cash flow of the business to be reasonably sure that there is enough cash generated to

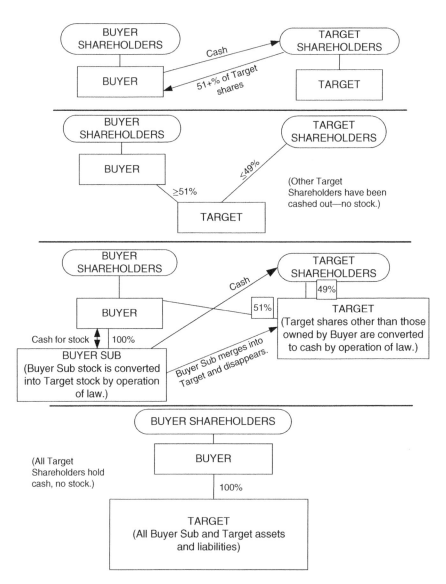

EXHIBIT 3.11   Squeeze-Out Merger: Stock Purchase for Cash Followed by Cash Merger

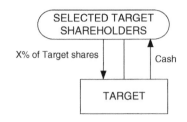

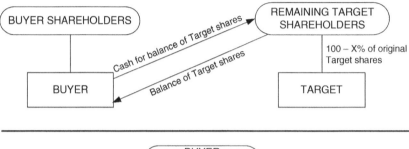

EXHIBIT 3.12 Direct Redemption Plus Sale

service the debt payments. That is the only way to properly manage the risk that using debt creates. Lenders would not lend the money otherwise. The business could be nicely increasing in value but not generating sufficient cash to pay its debts. If that were the case, perhaps the Buyer could refinance the business by, for example, raising more equity at a good valuation because the business is doing well. However, it is not that simple. The increase in value of the business may be unclear, or additional financing may not be available for multiple reasons, or may not be available soon enough to keep the lenders at bay.

Another advantage of the use of leverage is that the government, in effect, pays part of the acquisition price. Subject to certain limitations, interest paid by the Buyer or the Target on debt is deductible and reduces the borrower's tax burden. If equity were issued by Buyer instead to finance the acquisition, the dividends would be taxable to the Buyer's and/or Target's shareholders and would not be deductible by the Buyer or the Target. In order to accommodate various levels of risk tolerance and return expectations, some debt instruments can have equity features and some equity instruments can have debt features, making the characterization of the financing transaction subject to uncertainty as to its tax treatment. Multiple tax code sections deny deductibility for debt, including those relating to certain subordinated acquisition debt, certain high-yield or junk-bond debt issued at a discount, and debt where the interest is required to be paid in equity. Debt can also be recharacterized as equity in circumstances where the ratio of debt to equity is extremely high.

The identity of the borrower can affect the tax treatment of the cash paid to the Target's shareholders. If the Target is the borrower, or if the Buyer is the borrower but the Target's assets are the real credit support for the loan, the cash may be characterized as a payment by the Target rather than a payment by the Buyer. That could possibly result in the payment being characterized as a dividend rather than sale proceeds.

There is additional explanatory material in Chapter 4 on the tax aspects of debt and equity used to finance an acquisition.

Subordination Terms and the Analysis of the Risks of Holding Debt

In addition to the obvious economic terms just discussed, the riskiness of debt is also measured to a significant degree by the ranking or seniority of the debt achieved by securing the debt or by issuing subordinated debt. *Rank* means who among the lending creditors gets paid first on liquidation. By *liquidation,* we mean that the debtor goes under and voluntarily distributes its assets to its creditors and to its shareholders if anything is left, or the debtor voluntarily or involuntarily is put into bankruptcy and the distribution takes place under the jurisdiction of the bankruptcy court. If one class of debt is entitled to be paid before another, it is *senior* and the other class is *junior.* If two classes of debt are of equal rank, they are called *pari passu* with one another. The ranking of debt is determined by whether it is secured debt, which party in the corporate chain issues the debt, and by the contractual provisions of the debt itself, which may be contracts between the debtor and the lenders or contracts directly between lenders, known as *subordination agreements* or *intercreditor agreements.*

In a complicated private company capital structure (say, following a leveraged buyout), the following tiers of capital may be present:

- Senior secured debt
- Subordinated secured debt
- Senior unsecured debt (someone has debt subordinated to yours)
- Senior unsecured subordinated debt (not a contradiction in terms—you have debt subordinated to someone else's debt and someone has debt subordinated to yours)
- Subordinated debt (frequently convertible into common stock)
- Preferred stock
- Common stock

So how do lenders (including the Target's shareholders receiving Buyer debt) assess risk associated with debt? Lenders assess risk based on a borrower's balance sheet—its assets and liabilities, and the excess of liabilities over assets (or *shareholders' equity*). Shareholders' equity combines the cumulative amount of the company's past earnings with the proceeds of the issuance of capital stock. Lenders also assess risk based on the borrower's income statement and statement of cash flows (i.e., the borrower's ability, on a reasonably predictable basis, to generate earnings and cash flows sufficient to repay the debt).

The safest loans, all else being equal, are *asset-based,* which means debt secured by (i.e., having a lien on) the assets of the borrower, including accounts receivable and inventory. The amount that can be borrowed under a typical asset-based line of credit is a specified percentage of the *borrowing base* of *eligible accounts receivable* (i.e., receivables that appear to be collectible and not delinquent) and inventory. The debt terms that the borrower receives (interest rate, etc.) are a function of perceived risk by the lender. Risk is based partly on anticipated performance by the business and the tier that the debt is in. Lenders like a lot of debt underneath them in a lower tier, such that the borrower is *well capitalized.*

Both senior lenders and junior (subordinated) lenders attempt to mitigate risk by debt covenants and rights to accelerate the scheduled payment of the debt on default. That is necessary because the interests of the equity holders and the holders of the debt diverge; equity holders and debt holders make different trade-offs on risk versus growth. Sample debt covenants include limits on the amount of other debt that the borrower can incur; a prohibition on dividends to equity holders; no prepayments of other debt, particularly junior debt that serves as a cushion for the senior debt;

a prohibition on granting liens to other debt holders; a prohibition on the issuance of debt of equal or greater rank; the maintenance of specified financial ratios or measures of financial health; and no transfers of assets to subsidiaries, which would create structural subordination. Events of default include nonpayment of the debt when required, a breach of the debt covenants, defaults (*cross defaults*) on other debt, and sometimes a material adverse change in the business.

Subordinated debt is debt that gets paid after debt that is senior to it first gets paid in full. Subordination can be created by the junior creditor entering into a subordination agreement with the senior creditor. Subordination also can be part of the terms of the note or other debt instrument that the junior creditor receives even before senior debt is issued. This latter approach is used, for example, in situations where the borrower does not have any senior debt but expects to have some in the future and wants the current issue of debt to be subordinated to unspecified future debt. This works fine and binds the junior creditor, but where the senior creditor is identified at the time the junior debt is issued, the senior creditor usually will insist that the junior creditor sign a subordination agreement directly with it.

Creation of Debt Tiers   So how are debt tiers created other than by subordination? You can agree to subordinate your debt to another creditor's and another creditor can agree to subordinate its debt to yours; but you can't subordinate another creditor's debt to yours other than by getting a senior security interest in the assets of the borrower.

A borrower and its creditors can make one class of debt senior to other classes of debt by securing the debt with a security interest in the assets of the borrower. Unlike subordination agreements, which are fairly complicated and involve a range of issues other than mere rank in liquidation or bankruptcy, a security interest does not affect any of the actual terms of the junior debt other than its rank in the absence of a subordination agreement. So if there is secured debt and no subordination agreement, the junior creditors can, for example, sue the company if their debt is not paid. Subordination agreements frequently prohibit that course of action because senior creditors believe that it gives the junior creditors too much control over a deteriorating situation.

In a corporate structure that involves subsidiaries, there is, as we have said, also something called *structural subordination*. What that means is that if a creditor lends money to the parent in a parent–subsidiary structure, in a liquidation scenario the creditors of the subsidiary, no matter how junior, are all senior to all of the creditors of the parent because the only way the creditors of the parent can get their hands on the assets of the subsidiary is via a distribution of a dividend to the parent in respect of the stock it holds in the subsidiary. Because that stock is junior to all forms of debt in liquidation, the creditors of the parent are structurally subordinated to the creditors of the subsidiary. Creditors try to circumvent structural subordination by having the subsidiary guarantee the parent's debt, thereby creating creditor status directly vis-à-vis the subsidiary. These arrangements can be effective, but may be overridden in bankruptcy or otherwise by fraudulent conveyance and transfer laws and similar provisions of the bankruptcy code that are designed to protect creditors from maneuvers like this one where the subsidiary is conferring a benefit on its parent without consideration or without adequate consideration to the detriment of the subsidiary's creditors.

There is also a concept in bankruptcy called *equitable subordination*. Equitable subordination arises in situations where, because of a creditor's inside status or where there is abusive behavior by the creditor, the court "equitably subordinates" the otherwise senior or pari passu debt to other debt of the company or even subordinates it to equity.

To understand better how subordination works in bankruptcy, it is helpful to lay out the sequence of the distributions to creditors out of bankruptcy. First, the secured debt is paid or otherwise taken care of. The balance, if any, is then distributed to the unsecured creditors pro rata to the amount of debt owed to them. Then, if there are subordination agreements in place among the debt holders, the junior creditors turn over their payouts to their respective senior creditors until those senior creditors are paid in full. There is senior subordinated debt, which is simply debt that is senior to one or more classes of debt in a company and is also subordinated or junior to yet other classes of debt in the same company (i.e., even though the debt in question is junior to someone else's debt, there are other debtors who have debt that is subordinated to such debt in question). This is all a bit over-simplified because in bankruptcy there are tiers and priorities created by the bankruptcy laws.

One of the more confusing disclosures used in public subordinated debt financings is the following customary sentence, which hopefully will be meaningful at this point.

> *By reason of such subordination, in the event of insolvency, [unsecured] creditors of the Company who are not holders of Senior Indebtedness of the Company may recover less, ratably, than holders of Senior Indebtedness of the Company and may recover more, ratably, than holders of the [subordinated] Notes.*

Other Aspects of Subordination

There is much more in a subordination agreement than the liquidation priority provisions. The reason for this complexity is that in a situation that has

An Example of a Turnover Balance Sheet

$600,000 in assets
No secured debt
$500,000 in senior debt
$500,000 in subordinated debt
$500,000 in trade debt
Who gets what?

Senior debt gets $400,000: $200,000 in the initial allocation pro rata among all creditors and $200,000 in turnover from the subordinated creditors.

Subordinated debt gets nothing. The subordinated debt holders had to turn over everything until the senior debt was paid in full (which it wasn't).

Trade debt gets $200,000: $200,000 in the initial allocation and no obligation to turn anything over because this debt is not subordinated.

become precarious from the creditors' point of view, the senior lenders want to have a lot more control than simply waiting for a liquidation or being forced to initiate one.

There are three principal issues dealt with in subordination agreements: (1) priority in liquidation; (2) *payment blockages*; and (3) limitations on the right to "pull the plug" or *remedy bars*. Again, that is why merely getting a security interest in the assets of a debtor is often not sufficient in the eyes of the senior creditor. The senior creditor wants a subordination agreement even though it does not need one to have priority in liquidation, but it also wants the control represented by payment blockages and remedy bars.

One of the more hotly debated terms in a subordination agreement is the terms under which the subordinated debt can get paid out either prior to or at maturity. In *deep subordination* or *complete subordination,* the subordinated debt can get paid out only when the senior debt has been paid in full. Obviously, senior creditors love this, and get it when they hold a very strong hand. More common, however, are provisions that provide that the junior debt can get interest paid to it by the borrower (and sometimes interim principal payments and sometimes payments on maturity) but only if there is *no default* or *event of default* on the senior debt. These last two terms mean that there is no actual default in the senior debt, or any "event which with the giving of notice or the passage of time would become a default." Another, less restrictive, form is that no payments can be made to the junior debt "upon the maturity of the senior debt, by acceleration or otherwise," until the senior debt has been paid in full. That means that the junior debt can receive its normal payments even if there is a default or an event of default, but would not receive these payments if the senior debt exercises its remedies and *accelerates* or calls due the senior debt.

Where the junior debt has some cards to play, the junior creditors argue that this blockage from getting paid after a default on the senior debt should not be allowed to last forever—the senior creditor has to *fish or cut bait* after some period of time. That is, if the senior creditor does not accelerate the debt for some period after a default gives it the ability to do so, say six months, then the payment blockage goes away.

A related concept is the so-called *remedy bar.* A remedy bar is a provision that says that a junior creditor may not receive normal payments upon a default or whatever provision in that regard was negotiated, and also that it cannot exercise its legal remedies and sue the borrower for failure to pay. In other words, even though the junior creditor has agreed that it will not be paid and will turn over anything it gets to the senior creditor, that does not mean that it has waived its right to sue the borrower. It could sue and pay over part or all of what it collects to the senior creditor. Senior creditors usually insist on remedy bars because it gives them more control over a deteriorating situation—only the senior creditor can *pull the plug* while the borrower and its creditors are trying to work their way out of the mess.

Some debt indentures or other debt documents have a clause that essentially acknowledges that there are no remedy bars agreed to, even though the junior creditor is subordinating its debt to the senior debt in liquidation. Here is another confusing clause from a debt document that now hopefully will make sense.

> *These provisions are solely for the purpose of defining the relative rights of the holders of Senior Debt, on the one hand, and Subordinated Debt, on the other hand, against the Company and its assets, and nothing contained herein shall impair, as between the Company and a holder of Subordinated Debt, the obligation of the Company, which is absolute and unconditional, to perform in accordance with the terms of the Subordinated Debt, or prevent the holder of Subordinated Debt, upon default thereunder, from exercising all rights, powers and remedies otherwise provided therein or by applicable law, all subject to the rights of the holders of Senior Debt under this agreement to receive cash, property or securities otherwise payable or deliverable to the holders of the Subordinated Debt.*

Debt with Equity Features Debt can also be structured to give the holder the best of both worlds—the security, relatively speaking, of a debt instrument over an equity interest plus the ability to participate in the increase in value of the business by providing that the debt may be converted into stock of the issuer of the debt instrument. Debt can also be issued together with warrants to purchase stock of the issuer of the debt instrument. One advantage to the holder of debt with warrants is that the debt can be repaid with the holder still retaining its equity interest via the continuing exercisability of the warrants. In convertible debt, the holder has a choice—debt or the stock that is issued on conversion of the debt. This type of debt is called *mezzanine debt,* and equity features are often associated with subordinated debt to compensate for the extra risk that subordinated creditors take.

CASH, STOCK, AND EARNOUTS

Acquisition consideration can take a number of forms other than debt.

Cash

Cash is rarely unwelcome to the Target's shareholders in an acquisition. The cash can come from the Buyer's cash on hand, from the Target's cash on hand, from borrowings by one or both, or from the issuance of new equity by the Buyer. In a stock acquisition, cash from the Target is likely to be treated as a redemption of shares. In an asset deal, for the Target's shareholders, cash from the Target received on liquidation of the Target should be liquidation proceeds; if the Target is not liquidated, the cash would be redemption proceeds if shares are actually purchased, or a dividend otherwise.

Stock

Stock of the Buyer is frequently used as acquisition consideration and has to be used to at least a certain extent if the transaction is to qualify as tax-free under the reorganization provisions of the tax code.

Where Buyer stock is issued, the principal elements of such stock are rights to dividends, voting rights, rights upon liquidation or sale of the company, rights to redemption (automatic, or at the option of the holder or the issuer), and conversion to equity features.

Stock can be voting or nonvoting, or it can be nonvoting that becomes voting upon the occurrence of certain events, like the failure to declare and pay dividends over a specified period, failure to redeem the stock when due, or default in the equivalent of debt covenants. Voting arrangements can be effected through provisions of the corporate charter, or by private voting agreements among the principal shareholders, which require them to vote in certain ways (like electing specified directors, including representatives of different constituencies, or if any of the specified events occur).

The two basic forms of capital stock are preferred and common stock. Preferred stock has the preferred right to dividends. Dividends are paid upon declaration by the board of directors, and if they are not so declared they *cumulate* or are *cumulative* such that no dividends can be paid on the common until the full accrued dividend is paid on the preferred. Dividends can be payable in cash or can be paid-in-kind (PIK) dividends in preferred stock similar to PIK debt.

Preferred stock also has a liquidation preference on a liquidation of the company, which is defined to include the sale of the company. In other words, the preferred gets the first crack at the acquisition consideration. Preferred stock is often issued in layers, like debt, such that one class or series of preferred may have a preference in liquidation over other classes or series. In many cases, each successively issued class or series of preferred stock has a liquidation preference over all previously issued classes or series.

The preferred may provide that it is automatically redeemable by the company on certain dates, or is able to be put by the holders to the company after a certain date (i.e., the holders can force the company to redeem the preferred stock). If the preferred is convertible, it may permit the company to call the preferred for redemption, thus forcing the holders to choose between converting to common or getting paid out.

Convertible preferred stock is a common instrument in the private company and LBO worlds. The preferred is convertible at the option of the holder into a specified number of shares of common stock, and is typically protected by *anti-dilution covenants*. Anti-dilution covenants that protect against such corporate events as stock splits of the common stock are universal. In the private company world there also is so-called *price anti-dilution,* where there is an adjustment in the number of shares of common issuable upon conversion of the preferred stock if stock is later sold by the company at a price lower than the price inherent in the preferred stock's conversion ratio. Conversion can also vary (favorably and unfavorably) based on other factors, like the future performance of the issuer.

Private company convertible preferred has two types of liquidation preference:

1. *Straight nonparticipating preferred stock,* where upon a sale or liquidation the holder has a choice between getting paid its liquidation amount (cost plus accrued dividends) or getting the amount it would have gotten

had it converted to common (which may not be known until later in the case of an earnout).

2. *Participating preferred stock*, where the preferred first gets paid out and then converts to common to share in the sale proceeds that are left for the common holders after the payment of the preferred's liquidation preference.

Senior securities, debt, and preferred stock are also sometimes exchangeable, rather than convertible. This means that preferred can be exchanged for debt (at the option of the issuer or the holder), and debt can be exchanged for preferred stock. The exchange feature is usually used because the tax consequences to both parties are different for debt and stock, and circumstances may change from the date of issue regarding which is more favorable. For example, the company may actually prefer to have convertible debt, rather than convertible preferred stock, since interest paid on the debt is deductible and dividends on the preferred are not.

Earnouts

An earnout is an acquisition structure that is used to bridge the gap in price negotiations. The negotiations go something like this: The Buyer says it will pay a certain (low) amount for the business because it does not really believe all of the fabulous things the Target says will happen in the future that justify a higher price. The Target insists that all of these fabulous things really will happen and that a higher price is justified. The parties cannot agree on the price because of their differing views of the prospects of the business. To bridge this gap, the parties sometimes agree that the Buyer will pay the lower price at closing, and if the fabulous things actually do happen, then an additional amount will be paid by the Buyer later.

The additional amount to be paid by the Buyer can either be a fixed amount or an amount based on a formula tied to post-closing performance goals for the acquired business. Earnouts generally are based on achievement of projected targets in income statement items—at the top line (revenue), or the bottom line (net income), or something in between, such as earnings before interest and taxes (EBIT). The earnout can also be based on other operating targets, such as number of customers.

Earnouts are complicated and frequently problematic, and the parties regret that they used an earnout rather than just compromising the difference in the purchase price. Earnouts have a conceptual attraction, but they are difficult to implement. Disputes are common. The lower down the income statement that the earnout target is, the more likely it is that there will be a dispute because there are a lot of accounting judgments (and arguable manipulations) that can happen to items above the net income line. There is also an initial negotiating issue of who is going to run the business. If the Target's management is to run it or have a significant hand in running it and also has an economic interest in the earnout, their incentive is to run the business to maximize the particular income statement item that is the basis of the earnout, which may not be what is best for the business. The converse is that if the Buyer runs it (as is normally the case), the business will be run based on what is best for the Buyer's overall business objectives (which may or may not coincide with the earnout measure) or it may be run largely to minimize the earnout adjustment that the Buyer will have to pay (which may or may not coincide with what is best for the business).

The point is that what is best for the business may or may not be the same as the income statement item that forms the basis of the earnout, or even if it is what the business needs, the decisions and methods used to achieve the performance goal may not be optimal.

To take an example, let us say that the earnout goal is tied to net income. As is often the case, even if the Buyer retains all rights to make decisions regarding the business, the managers who previously worked for the business and had equity have a personal economic interest in the earnout outcome. So, in order to maximize the earnout amount, management will be tempted to take imprudent actions, such as deferring expenses that otherwise would not be deferred for business reasons; pushing into the market a product that is not ready, with attendant risk to the company's reputation; or pricing to maximize margins when lower margins may help to establish the product for the company's longer-term benefit.

In order to avoid these pitfalls and the potential accounting disputes that may arise from a bottom-line earnout target, the parties may choose the simpler route of having the earnout tie to top-line revenue. But that creates its own set of problems. What is best for the business, more often than not, is to maximize net income (in prudent and legitimate ways), not to maximize revenue. An extreme example of the latter would be to set pricing so low that the product flies off the shelf and generates a lot of revenue, but the company loses money on every sale. The obvious fix to that is to have both a revenue and a net income test.

If the earnout route is chosen, the acquisition documents will set up complex rules and implementation procedures.

Targets may assert that the earnout payments should be accelerated under certain circumstances. These circumstances may include:

- Termination of members of management without cause
- The sale of the business by the Buyer, or the sale of the Buyer itself
- Breach by the Buyer of any of its post-closing obligations

Certain operating rules need to be established. For example:

- Is the Buyer required to fund the business to a specified extent?
- Are the other business units of the Buyer prohibited from competing with the acquired business?
- If the Buyer's other business units sell products that cannibalize the products of the acquired business, are there to be any restrictions on those sales, or should those sales be hypothetically assumed to be part of the acquired business for earnout purposes?
- What happens if the acquired business wants to acquire another business? How is it to be financed, and how are the financing expenses to be allocated? Should the acquired business have the first opportunity to purchase businesses that will have an impact on the earnout calculation?

Accounting principles need to be specified. For example:

- It is normally specified that new items of expense allocated to the business from the application of acquisition accounting need to be excluded on a pro forma basis from the income statement of the business. For example, the application of these accounting principles normally requires a write-up in the values of the Target's assets, and that write-up creates additional depreciation expense that reduces net income. Often debt incurred at the parent level to run the business is pushed down to the subsidiary level since it properly is regarded as an expense of the company where the business is located.
- If goodwill has to be written off or if acquisition reserves have to be created, those should be excluded as well.
- How is Buyer overhead to be allocated to the business, if at all?
- A related question is, if the Buyer performs certain functions for the business that were formerly paid for by the business, such as finance or benefits administration, what adjustments need to be made to the net income of the business for the benefit of the Buyer?
- Are the effects of *extraordinary items,* such as the sale of capital assets, to be excluded?
- Who pays the cost of preparing the financial statements used to determine the earnout amount?
- How are intercompany transactions priced, and do they require any special approvals?
- Are restructuring or severance expenses to be excluded?
- If the employees of the Target receive different and more expensive benefits from the Buyer, is the increase to be excluded?
- What happens if the Buyer substantially changes the business plan of the acquired business?

Governance principles also need to be included. For example:

- No commingling of the assets or business of the Buyer and the Target are permitted.
- The Buyer will be obligated, in general terms, not to take any action that would have the effect of materially reducing the amount of the earnout payment, other than in the ordinary course of business.
- Certain specified major actions require the consent of the former owners of the business, or their appointed representative.
- The parameters of the ability of management to make operating decisions need to be specified, including compensation, pricing, hiring/firing, and the like.

There are also a number of tax issues involved in earnouts. If earnout payments are linked in any way to continued employment, then compensation income may need to be recognized. How is imputed interest handled? What are the implications relating to the installment method of tax reporting, and how is tax basis allocated for purposes of calculating interim gain? How does the earnout affect a tax-free reorganization, particularly if the earnout is to be paid in cash?

SUCCESSOR LIABILITY AND THE DE FACTO MERGER DOCTRINE

At least in the initial analysis, the rules as to the status of creditors and other outside parties in the three basic forms of acquisition are quite clear. In a merger, the merging corporations become one corporation with all of the assets and liabilities of both. In a stock purchase, the Target remains intact with its assets and liabilities; the Buyer, in the absence of the applicability of the doctrine of "piercing the corporate veil," does not become responsible for the debts of the Target, now its subsidiary.

Responsibility for liabilities in an asset purchase is dictated by the asset purchase agreement. The general rule is that where an acquirer acquires assets from a selling corporation, the acquirer is not responsible for the liabilities of the Target unless the acquirer expressly assumes those obligations.

But it is not quite that simple. In an asset purchase, there are statutes such as fraudulent conveyance and transfer laws that may impose liabilities in a manner other than as agreed by the parties. Essentially, the transferred assets are reachable by the creditors of the entity that transferred the assets if the Target's assets were not sold at fair market value and certain other conditions apply. These laws are explored in Chapter 7.

A fraudulent transfer may even take place in a stock purchase or a merger. This occurs where the assets of the Target are themselves used to pay part of the purchase price or where the return to the Target's shareholders is in the form of a dividend and the dividend is deemed to be improper because the Target is insolvent under the applicable corporate statute. This type of financing technique is used in an LBO. The state corporation statutes themselves protect creditors in the situation where a corporation sells all of its assets, does not pay its creditors, and distributes the proceeds of the sale to its shareholders in connection with a formal dissolution. In that case, the creditors who were harmed have rights to proceed against the shareholders who absconded with the proceeds—if they can find them. Also, creditors whose claims are contingent at the time of the acquisition may not have adequate means to protect themselves once their claims become known. For one thing, the state corporate statutes provide for rights against shareholders in a dissolved corporation only for a limited period of time.

In addition to the statutory aspects, there is case law supporting the notion that certain acquisition transactions be treated as *de facto mergers* even though not a merger in form. The essence of these decisions is that mere form should not dictate economic results in certain situations, and that the transaction should be recharacterized as a merger where the assets and liabilities of the two involved entities are pooled and where the business continues substantially unchanged.

Other cases form the effective equivalent of fraudulent transfer law, holding that a transaction itself was effectively fraudulent. This occurs where the acquirer is a mere continuation of the Target and where the Target's transfer of assets was fraudulent in that its only purpose was to escape liability for its debts.

One court set forth the following elements that must be present for application of the de facto merger doctrine:

- There is a continuation of the enterprise of the seller corporation, so that there is a continuity of management, personnel, physical location, assets, and general business operations.
- There is a continuation of shareholders that results from the purchasing corporation paying for the acquired assets with shares of its own stock, this stock ultimately coming to be held by the shareholders of the seller corporation so that they become a constituent part of the purchasing corporation.
- The selling corporation ceases its ordinary business operations, liquidates, and dissolves as soon as legally and practically possible.

■ The purchasing corporation assumes those liabilities and obligations of the seller ordinarily necessary for the uninterrupted continuation of normal business operations of the seller corporation.

In practice, the de facto merger doctrine is applied only in egregious cases. Trouble begins when creditors do not get paid after the acquisition. The parties should be aware of the risks in any structure that essentially is meant to avoid full payment of creditors.

One scenario goes as follows. The business of Company X is running at a loss and is essentially insolvent—the value of its assets is less than its liabilities (the balance sheet test) or it is unable to pay its debts as they become due (the income statement test). Management of Company X approaches management of Company Y and proposes that Company X sell its assets to Company Y for a very attractive price that is likely well below what Company X would get for its assets in a *bona fide* sale, together with Company X management and shareholders getting an equity position in Company Y. The attractive price paid to Company X is insufficient to pay the debts of Company X, and Company X creditors ultimately get shortchanged. The elements of a fraudulent transfer (discussed in Chapter 7) are probably here, but even if they are not, there is a substantial risk that a court would apply the de facto merger doctrine or successor liability because of the inherently fraudulent nature of the transaction. More likely, the creditors who were not paid would put Company X into bankruptcy so that the bankruptcy court could sort out what was properly done and what was not. The bankruptcy court has the ability to reverse prior transactions if it determines them to be improper.

Even in situations that are not an egregious attempt to avoid debts, courts have imposed liability where the court felt compelled to take into account (or even legislate?) public policy in areas of specific concern, like products liability.

Labor law is another area where successor liability has been found. Among the possible liabilities are:

■ Union recognition and the obligation to bargain.
■ Obligations under the collective bargaining agreement.
■ Contractual obligation to arbitrate.
■ Obligations to remedy past unfair labor practices.

There is statutory liability under ERISA for benefit plan liabilities, including liability of a parent in a consolidated group. However, asset sales are generally respected.

Environmental liabilities are another area where there is statutory and case law support for successor liability (and parent liability).

SECURITIES LAW COMPLIANCE

Overview

The principal securities laws affecting acquisitions are as follows:

- *Securities Act of 1933.* The Securities Act of 1933 (Securities Act or '33 Act) regulates the offer and sale of securities, including shares issued in connection with acquisitions. The '33 Act not only regulates the sale by a Buyer of its securities, it also regulates the sale of the Buyer's securities by the shareholders of the Target who receive them. Offers and sales of securities have to be registered with the SEC or be exempt from registration. If they are registered, extremely onerous and complicated filings must be made with the SEC. As we will see later, in certain circumstances, in order to qualify as a private placement, exempt acquisitions of private companies for stock may require elaborate disclosures as well. In representing a Buyer, the Buyer's counsel must also investigate whether the Target complied with the Securities Act when it did its private placement financings; if it did not, those purchasers may have rescission rights.
- *Securities Exchange Act of 1934.* The Securities Exchange Act of 1934 (Exchange Act or the '34 Act) regulates multiple aspects of public companies:
  - Public companies must file periodic disclosure reports with the SEC. When a public company makes a significant acquisition, it must file a description of the transaction promptly on Form 8-K. If the transaction is large enough, the Target's financial statements must be filed by the Buyer with the SEC. Care must be taken to make sure these financials are available. Whether and when preliminary negotiations require public disclosure is a complicated topic discussed in Chapter 6.
  - Solicitations of a public company's shareholders for votes are regulated by the SEC's proxy rules under the Exchange Act. If a public company must solicit its shareholders for approval of a merger, elaborate SEC rules relating to the solicitation must be followed.
  - The Exchange Act also regulates takeovers of public companies. Shareholders who acquire more than 5 percent of a public company's stock have to file a special disclosure schedule with the SEC. The Exchange Act and the rules under it also contain substantive and disclosure regulation of tender offers for the securities of public companies.
  - The antifraud provisions of the Exchange Act, and the rules under it, particularly Rule 10b-5, prohibit fraud in connection with the

purchase and sale of securities. More precisely, Rule 10b-5 prohibits a misstatement of a material fact or the omission of a fact, which omission makes the statement misleading in light of the statements made. The antifraud rules apply with equal force to public and private acquisitions. Also, public companies cannot make misleading statements or omissions regarding the potential or actual acquisition of a private or public company.

■ *Sarbanes-Oxley Act.* This ill-conceived law, which has made the lives of public company executives miserable, has little direct applicability to private companies. The most onerous requirement is the extensive internal financial controls that public companies must now have and the related certifications of the public company's financial statements by its senior officers. When public companies acquire private companies, even for cash, they need to make sure that the Target's internal controls and related procedures are in decent enough shape so as not to cause later problems after the acquisition because of the certifications that have to be made with respect to the combined business.

■ *State blue-sky laws.* To the frequent chagrin of practitioners, each state also has a separate regulatory scheme for the offer and sale of securities. Like the federal scheme, the issuance of securities has to be either registered with the blue-sky commissions that have jurisdiction (state of residence of the Target's shareholders) or be exempt from registration. Fortunately, the blue-sky registration/exemption process has been preempted to a significant degree by federal law. In addition to the regulation of the purchase and sale of securities, many states have enacted their own version of anti-takeover legislation.

Private Placements

An acquisition where the acquisition consideration consists, in whole or in part, of securities involves an offer and sale of securities that has to be either registered under the Securities Act or be exempt from registration, generally under the so-called private placement exemption. *Securities* for this purpose means stock of the Buyer, Buyer notes, and the like. An earnout, because the Target's shareholders are relying on the future performance of the business, may (or may not under SEC no-action guidelines) constitute a security.

If the transaction is an offer and sale of securities, there are two basic ways to achieve securities law compliance: Register the offered securities on a registration statement filed with the SEC, or structure the transaction to be exempt. As mentioned previously, Buyers want to avoid going through the SEC filing process if at all possible because it is extremely expensive and involves significant delays. For acquisitions of public companies, registration with the SEC is the only practical alternative since it would be impossible to find a private placement exemption where there are hundreds or thousands of public shareholders. (The securities laws aspects of the acquisition of public companies are discussed in Chapter 6.) In acquisitions of private companies, whether the Buyer is a public or a private company, the most expedient route is to attempt to comply with the private placement rules.

What are the basic legal parameters that an issuance of securities in an acquisition must comply with in order to be a valid private placement—i.e., an exempt offer and sale of securities of the Buyer?

The principal exemption from registration is Section 4(a)(2)[1] under the Securities Act, which exempts securities issued in a transaction not involving a public offering. The SEC has adopted a safe harbor implementing various statutory provisions in the form of Regulation D (Reg. D). Lawyers attempt to comply with Reg. D for all offers and sales of securities by private companies, including in acquisitions structured as private placements. Where compliance with Reg. D is not possible as a practical matter, lawyers may be comfortable with relying on the exemption contained in Section 4(a)(2) itself where the transaction fits within the case law defining the underlying principles of investor protection, including the sophistication of the offerees/purchasers. Because you cannot choose the purchasers in an acquisition transaction (i.e., the shareholders of the Target) and thus limit purchasers to those who will not jeopardize compliance, use of the Section 4(a)(2) exemption becomes difficult.

Section 4(a)(2)   Whether offers and sales amount to a nonexempt public offering depends on a number of factors, particularly the identity of the offerees/purchasers and the manner in which the offering is conducted. The offering must be conducted in a manner to make the offering private rather than public—hence, the term *private placement*. The case law has defined the parameters of what constitutes a private placement:

- *Access to material information.* Offerees have access to the same kind of information about the company that a prospectus meeting SEC requirements would provide.
- *Investors are sophisticated.* Offerees have "such knowledge and experience in business and financial matters" (sophistication) to be able to evaluate the merits and risks of the investment.
- No *general solicitation or advertising.* There is no general solicitation of investors or advertising in connection with the offering. This means,

---

[1]Formerly Section 4(2) but changed to Section 4(a)(2) under the JOBS Act.

among other things, that the issuer cannot make mass mailings of offering materials, place ads in the media or on the Internet, or hold public meetings about the offering. In addition, it means that issuers should limit the number of offers because making a large number of offers could be deemed to involve a general solicitation.

- *No purchaser intent to resell.* Investors must purchase the stock for investment (i.e., they must intend to hold on to it for an indefinite period and not resell it without an exemption for the resale). Plus, they must represent to that effect in one of the subscription documents called an investment letter.

Regulation D—The Safe Harbor Reg. D provides a safe harbor for the Section 4(a)(2) nonpublic offering exemption under the '33 Act. Reg. D consists of Rules 501 through 508. Rule 501 provides definitions of terms used in Reg. D. Rule 502 contains general conditions applicable in each of the exemptions provided by Rules 504, 505, and 506. Rule 503 contains a filing requirement with the SEC (Form D). Rule 504 provides an exemption for offerings not exceeding $1 million. Rule 505 provides an exemption for certain offerings not exceeding $5 million. Rule 506 provides an exemption for certain offerings without regard to the dollar amount of the offering.[2] Rule 507 states that parties are prohibited from relying on the exemptions if a court has enjoined them from doing so. Rule 508 permits reliance on the exemptions in the event of insignificant deviations from their requirements. Some additional details are:

- Rule 501, definition of *accredited investor.* The key definition in Rule 501 is *accredited investor.* Offers and sales to accredited investors are not subject to the informational and certain transactional restrictions of Reg. D. Accredited investors include:
  - Banks, broker-dealers, insurance companies, and various other institutional investors.
  - Corporations and various other entities (provided that they have not been formed for the specific purpose of acquiring the securities offered) with total assets in excess of $5 million.
  - Any director, executive officer, or general partner of the issuer of the securities being offered or sold.
  - Any individual with a net worth, or joint net worth with spouse, at the time of purchase exceeding $1 million, excluding the value of one's primary residence.

---

[2]The dollar limits and other provisions of Reg. D are under examination by the SEC. The regulation in effect at the time of the acquisition should always be checked.

- Any individual with an income in excess of $200,000 in each of the two most recent years or joint income with spouse in excess of $300,000 in each of those years and who has a reasonable expectation of reaching the same income level in the current year.
- Any trust, with total assets in excess of $5 million, not formed for the specific purpose of acquiring the securities offered, whose purchase is directed by a sophisticated person, as defined.
- Any entity in which all of the equity owners are accredited investors.

- Rule 502, general conditions.

  - *No integration.* This term means that certain offerings will be combined for purposes of establishing an exemption if the offerings, although technically separate, are really part of the same offering.
  - *Information requirements.* Special information must be furnished to nonaccredited investors in offerings under Rule 505 and 506, but not Rule 504. These information requirements are quite onerous and require in most cases IPO prospectus-level disclosure and in some cases audited financial statements. As a practical matter, these requirements are very difficult to comply with, as is discussed later.
  - *Access.* Mimicking the case law under Section 4(a)(2), the issuer must make available to each prospective purchaser the opportunity to ask questions of the issuer concerning the terms and conditions of the offering and to obtain any additional information that the issuer possesses or can acquire without unreasonable effort or expense to verify information provided to the investor.
  - *No general solicitation or advertising.* The offerees must be restricted to a reasonably limited number of persons with a prior relationship to the issuer in some manner. Note that under Reg. D, there is no other requirement relating to the identity of the offerees. In other words, there is no restriction on the sophistication of the offerees or the number of offerees per se (other than if there is a general solicitation). Compliance is measured by the sophistication and number of actual purchasers in the offering.
  - *Limitations on resale.* The issuer must exercise reasonable care to assure that purchasers do not resell securities in a nonexempt transaction, including reasonable inquiry regarding the purchaser's investment intent; written disclosure to the investor prior to sale that the securities have not been registered and cannot be resold unless registered or exempt from registration; and placement of a restrictive legend on the certificate evidencing the security.

- Rule 503, Form D filing requirement. The SEC Form D must be filed no later than 15 days after the first sale of securities (which occurs whenever the issuer takes money or has investors sign subscription agreements even if the closing has not occurred).

- Rule 504, small offering exemption. The aggregate offering price for offerings under Rule 504 must not exceed $1 million. Under Rule 504, no special information must be disclosed to unaccredited investors.
- Rule 505, exemption for offerings of $5 million or less. Maximum of 35 unaccredited purchasers, plus the informational and other transactional requirements of Reg. D.
- Rule 506, exemption for offerings of any size. The same as Rule 505, but each unaccredited investor either alone or with his "purchaser representative(s)" must have "such knowledge and experience in financial and business matters to be capable of evaluating the merits and risks of the prospective investment"—mimicking the investor sophistication requirements of the Section 4(a)(2) case law.

Section 3(a)(10) of the Securities Act   Section 3(a)(10) of the Securities Act is available to exempt from registration securities that are issued in an "exchange," where the terms of the exchange are approved by a court or authorized governmental entity after a hearing regarding the fairness of the exchange. The exchange must be an exchange of securities for securities, claims, or property interests, although cash and securities together may be offered in the exchange and options and warrants may be assumed (their underlying securities must be separately registered (e.g., on a Form S-8) or an exemption from their registration must be available (e.g., Rule 701). Earnout shares may be covered by the Section 3(a)(10) exemption.

The exchange securities may be issued upon a domestic or foreign court order or upon an order of a state entity if the state has enacted specific enabling legislation providing for a fairness hearing. A small number of states have approved fairness hearing procedures, most importantly California. A transaction must have a nexus to the state in which it seeks a fairness hearing.

State Securities or Blue-Sky Laws   Burdensome though it may be, all offerings and sales of securities must also be exempt from registration under the securities (or so-called blue-sky) laws of the states. Most states have adopted a limited offering exemption patterned after Section 4(a)(2) of the '33 Act. A federal law, the National Securities Markets Improvement Act of 1996 (NSMIA), preempted state registration/exemption provisions for transactions qualifying under Rule 506.

Each state usually has other limited offering exemptions based on the number of purchasers in the state or based on the investors being *institutional investors,* as defined in the applicable state regulations. Important traps for the unwary in complying with blue-sky laws are often present where a non-Rule 506 offering involves the payment of commissions on sales (and particularly where the commissions are paid to an unregistered broker-dealer) or where the offering is to persons in states such as New Hampshire, which has its own unique view of its securities laws and their preemption. In those cases, it is important to check the state law requirements for such compliance items as a required filing that must be made before offers or sales are made. Compliance with the blue-sky laws often requires filing a copy of the SEC Form D and payment of a filing fee—even for offerings exempted under NSMIA.

Private Placements in the Acquisition Context

SEC Rule 145 says in effect that an offer includes, so far as the security holders of a corporation are concerned, the submission to a vote of such security holders, a merger where stock is issued as acquisition consideration. According to the introductory note to Rule 145, an offer occurs when there is submitted to security holders a vote where they must elect, in what is a new investment decision, to accept a new security. Technically, a stock-for-stock exchange does not fall under Rule 145, but that is because such a transaction is unambiguously a purchase and sale, as opposed to a merger.

So, where an acquisition is partly for stock or other securities of the Buyer, the offer of that stock or those securities in any form of acquisition where the Target shareholders have to make an investment decision involves first the offer and then the sale of securities. We generally speak only of stock in this section, although the rules apply equally to other securities.

In acquisitions of private companies, a private placement is possible depending on the number and characteristics of the selling shareholders of the Target. Offers and sales can be made only to accredited investors; sales can otherwise be made in satisfaction of the disclosure and other requirements of SEC Reg. D, or the offer and sale can be exempt under Section 4(a)(2) of the Securities Act. If an offering is made to unaccredited investors, the informational requirements under Reg. D technically are nearly as strict as they are for a public offering prospectus, although there is no SEC review of the private placement memorandum.

Acquisitions present unique private placement structuring challenges because you cannot choose to whom you are going to offer the securities; you are stuck with offering them to the shareholders of the Target, and in many private companies the shareholder base is sizable and is composed of multiple shareholders who are neither accredited nor sophisticated (e.g., option holders who are lower-level employees who acquired the underlying stock under SEC Rule 701). Even worse, option holders under the Target's stock option plan under certain circumstances may be required to make an investment decision and so must be counted as offerees/purchasers of securities.

The first task in determining whether an acquisition where the Buyer issues securities can fit into the Reg. D exemption is to analyze the size and composition of the shareholder base of the Target. This should be done at the outset. If, for Reg. D purposes, you have some, but fewer than 35, unaccredited Target shareholders, Reg. D requires that an offering memorandum containing extensive information about the Buyer and the Target must be sent to the Target's shareholders to assist them in their investment decision.

If, for Reg. D purposes, you have more than 35 unaccredited shareholders of the Target, what do you do? If all of these shareholders were to be offered Buyer securities, it would be impossible to comply with Reg. D.

There are several tricks you can use that may solve the problem. The key to the solution involves using the Rule 145 concept that an investment decision is what constitutes the offer/sale in this context, and then structuring the transaction so that the nonaccredited investor/shareholders of the Target do not have to make an investment decision as to whether to take new securities.

One trick is to structure the deal so that unaccredited investors get all cash and no stock. Cash is not a security, so there is no investment decision to be made involving a new security. Delaware case law supports offering different consideration to different classes of shareholders in a merger, but only where there is a valid business purpose. Law firms usually will not give an opinion that this structure complies with Delaware law (and/or that there is a valid private placement), because of the subjectivity involved. In the right circumstances, it seems reasonably clear that there are valid business reasons here in using this structure and that the structure does not involve a Rule 145 investment decision. In short, the deal may not be cost-effective or otherwise practical if full-blown SEC registration is required. One must be careful, however, because the use of cash above a certain amount may disqualify an otherwise tax-free deal. Also, the acquirer may not want to use its available cash for the deal.

Another technique that can be used where the use of cash is not desirable for business or tax reasons is to solicit votes approving the transaction by a written consent submitted only to shareholders who are accredited investors, assuming you can get the requisite shareholder approval just from accredited investors. There is some discomfort with this approach on the theory that even though the nonaccredited investors do not vote, they still have to make a decision as to whether to take the merger consideration or to exercise their appraisal rights. Some think that this is an investment decision that destroys the exemption. The better view, in our opinion, is that even though a decision has to be made whether or not to seek a court appraisal, that decision is not an investment decision relating to taking a new security within the intent and language of the rule. For one thing, as was said previously, the decision to seek an appraisal is rarely made since the overwhelming factor is the expense of the process. It would be a rare case where the prospective increase in the acquisition price would justify the risk and expense of the proceeding.

Compliance with the federal securities laws does not necessarily equate to a board fulfilling its fiduciary duties under Delaware law. There are a number of cases to the effect that the board has a duty to make available to the shareholders all information necessary to make an informed decision about an acquisition, including whether to exercise appraisal rights. The logic of those decisions applies to cash and stock mergers.

In summary, if the acquisition involves the issuance of stock or other securities by the Buyer, you have to consider the securities law aspects as one of the structuring parameters.

Securities Laws from the Target's Perspective

Attempting to structure the acquisition of a private company as a private placement is not necessarily in the Target shareholders' interest. In a private placement, the recipient gets *restricted securities* that may not be sold unless subsequently registered with the SEC or exempt from registration. The principal exemption from registration in this context is Rule 144.

Rule 144 is a *safe harbor* exemption. To utilize this safe harbor, a seller is prohibited from selling restricted securities until at least one year has elapsed since the specific shares were acquired from the issuer or an affiliate of the issuer and fully paid for. Such sales are also subject to quantitative and qualitative restrictions, described in the next few paragraphs. Restricted securities held by persons other than affiliates for longer than two years, however, may be freely sold under the securities law without restriction. Sales by affiliates are subject to the rule until the seller is no longer an affiliate for three months.

The qualitative restrictions generally require that the sale be handled as a routine open-market brokerage transaction, although the seller also may deal directly with an over-the-counter market maker that deals as a principal for its own account rather than as a broker. Also, the issuer must be current in its reporting obligations to the SEC at the time of the sale (i.e., having filed its periodic reports).

The quantitative restrictions limit sales by the holder during each three-month period to an amount of securities equal to the *greater of:*

- One percent of the number of shares of the issuer's common stock outstanding; and
- The average reported weekly trading volume during the four calendar weeks preceding the date placing the order to sell.

Acquisitions of Private Target by Private Buyer If a private company is acquiring another private company for stock, the expectation must be that the securities cannot be sold until the Buyer goes public or is sold itself. The Target's shareholders should see themselves as investors in the Buyer much the same as venture capital or other investors. These investors typically demand a number of contractual provisions for their protection, and many of these are appropriate for investors via an acquisition.

The Buyer's shareholders should ask to become parties to any shareholders agreements, right of first refusal, and co-sale and investors rights agreements that the other investors are party to. Among the rights demanded are registration rights to have their securities registered with the SEC. These rights take two forms: *demand* registration rights, where a minimum number of investors can force the issuer to register their shares for resale with the SEC, sometimes (but rarely) before the issuer's IPO; and *piggyback* registration rights, where the investors have a right to have their shares registered for resale with the SEC if the issuer is filing a registration statement with the SEC for another purpose. There are multiple nuances to these agreements that are beyond our scope of consideration, such as whether and to what extent the underwriters in a company offering can cut back the participation of investors with piggyback registration rights, and when the agreements expire—either when the shares become tradable with volume restrictions under Rule 144, freely tradable under Rule 144(k) without volume restrictions, or some longer period in order for the shareholders to have more time to participate in a piggyback registration that may afford more practical liquidity than sales under Rule 144.

Acquisition of Private Target by Public Buyer If a public company is acquiring a private company for stock, the first question is whether the Target's shareholders want or will permit the transaction to be structured as a private placement. In these transactions, unlike a private/private acquisition, registration with the SEC is possible, although complicated and expensive.

Because resale restrictions significantly reduce the value of the shares received, given the risk inherent in the holding period, sellers usually insist on obtaining *shelf* registration rights. Shelf registration rights require the Buyer to register for resale the Target's shareholders' shares with the SEC without requirement of a demand or a requirement that the company be filing a registration statement for another reason. The obligation is typically to file this registration with the SEC within a prescribed period of time after the closing. This time period is usually quite short—say, 10 days—because the form of registration statement for this type of transaction is quite simple to prepare. Once the registration statement is filed, the obligation becomes one of best efforts by the issuer to cause the registration statement to be declared effective by the SEC. This is a best-efforts obligation because it is the SEC that must declare the registration statement effective, and the issuer can only do so much to expedite the process. Nevertheless, sometimes there are financial penalties imposed on the Buyer if the registration statement is not declared effective by the SEC within some relatively long period of time—say, three months. With a little luck, this form of registration statement can be declared effective within a week or two after filing.

As was noted above, acquisitions of private companies for stock of public companies do not have to be structured as private placements. They can be registered with the SEC from the outset, and the shares are freely tradable at the closing, unless contractual restrictions on sales are agreed to. Because of the necessary lag in the time the shares are received in a private placement and the time the shares can be sold pursuant to an effective registration statement, the Target's shareholders may not want to take the risk of a delay and will attempt to require the Buyer to register the shares from the outset. It is also possible that the transaction cannot be structured as a private placement at all, or cannot be so structured without adverse tax consequences. In that event, there is no choice. The Buyer will usually strongly resist the filing of a registration statement because of the expense and because that route will result in a significant lag in the time from signing to closing, with all of its inherent complications and risks. The Target's shareholders may well think that the risk of a delay to closing from a fully registered offering is a greater risk to them than the risk of the lag between signing and liquidity for the shares.

ANTITRUST COMPLIANCE: HART-SCOTT-RODINO ACT

Antitrust compliance in the United States consists of two aspects: whether the transaction is illegal under Section 7 of the Clayton Act because its effect might be to lessen competition or tend to create a monopoly, and whether a filing must be made under Section 7A of the Clayton Act, the so-called Hart-Scott-Rodino Act (HSR). This discussion covers only premerger notification in the United States. Many other jurisdictions have their own premerger notification procedures.

If a filing is required, then the deal cannot close until the waiting period has expired. HSR does not change or add to the substance of the antitrust laws; its only purpose is to give the government a chance to review acquisitions before closing and enforce the antitrust laws preemptively where necessary. Certain cooperative activities that could violate substantive antitrust law (primarily where the parties are competitors) must be avoided before closing, and the acquiring party must avoid assuming beneficial ownership of the acquired party (in any transaction, even one raising no competition concerns) until the HSR waiting period has expired. Failure to comply with HSR, even absent any substantive antitrust problems, can cause the violator to incur severe monetary penalties.

Filing Requirement

Hart-Scott-Rodino can apply to transactions that are obviously acquisitions as commonly understood, like a merger, but it can also apply to any transaction that results in one person or entity acquiring voting securities, assets, or other noncorporate interests of another entity, directly or indirectly. Note that voting securities include only those that have current voting rights, and do not include options, warrants, and nonvoting convertibles.

Hart-Scott-Rodino outlines a three-part test (the "Test") of proposed transactions. If the Test is satisfied and the transaction is not otherwise exempt, HSR requires the filing of a Notification and Report Form with the Federal Trade Commission (FTC) and the Antitrust Division of the Department of Justice (DOJ), and expiration of the applicable waiting period (typically 30 days), prior to consummation of the proposed transaction. The three elements of the Test are as follows (note that the various dollar thresholds are indexed for inflation, and change on an annual basis):

1. *Commerce Test.* The Commerce Test is satisfied if either the acquiring person or the acquired person is engaged in U.S. commerce or in any activity affecting U.S. commerce. Since the provision reaches to the full extent of Congressional power to regulate commerce, this test will be satisfied in almost all situations.
2. *Size of the Transaction Test.* The Size of the Transaction Test addresses the amount of voting securities or assets held after the proposed transaction. This test is satisfied if, as a result of the acquisition, the acquiring person would hold (not acquire) an aggregate total amount of the voting securities and assets of the acquired person in excess of $80.8 million. For transactions valued at greater than $80.8 million up to $323 million, the Size of the Parties Test (described next) must also be satisfied for a filing to be required. Transactions valued in excess of $323 million need only meet the Commerce and Size of the Transaction Tests. For purposes of the Size of the Transaction Test, the value of assets or voting securities is the greater of the market price (or fair market value) and the acquisition price, if determined. The fair market value shall be determined in good faith by the board of directors (or board designee) of the acquiring person. Assumed liabilities are part of the purchase price.
3. *Size of the Parties Test.* The Size of the Parties Test addresses the magnitude of the sales or total assets of the acquiring and acquired persons.

This test is applicable only to transactions valued in excess of $80.8 million up to $323 million, and is satisfied if any one of the following conditions is met:

- Any voting securities or assets of a person engaged in manufacturing that has annual net sales or total assets of $16.2 million or more are being acquired by any person that has total assets or annual net sales of $161.5 million or more.
- Any voting securities or assets of a person not engaged in manufacturing that has total assets of $16.2 million or more are being acquired by any person that has total assets or annual net sales of $161.5 million or more.
- Any voting securities or assets of a person with annual net sales or total assets of $161.5 million or more are being acquired by any person with total assets or annual net sales of $16.2 million or more.

For purposes of these thresholds, the total assets of a person (except a newly organized entity) shall be as stated on the last regularly prepared balance sheet of that person, and the annual net sales of a person shall be as stated on the last regularly prepared annual statement of income and expense of that person. If the financials are over 15 months old or fail to consolidate entities within the reporting person, new financials are required.

The initial task under HSR is identifying the *acquiring person* and *acquired person*. Person is defined in the rules as the *ultimate parent entity*, which, in turn, is defined as the entity that is not controlled by another entity. Control of a corporate entity means either holding 50 percent or more of its outstanding voting securities, or having the contractual power presently to designate 50 percent or more of its directors. Control of noncorporate entities, such as partnerships or limited liability companies (LLCs), resides in anyone with a right to 50 percent or more in profits or 50 percent of the assets of the entity on liquidation. There are additional control rules for trusts and attribution rules among spouses and minor children. If the entity making the acquisition is controlled by another entity, the acquiring person also includes that entity and any entities that it controls. Accordingly, the acquiring person consists of this ultimate parent entity and all entities that it directly or indirectly controls. Similar to the acquiring person, the acquired person consists of the ultimate parent entity of the entity being acquired and all entities that it directly or indirectly controls.

Other Possible HSR Transactions

Other possible transactions under HSR include:

- Contributions of assets to a newly formed partnership or LLC, or a transfer of partnership or LLC interests, such as in a joint venture explained in Chapter 9. These are generally only reportable by persons obtaining control of the entity. By contrast, contributions of assets to a new corporation, or transfer of corporate voting securities, may be reportable where the size tests are met even by a noncontrolling person.

- Secondary acquisitions (acquisitions of noncontrolling voting securities held by a Target). These may require separate reporting by the issuer and the acquirer.
- Distributions of assets or voting securities.
- Recapitalizations where an investor increases its share.
- Entering an exclusive license.

There are numerous exemptions from the filing requirements, including passive acquisitions of 10 percent or less of an entity's voting securities and acquisitions of goods in the ordinary course of business.

The HSR requirements are directed to acquisitions of U.S. entities. They apply, however, to acquisitions of foreign assets where those assets generate a specified amount of sales in the United States and other U.S.-connection tests are met. A similar test applies to acquisitions of voting securities of foreign persons.

Once it has been determined that the submission of a filing will be required, both the acquiring person and the acquired person must prepare the necessary premerger notification. Although there is no explicit time deadline for making the filing, the proposed acquisition may not be consummated until the waiting period (usually 30 days) has expired or been terminated early. If a filing is required, the transaction is put on hold while the FTC and DOJ review it. If they take no action, the transaction may be consummated when the waiting period is over.

Waiting Period

The waiting period prior to consummation of an acquisition is the cornerstone of HSR. During this waiting period, the FTC and DOJ examine whether the proposed transaction is likely to violate the antitrust laws. While the waiting period preserves the status quo, the agencies, armed with the information obtained from the parties and their own research, can and do challenge proposed mergers. Complex remedial problems of undoing anticompetitive transactions are thereby avoided.

The actual waiting period for a particular transaction may be less than the statutory 30 days. The agencies may in their discretion grant a request for early termination of the waiting period. Parties usually but not always request such early termination when making their HSR filings. The price of receiving it, however, is a partial waiver of the Act's confidentiality provisions: When the agencies grant early termination, the FTC publishes notice of this action in the Federal Register and on the FTC's website.

If, however, the waiting period expires on its own, both the fact and the content of filings under the Act are confidential (except in subsequent administrative or judicial proceedings). Either party, as an entity required to file the premerger notification, may request early termination of the waiting period on the HSR form.

The FTC and DOJ may also decide to extend the waiting period by requesting additional information before the end of the waiting period. Such a request—commonly called a second request—extends the waiting period for designated additional time (not more than 30 days) after the additional information has been received. Generally, the parties must produce a large volume of documents and answer numerous interrogatories in order to comply with a second request. This process may postpone the ultimate termination of the waiting period by weeks or even months.

The FTC or DOJ may also seek a further extension of the waiting period in federal court if it believes that a person has failed substantially to comply with the Act's notification requirements. If the agency can make such a showing, the court will extend the waiting period until there is substantial compliance. Similarly, if either agency believes that the transaction would violate Section 7 of HSR, it can go to court seeking a preliminary injunction.

In addition to filing the proper notification, the Act requires payment of a filing fee determined in amount by the transaction value, as set forth below:

- For transactions valued at greater than $80.8 million but less than $161.5 million, a $45,000 fee.
- For transactions valued at $161.5 million or more but less than $807.5 million, a $125,000 fee.
- For transactions valued at $807.5 million or more, a $280,000 fee.

Filing fees must be paid by persons acquiring voting securities, assets, or noncorporate interests who are required to file premerger notifications by the Act. The acquired person is not required to pay a filing fee unless it or one or more of its shareholders is also deemed an acquiring person under the Act (e.g., by acquisition of shares in the acquiring person).

Filing Requirement Flowchart

Exhibit 3.13 summarizes the analysis as to whether an HSR filing is required.

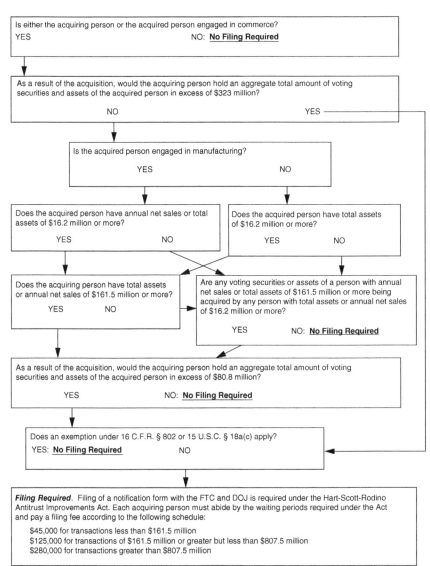

EXHIBIT 3.13 HSR Filing Analysis

Gun Jumping: Impermissible Activities during the Waiting Period and before Closing

Merging parties must exchange some information to conduct due diligence and plan for the transition. Nevertheless, as previously indicated, when the parties merging are competitors they must, in the preclosing period, not allow their cooperative actions to rise to the level of substantive antitrust violations. Even when the parties do not compete, however, until termination of the HSR waiting period, they must refrain from acquiring beneficial ownership of the other. The agencies interpret HSR's ban on acquiring voting securities or assets prior to clearance as prohibiting acquisition of beneficial ownership by managerial control.

Coordination of prices and allocation of accounts prior to merger are forbidden by antitrust law. However, a covenant by the acquired firm not to make extraordinary capital expenditures or disposition of assets is generally supportable as reasonably ancillary to the acquisition agreement. In some cases, antitrust problems may be avoided by walling off the acquiring person's planning personnel, considering for example post-merger pricing, from sales and marketing personnel setting current prices. While joint marketing of products before merger is forbidden, joint ads or calls on customers to tout the merger are generally permitted.

Even in mergers not involving competitors, an interim management agreement combining management of the parties that takes effect before HSR clearance likely violates HSR as a transfer of beneficial ownership. Care must be exercised, for example, not to distribute new business cards with new titles or new phone lists for the combined operations before termination of the HSR waiting period.

EQUITY COMPENSATION

Executive compensation and employment arrangements are an integral part of the acquisition process. In most acquisitions, the Buyer will want to retain some, most, or all of the Target's employees. If a business is purchased as a complete business, it is hard to imagine how it will be run without the participation of at least some of those who have been running it historically. In certain acquisitions, the technical and management employees of the Target may be one of the principal reasons for the acquisition.

If the Buyer is a public company, it will already have equity compensation plans in place. Little will be negotiable except for the number of options or restricted shares to be granted as incentives. In a private acquisition, particularly in an LBO, a new shell company is formed to acquire the business, and the equity compensation plans are drafted with a clean slate. The participation of management may be in the form of rolling over some of their existing equity in the Target into the equity of the Buyer. Normally, they would receive the same preferred securities as the other investors in the Buyer. But, in addition, *founders' stock* will be granted to management and other employees, for nominal consideration, with vesting provisions, as an incentive to stay with and pay attention to the business.

In these transactions, the layers of senior and subordinated debt and preferred stock will have the effect of driving down the fair market value of the investee company's common stock. As a result, the company may issue to management shares of restricted stock at a substantially reduced price per share or grant options having a low exercise price, relative to the preferred securities. The option holder or shareholder has the prospect of relatively rapid appreciation in the value of the restricted stock or options and the realization of that appreciation by going public or another sale of the company.

There are several common forms of equity compensation in private companies. The most common are *restricted stock* purchases and stock options—with the options being either in the form of incentive stock options (ISOs) or nonqualified stock options (NQSOs). A restricted stock purchase is simply the purchase of a company's stock in a private transaction, with the stock typically being subject to declining *vesting* (forfeiture) provisions and to sale restrictions. Upon termination of employment, the company can buy back the unvested portion of the stock at its original, and presumably low, purchase price. The other form of equity compensation is a stock option, where the employee is given the right to buy the stock at a fixed price for a specified period of time. The optionee is given the opportunity to exercise only a portion (or none) of the option at the outset, with that portion increasing (i.e., vesting) over the first several years of employment. When employment ceases, vesting ceases. In effect, companies granting equity to employees or others rendering services to the company provide that the equity holder must earn this equity over time by continuing to remain in the employment/service relationship. This is what is known as *sweat equity.*

One disadvantage of options, other than tax disadvantages, is that employers frequently provide that the employee must exercise the vested portion of the option within a certain number of days after termination of employment. This requires the employee to make a difficult investment decision and to pay the cash exercise price, which can be significant, particularly where the company is past the startup stage. In the case of a nonqualified stock option, because the difference between the fair market value of the stock received on exercise over the exercise price is compensation income, the employee also incurs a tax liability on exercise that cannot be funded by a sale of the stock because of the legal and practical restrictions on selling stock in a private company.

Vesting schedules vary. Sometimes a portion of the equity is vested up front—this is usually the case for founders and often for senior executives; the rest vests over a period of three or four years. Often the first vesting installment is after a year of service, with monthly or quarterly vesting thereafter. Another provision that is negotiated by senior management, but rarely by others, is to provide more favorable vesting if the employee is terminated *without cause*, or if the employee terminates the employment relationship for *good reason*, meaning that the employee has been effectively forced out by a pay cut or otherwise.

Vesting tied solely to tenure with the company is by far the most common form of vesting. The reason for this is that, historically, time vesting was the only form of vesting that was eligible for favorable accounting treatment. Under the old accounting rules, options granted at fair market value with the vesting being tied to tenure resulted in no accounting charge (expense). Under new rules, options are valued based on certain standard mathematical formulas (such as *Black-Scholes*) and that value is charged to (deducted from) earnings over the vesting period of the option, whether time-based or based on some performance measure. Because all options now result in an earnings charge, companies are much more frequently structuring vesting to tie more closely to individual and companywide performance goals. Achievement of performance goals is what the company really wants to provide incentives for.

Other than stock issued upon incorporation, restricted stock and options typically are issued to employees pursuant to what is known as an *omnibus* stock plan—a plan that permits the issuance of restricted stock, stock options, and other forms of equity compensation. A sample omnibus stock plan can be found in the appendixes.

In order to avoid compensation income, restricted stock must be sold to the employee at its fair market value, and stock options must be granted with an exercise price equal to fair market value. In a private company, fair market value is largely in the eye of the beholder. In venture capital-backed startups, the venture capitalists always buy convertible preferred stock that has a liquidation preference over the common stock. That means that upon a liquidation (defined to include a sale) of the company, the preferred stockholders get their money back (or more) before the common stockholders get anything. In a big success story, where the stock is sold for multiples of the liquidation preference of the preferred stock, the value of the common stock equals or approaches the value of the preferred.

Because of the inherently greater value of preferred stock, the common stock is usually sold, or the option exercise price is set, at a price that is a discount to the price per share of the preferred. In the early stages of the company, this is usually from 10 to 25 percent of the preferred stock price. This practice was so common that many boards of directors came to believe that the formula automatically was a fair reflection of the value of the common stock. Occasionally, the company's accountants would challenge the price because the pricing of options has accounting consequences, and the SEC in an IPO would often challenge the price of the common stock if it was set at a significant discount to the IPO price, particularly if the price was set within a year or maybe two before the IPO.

New tax and accounting rules, including Internal Revenue Code (IRC) Section 409A, have resulted in more attention being paid to the price of restricted stock and the exercise price of employee stock options. These developments have effectively forced boards of directors to make a much more professional analysis of fair market value. In many cases, boards are involving outside valuation experts to support the company's equity pricing. In the very earliest stages of a startup, however, the old rules of thumb continue to be used since valuing the company at that stage is as much guesswork as anything else.

There are also more exotic forms of equity compensation, including stock appreciation rights (SARs), phantom stock, and other forms of compensation tied to equity value. Stock appreciation rights are issued by some public companies and represent the right to have the company cash out the difference between the original value of the stock and the current fair market value (in other words, the stock appreciation). The employee never owns the stock itself. Phantom stock is sometimes issued by private companies. It is a contractual right to be treated *as if* the employee were the holder of a specified number of shares, so that the employee would be entitled to dividends and the proceeds of sale if the company were sold. Phantom stock is issued by private companies where the existing owners of the business want to limit the number of people who have the technical rights of stockholders (i.e., voting, etc.). None of these alternative forms of equity compensation entitle the holder to capital gains treatment—the income from gains is treated as compensation income taxed at ordinary rates.

Accelerated Vesting on an Acquisition or IPO

Companies sometimes provide, particularly for senior executives, that all or a portion of the options or restricted stock will vest on an acquisition of the company. Rarely will a portion vest on an initial public offering (IPO). Accelerated vesting is a provision that has important employee morale implications, as well as being a potential impediment to an acquisition.

Equity rarely accelerates on an IPO. There is a perception that it would impair the marketing of the stock in the IPO. The buyers of the stock in the public offering want the founders to continue to sweat.

With respect to accelerated vesting on an acquisition, there are competing considerations:

- From the Target shareholders' and a potential acquirer's point of view, no acceleration is best because what the acquirer is paying for in an acquisition is, in part, the expected continuing contribution of the Target's employees; this is particularly true in the acquisition of a technology company. The Buyer wants the key employees to have an incentive to continue working, and does not want them to get so rich via accelerated vesting as to lose the incentive to continue to work.
- The competing viewpoint is that the employee has earned something from the venture investors and other shareholders of the Target by delivering an acquisition and allowing them to realize value. Why should the investors cash out, with the employees being required to continue to earn out their equity?

The normal solution, at least for senior management, is a compromise between no vesting and complete accelerated vesting (i.e., partial acceleration on an acquisition). A portion of the options are accelerated on an acquisition, with the balance continuing to vest, perhaps at an accelerated rate or with a shortened vesting period, provided the employee remains employed by the acquirer. A fixed number of options can vest; a percentage of the unvested options can vest; or you can provide that a specified additional vesting period shall be deemed to have elapsed—there are subtle differences between these alternatives. In addition, you can provide for full vesting after a transition period—say, six months or one year. Frequently in that case, the employee is also relieved from the threat of loss of unvested equity if the employee is terminated without cause—in that event, there is full vesting.

Some might argue that if the employee is never offered a job with the survivor/acquirer, then there should be full accelerated vesting, either on general fairness principles or because the acquirer should not care—if the employee is not wanted, then incentives are not needed to keep him on board. The irony in this approach is that employees who are not hired are treated better than those who are hired.

Tax Aspects of Stock Options and Restricted Stock

Historically, there has been a significant disparity under the federal income tax laws between the maximum ordinary income rate and the maximum long-term capital gains rate. This disparity results in the employer and the employee attempting to structure equity-based compensation arrangements in a manner that will produce capital gains.

A stock option generally allows for the taxation of pre-exercise appreciation in the value of the underlying stock at long-term capital gain rates only if the option is an incentive stock option (ISO) and the grantee satisfies a holding period requirement with respect to the stock after exercising the option. Not all options, however, qualify for treatment as ISOs. In addition, while the exercise of an ISO is not a taxable event for the optionee under the regular tax regime, the exercise may subject the grantee to the federal alternative minimum tax (AMT). In practice, the ISO qualification rules, the holding period requirement, and the potential AMT liability often serve to render the capital gains advantages of ISOs unavailable.

Nonqualified Stock Options

The grantee of an option that is *not* an ISO (called a nonqualified stock option, or NQSO) generally recognizes ordinary compensation income upon exercising the NQSO in an amount equal to the excess of the fair market value of the stock received upon exercising the NQSO (measured as of the time of exercise) over the exercise price of the NQSO (the excess is sometimes referred to as the *spread*). (Where the exercise price is so low as to be a sham, this treatment does not apply.) The grantee then receives the underlying stock with a fair market value basis and a capital gains holding period beginning on the date of exercise. However, if the stock received upon exercising the NQSO is restricted (i.e., nontransferable and subject to a substantial risk of forfeiture—see discussion of restricted stock in the next sections), the grantee is deemed to exercise the NQSO when or as the restriction lapses unless the grantee makes a Section 83(b) election with respect to the stock (in which case the restriction is disregarded and the exercise of the NQSO is the relevant tax event).

Subject to any applicable deductibility limitations, the company granting the NQSO has a compensation deduction that mirrors the compensation income of the grantee in both amount and timing if it properly reports the grantee's compensation income on a Form W-2 or 1099, as the case may be. The company must also withhold and pay employment tax with respect to the grantee's compensation income if the grantee is an employee.

Nonqualified stock options may be attractive because they are not subject to the various requirements and limitations applicable to ISOs (see the next section), they may be granted to nonemployees, and they entitle the granting corporation to compensation deductions. In the absence of special circumstances that would preclude ISO treatment, however, an employee generally will prefer to receive an ISO so as to avoid taxation of pre-exercise appreciation in the value of the underlying stock at ordinary income rates at the time the option is exercised. If an NQSO is required to be exercised by the terms of the option agreement within a specified period after the employee's employment terminates (usually 90 days by analogy to ISO requirements), the grantee is put in an extremely difficult position—not only does the grantee have to come up with the cash to pay the exercise price, but, in addition, the grantee is taxed on the appreciation in the stock at the time of exercise.

INCENTIVE STOCK OPTIONS

An option may qualify as an ISO only if:

- It is granted pursuant to a plan that specifies the aggregate number of shares that may be issued and the employees or class of employees eligible to receive grants and is approved by the stockholders of the granting corporation within 12 months before or after the date on which the plan is adopted.
- It is granted within 10 years after the earlier of the date of the adoption of the plan or the date of the approval of the plan by the granting corporation's stockholders.
- It is not exercisable more than 10 (or, if the grantee is a 10 percent stockholder, 5) years from its grant date.
- The exercise price of the option is not less than the fair market value (or, if the grantee is a 10 percent stockholder, 110 percent of the fair market value) of the underlying stock as of the grant date.
- The option is not transferable by the grantee other than by will or the laws of descent and distribution and is exercisable during the grantee's lifetime only by the grantee.
- The grantee is an employee of the granting corporation (or of a parent or subsidiary corporation) from the date of the grant of the option until the date three months (or one year, in the case of the grantee's death or disability) before the exercise of the option.

In addition, an option will not qualify as an ISO to the extent that the underlying stock with respect to which the option is exercisable for the first time during any calendar year has a value exceeding $100,000 as of the grant date. For example, if an employee is granted an option to acquire stock worth $500,000 on the grant date and the option is immediately exercisable, only 20 percent of the option (\$100,000/\$500,000) may qualify as an ISO. If the option vests 20 percent per year over five years, the option may qualify as an ISO in its entirety.

The exercisability of an ISO may be made subject to conditions that are "not inconsistent" with the rules just described. Accordingly, ISOs (like NQSOs) may be granted subject to vesting provisions.

Many are under the misimpression that an option agreement relating to an ISO is required to provide that the option must be exercised within 90 days after termination of employment. This is not the case. The ISO rules require that *in order to receive ISO treatment*, an option must in fact be exercised in the 90-day period. An option agreement for an ISO can provide, without violation of the ISO rules, that the option will not expire for a specified period of time, whether or not employment has been terminated. In that case, the ISO is effectively converted into an NQSO if it is not exercised within 90 days of termination of employment.

With two caveats, the grantee of an ISO is not taxed upon exercising the ISO. Instead, the grantee reports long-term capital gain upon selling the underlying stock equal to the excess of their amount realized in the sale over the exercise price of the ISO. The corporation granting the ISO reports no compensation deduction with respect to the ISO.

The first caveat is that the grantee must hold the underlying stock until at least two years after the grant of the ISO *and* at least one year after the exercise of the ISO. A disposition of the underlying stock before the holding period has run (referred to as a *disqualifying disposition*) requires the grantee to recognize ordinary compensation income for the year of the disposition equal to the lesser of the spread on the option at the time of exercise or the gain realized by the grantee on the disposition. If the grantee fails to satisfy the holding period requirement, the granting corporation can deduct the compensation reported by the grantee subject to any applicable deductibility limitations and the compliance by the granting corporation with applicable reporting rules. Often, employees do not understand this rule, resulting in surprise to find out the cashing out of previously unexercised options in an M&A deal results in ordinary income and not capital gain like common shareholders.

The second caveat is that the AMT rules accord no special treatment to ISOs. Thus, the grantee must include the spread on the ISO at the time of exercise in computing his alternative minimum taxable income for the year of exercise. Depending on the size of the spread and the grantee's other adjustments and preferences, the AMT rules can subject the grantee to tax for the year of exercise at a specified maximum rate on some portion of the spread at the time of exercise.

Restricted Stock

As an alternative to stock options, companies sometimes offer restricted stock to employees, consultants, and other service providers. The term *restricted stock* means that the stock that the service provider purchases is subject to a right of the company to repurchase the stock at the service provider's cost (or some other amount that is less than fair market value at the time of repurchase) if specified service-related or performance-vesting conditions are not met. Technically, the applicable tax regulations refer to stock that is both nontransferable and "subject to a substantial risk of forfeiture," as defined therein, upon its issuance to the recipient as "substantially nonvested" stock. The restricted stock we have been discussing is stock that is "substantially nonvested" within the meaning of those regulations.

Restricted stock can be made subject to the same time- or performance-based vesting conditions as might apply to options. In the case of an option, vesting permits the grantee to exercise the option and thereby purchase the underlying stock at a price fixed on the grant date. In the case of restricted stock, vesting allows the stockholder to retain the vested stock on termination of the service relationship; if the company retains any right to repurchase vested stock, the repurchase price is typically the fair market value of the stock at the time of the repurchase (or some formula price intended to approximate fair market value). Unvested stock is repurchased at a "forfeiture" price, generally original cost.

Thus, vesting in each case establishes the right of the service provider to receive any value of the stock in excess of the price established at the outset. The difference between restricted stock and stock options is that, under a restricted stock arrangement, the stock is actually issued to the service provider up front, subject to a right of the company to repurchase unvested stock at the service provider's cost if the shares fail to vest. Because of the additional complexity, companies often hesitate to make restricted stock available to a broad pool of employees and other service providers. Also, the company wants to avoid the bookkeeping and procedural complexities of keeping track of a large number of shareholders, each of whom is entitled to participate in corporate governance.

A recipient of restricted stock generally has two choices for tax purposes. On the one hand, the recipient may, within 30 days of issuance, make a Section 83(b) election with respect to the stock. In that case, the receipt of the stock is the relevant tax event, and the grantee is taxed at ordinary income rates on any excess of the value of the stock at the time it is received (without regard to the service-related restrictions) over the amount paid for the stock. Because the restricted stock is almost always sold at its fair market value, there is no excess value that is taxed. The grantee takes a fair market value basis in the stock, and the capital gain holding period begins. The grantee then suffers no tax consequences upon vesting. Instead, the grantee reports capital gain upon the later sale of the stock (assuming that the capital gains holding period is met) equal to the amount received in the sale over the basis in the stock. If the stock is forfeited by failing to vest, however, the loss (which is generally a capital loss) is limited to the excess of the amount received on forfeiture over the amount paid for the stock (thus, the grantee is not entitled to recoup any income reported upon receiving the stock by taking a corresponding deduction upon forfeiture). The forfeiture rule may be even more harsh if the corporation is an S corporation and the recipient has had to report a share of the granting corporation's income without receiving a corresponding tax distribution. Subject to any applicable limitations and the compliance with applicable reporting rules, the granting corporation's compensation deductions mirror the recipient's compensation income in both amount and timing.

On the other hand, the recipient may forgo making a Section 83(b) election. In that case, the grantee is taxed at ordinary income rates when (or as) the stock vests (i.e., ceases to be nontransferable and subject to a substantial risk of forfeiture) on the excess of the value of the stock at the time of vesting over the amount he paid for the stock. The post-receipt appreciation in the value of the stock is taxed at ordinary income rates (and at the time of vesting). The capital gains holding period begins at the time of vesting. Again, subject to any applicable limitations and compliance with the applicable reporting rules, the company's compensation deductions mirror the recipient's compensation income in both amount and timing.

In practice, Section 83(b) elections are always made in the private company context. The board purports to grant the restricted stock at fair market value, and the grantee buys at fair market value. The grantee fills out the Section 83(b) election form to show that the purchase price and the fair market value are the same. Violà!—no tax. Because the actual fair market value of a startup technology company is almost impossible to fairly determine, it is extremely unlikely that the price set by the board and used by the grantee will be challenged as not being fair market value. The Section 83(b) election must be filed with the Internal Revenue Service (IRS) by the recipient within 30 days after receipt of the stock. The grantee must also provide the corporation (and others in certain instances) with a copy of the election and attach another copy to the grantee's tax return for the year of receipt of the stock.

If the Section 83(b) election is not made, the grantee must pay tax equal to the fair market value spread of the stock on each vesting date over the purchase price. This creates an impossible situation for the grantee—that spread may be significant and the grantee is unable to sell the stock to pay for the tax because of restrictions on transfer.

The use of restricted stock raises a number of practical issues, including these:

- Typically, the recipient must pay for the stock upon receiving it. If the recipient borrows the purchase price from the corporation, the IRS may attempt to treat the recipient as having only an NQSO if the recipient is not personally liable for a "substantial portion" of the debt. Arrangements that obligate the corporation to repurchase the stock can undermine the tax objectives sought in using restricted stock. In addition, under SEC rules under the Sarbanes-Oxley Act, loans from the corporation to officers must be repaid before the filing of the IPO registration statement, even though the IPO may never get to a closing.
- Often, restricted stock is issued to a service provider solely to accommodate the service provider's tax objectives. If not for the tax laws, the corporation would have granted options to the service provider to condition the service provider's right to hold shares on the satisfaction of vesting requirements. For state law purposes, however, the recipient is a shareholder despite the fact that the recipient might not yet have fully earned the shares. Issues may arise as to the extent to which the recipient is to be accorded rights of a shareholder under a shareholders' agreement. In addition, consideration is often given to whether voting agreements or other arrangements with respect to the voting of nonvested shares are appropriate.
- If the recipient does not make a Section 83(b) election, the recipient is not deemed to own the stock for tax purposes until vesting. Any distributions made to the recipient with respect to the stock before vesting are treated as compensation payments and not a dividend. If the corporation is an S corporation, the recipient does not report any of the corporation's undistributed income, even though the recipient might be entitled to receive a share of the income if later distributed. It is not unusual, therefore, for S corporations to require recipients of restricted stock to make Section 83(b) elections.

EMPLOYMENT AGREEMENTS AND NONCOMPETITION COVENANTS

Employment agreements, at least long fancy ones, are relatively rare in the private company world. Almost all employees, other than senior employees, are usually given a simple offer letter that describes their compensation and other employment basics. Such offer letters always provide (or should provide) that the prospective employee will be an employee "at-will" (i.e., that the employee may be fired at any time with or without cause). In addition, all employees and consultants (and anyone who may come into contact with any of the company's trade secrets) also must be required to sign a confidentiality/invention assignment/noncompetition agreement. A sample employment agreement is included in the appendixes.

Most provisions of employment agreements are relatively uncontroversial. The agreement specifies a salary and benefits, and may specify a formula for a bonus. If not already the subject of a separate agreement, the employment agreement will also contain relatively customary confidentiality, assignment of inventions, and noncompetition agreements.

There are, however, several critical areas of negotiation. The most important point to remember with respect to employment agreements is that they should *never* guarantee the employee the right to remain an employee or in a specified position for a fixed or minimum period of time. This is highly imprudent from the company's point of view. If the board decides that the employee must be fired, then the company must be able to carry that out for the well-being of the company. The company always needs to be protected from incompetent or nonperforming employees. There really is no such thing (or should not be) as a true two-year employment contract.

What is properly understood by a two-year employment agreement is that if an employee is fired within two years, he has to leave immediately but is entitled to some amount of severance. When and under what circumstances severance is paid is a critical element of negotiation. What many people mean by a two-year employment contract, for example, is that if the employee is fired within the first two years of employment, the employee continues to receive a salary for the remainder of the term, in a lump sum or paid in accordance with ordinary payroll, even though no longer employed by the company—or is entitled to receive the greater of a specified lump sum or a specified number of months' installments. The employee's viewpoint is that he or she is entitled to the greater of the lump sum or specified installments, or the balance of the two years' salary. This is a key negotiating point.

The other key negotiating points are whether there is a difference in the employee's treatment if the employee is fired "*with cause*," fired "*without cause*," quits for "*good reason*," or quits without good reason. Generally speaking, the employee is entitled to nothing other than accrued salary if fired with cause or if he quits without good reason. The employee typically gets severance only if fired without cause or if the employee quits for good reason. Because this is the case, the definitions of cause and good reason become critical in the employment agreement.

Astute lawyers for employees will make sure that the definition of cause does not include failure to perform according to expectations as long as the employee is making a reasonable effort. Such lawyers take care to limit the definition of cause to egregious acts where the malfeasance is clear and is not the subject of reasonable differing interpretations.

Examples of Cause Definitions

Following are six increasingly onerous (to the employee) definitions of cause. The real dividing line is between numbers 5 and 6—the reason being that the ones before the dividing line are within the reasonable control of the employee, but the one after the line may well not be. This is a huge distinction.

1. The employee's indictment for or the pleading of the employee of *nolo contendere* to a felony.
2. The commission by the employee of an act of fraud, embezzlement, or any other illegal conduct in connection with the employee's performance of his duties.
3. Disregard of the material rules or material policies of the company that have not been cured within 15 days after notice thereof from the company.
4. Gross negligence in the performance of the employee's duties, willful misfeasance in connection with the employee's work, or a breach of fiduciary duty by the employee.
5. Willful failure to perform the employee's employment duties, or willful failure to follow instructions of the board of directors, if such failure is in any way significant, but only if such failure does not result from an ambiguity in such duties or instructions; provided, however, that such duties or instructions are specific in nature and not in the nature of performance goals or objectives.
6. Unsatisfactory performance by the employee as determined in the sole discretion of the company's board of directors (or failure to meet performance goals and the like).

Another issue is whether the employment agreement will contain provisions dealing with the situation where the employee quits for good reason. The argument for the employee is that, to take an extreme example, if the employee's salary is reduced to minimum wage, then the employee is forced to quit, which is not substantively different from being fired without cause.

This is tough to argue against. The only issue is how broadly *good reason* is defined. Here is a sample of a definition of *good reason:*

> *"Good Reason" shall mean any of the following: (i) a material diminution in the Employee's responsibilities, duties or authority to which the Employee has not consented and which remains unremedied for thirty (30) days after written notice from the Employee* [Question: *What does this phrase mean if the company is acquired by a substantially larger company—does the employee have the right to be an executive officer of the acquirer?*]; *(ii) the relocation of the Employee by the Company outside the Company's main office without the Employee's written consent [or a change in the location of the Employee's office by more than a specified number of miles]; or (iii) a material decrease in the Employee's compensation or aggregate benefits without the Employee's written consent [sometimes with an exception for across-the-board reductions among all senior executives up to a limit].*

It is generally accepted that, from the viewpoint of the employer, the shorter and simpler the agreement, the better. Generally, other than confidentiality, invention assignment, and noncompetition provisions, an employment agreement is viewed as being for the employee's benefit.

Examples of Negotiating Points

From the employee's viewpoint, in addition to the critical issues already discussed, there are a myriad of negotiating points to consider. The following is a list of issues for prospective employees to consider in negotiating an employment arrangement with a new employer.

Term   A stated term is not necessary. The key issue to consider is the amount of severance, when it is paid (up front or periodically), and how the circumstances of termination affect or don't affect the severance provisions.

Compensation
- Salary, payment periods, and any agreed periodic changes in base salary
- Bonus opportunity—clear definitions of metrics and ability to earn pro rata, assuming not-for-cause termination
- Benefit arrangements
- Vacation, expenses, and so forth—a stated initial agreement relating to these items
- A statement that the executive is entitled to participate in all benefit programs for which other executives of the same level are eligible

Position/Responsibilities

- Scope
- Clear definition of duty of loyalty (i.e., devote full time, best efforts, non-competition, etc.), which defines what activities can be pursued without violating the duty (e.g., service on other boards, serving nonprofits, private investing, etc.)
- Location of office or duties, which ties into executive's voluntary termination for good reason if the location of office or duties is materially changed
- Board duties
- Reporting structure (i.e., to whom will executive report), tying into a voluntary termination for good reason (which may include demotion)

Termination For cause definition:

- Narrow and clearly defined
- Elimination of any provisions that are performance standards or disguised performance standards
- Notice and opportunity to cure as to the others
- Materiality qualifications
- Willfulness/knowing qualifications as to misconduct provisions
- Opportunity to be heard for any termination decision

The agreement might include a provision for voluntary termination by executive for "good reason":

- If the contract makes any distinction as to consequences of a cause/no cause termination, then a good reason provision is usually regarded as a corollary.
- Components of good reason: Diminution of title or duties; diminution of salary or benefits; relocation; change of control or sale of assets.

Death will certainly terminate employment; disability might. The agreement should spell out benefits and any pertinent details regarding what might constitute disability.

Severance Arrangements The agreement should address triggers/entitlement/amounts:

- Payable if voluntary termination for good reason. What if the employee quits without good reason?

- Is severance payable for balance of a stated term or for x months, if greater?
- Is the severance payable up front as a lump sum?
- Does periodic severance cease or become reduced if other employment is obtained during the severance period?
- Does periodic severance cease or become reduced upon death or disability?
- Does severance include provision of health benefits during severance period or payment of Consolidated Omnibus Budget Reconciliation Act (COBRA) premiums?
- Will employer include payment for outplacement services of employee's choice?
- Will arrangements be made for use of offices, technology, and/or voicemail upon termination?
- Will employer agree to reasonable reference arrangements?

Equity Compensation

- Stock/restricted stock. Restricted stock is much better for the employee as a tax matter. If restricted stock is purchased and requires a substantial outlay of cash, consider using a note for all or part of the purchase price, and also maximize the nonrecourse portion of note. Is buyout at termination automatic or at option of the company? (It should be automatic if a real-money purchase price.)
- Options (ISO/NQSO). Both ISOs and NQSOs should provide for a fixed term to exercise and not terminate within a specific period after termination. As discussed earlier, this is not an ISO requirement. This provision is particularly important for NQSOs because exercise is a taxable event.
- Vesting schedule. How much up front? Specify vesting period and timing of balance. Is there accelerated vesting if termination without cause?
- Acceleration upon change of control. If not full acceleration, try to obtain a specified amount of vesting on a change in control and a so-called double trigger clause stating that if the executive is not offered employment, or if the executive remains for a transition period, or if the executive is terminated without cause during the transition period, then there is full acceleration.
- Antidilution. Examine (highly unlikely) possibility of protection against dilution from extraordinary preferred stock terms and/or *down round* financings—so-called *make whole* provisions. For example, the executive is entitled to a bonus equal to a fixed percentage of sale proceeds on an as-converted basis.

Restrictive Covenants

- Noncompete, nonsolicit, antipiracy:
  - Preferable to define precisely a competing business, rather than just saying that the employee will not compete with the business of the employer.
  - Does covenant terminate on substantial cessation of business?
  - Is period shorter (or nonexistent) if terminated without cause?
  - Make sure the definition of *competing business* does not generically include the business of a successor.
  - Can the employee go to work for a large company that competes but may not work in the competitive division?
- Invention assignment:
  - Avoid invention assignments that cover post-termination inventions.
- Nondisparagement:
  - If the employer asks for a nondisparagement clause, employees should ask that this be mutual.

280G Does the employee get protection if IRC Section 280G is triggered? (This is a tax code provision that imposes severe penalties for *excess parachute payments*.) Consider up-front shareholder approval of parachute provisions if a private company, or a tax "gross up" for parachute taxes.

Attorneys' Fees Determine whether attorneys' fees will be reimbursed in connection with the negotiation of the agreement by employer.

Merger Clauses Ensure that the employer is obligated to require assumption, in writing, of employment agreement in the event of a sale of the company.

INDEMNIFICATION

Consider obtaining provisions requiring employer to indemnify the executive under the company's existing bylaws and provide that the executive is entitled to the fullest indemnification permitted by law if the bylaws are inadequate or are amended. Consider a requirement for insurance coverage under directors' and officers' (D&O) insurance or other policies.

Noncompetition Covenants

A noncompete agreement signed by key employees is usually an essential component of an acquisition from the point of view of the Buyer. There is no way the Buyer will buy the business if it is at risk of key employees of the Target leaving and competing with it.

A noncompete agreement needs to be supported by consideration. A noncompetition agreement entered into upon commencement of employment is usually not problematic, but in some states, like California, such an agreement is unenforceable. Employers sometimes forget to get one at the outset and ask an employee to sign one later. That risks unenforceability because of the consideration issue.

In most acquisitions, the key employee is being paid out on his stock in the acquisition and/or is being given a new employment agreement or a retention bonus. Those agreements are typically enforceable. Regardless of consideration, noncompetition agreements must be reasonable in scope and length. Agreements that are too broad or too long can be thrown out by the courts.

In drafting noncompetition agreements, care must be taken to make them as narrow as possible. Employers prefer to define scope as anything that competes with the employer at the time of termination. That may be enforceable, but it creates some risk that a court would determine that it unfairly deprives the employee of the right to make a living. Consideration should be given to drafting a clause that describes the employer's business in specific terms that limits the scope of what is competition. Properly drafted, this should be sufficient for both parties.

These agreements usually contain a nonsolicitation clause that prohibits, for a period of time, the departing employee from soliciting his co-workers to leave employment or from soliciting the employer's customers in a way that is detrimental to the employer. Again, the narrower the better from the viewpoint of enforceability. Thus, these types of clauses might be limited to customers with whom the departing employee dealt during his tenure with the employer.

Additional Considerations

Part of the Buyer's due diligence should include an analysis as to whether the Target has remained current in its employment withholding obligations. This is particularly true in the case of a distressed business. If the Buyer has plans to do layoffs, it must examine whether the Worker Adjustment and Retraining Notification (WARN) Act plant closing/mass layoff law is applicable, or if a state equivalent is applicable. These laws typically require a notice period before the layoff can occur. If feasible, notice should be given by the Target before the closing if the Buyer wants to initiate an immediate layoff.

One other issue is to determine whether any of the Target's employees are unionized. In that case, even in an asset sale the Buyer may be liable under the Target's collective bargaining agreement.

EMPLOYMENT AND BENEFITS LAW

General Employment Issues

The preceding two sections assumed that there was a blank slate to create an equity compensation program and employment agreements for key executives. In an acquisition, both the Buyer and the Target need to focus on how the Target's *existing* compensation arrangements and benefit plans are to be handled. Some or all of the nuances in this area may be present in the Target's plans, and the Buyer's response to handling existing arrangements can make or break a deal.

The first task is to examine and categorize the Target's employment and benefits landscape. That includes obtaining a list of all employees with salary and benefits for each (or at least, for lower-level employees, selected categories). Benefit plans need to be analyzed both for the level of benefits but also for special arrangements that may have been made in the event of a change of control.

As a general matter, the Buyer must make a determination as to how many employees of the Target will be offered continuing employment with the surviving corporation. In many businesses, but not all, a significant component of what the Buyer is actually acquiring is the employee base of the Target. That is particularly true in technology company acquisitions. Inevitably, the Buyer will not intend to maintain the exact workforce in place with the Target. The Buyer may want to trim costs, may have its own managers that it thinks are better than existing managers, and there are usually redundancies with the Buyer's existing staff functions. For example, financial, legal, and accounting personnel at the Target do not survive the acquisition if the Buyer's existing staff in those areas can handle the incremental work relating to the business of the Target (unless the Buyer's CEO likes the Target's staff better).

A delicate negotiating issue is when these issues are brought up, and by whom. As for employment arrangements, the board and management owe their first duty to the shareholders of the Target. So one might argue that dealing with employment arrangements is not appropriate until the purchase price and other key terms have been settled. Frequently, this issue arises because the Buyer itself raises the issue, both because it knows it will enhance its prospects of getting the deal and because the Buyer usually wants to keep at least some of the key people at the Target as a condition of doing the deal.

As for the general employee base, as opposed to key employees, the practice varies widely. In some cases, the Target's board and management never even raise the issue of what will happen to the Target's employees post-acquisition. As long as the Target shareholders get their money, the

Buyer can do whatever it wants with the employee base. Other boards and management feel an ethical responsibility to the Target's employees and will negotiate in advance what will happen to them. There may be a deal that ensures that all or a substantial portion of the Target's employees will at least be offered initial employment at their current compensation. In addition, the Target may negotiate a few specifics, like whether employees will be given comparable benefits after the deal, and whether they will be given credit for eligibility and vesting purposes under the Buyer's benefit plans for their years of service with the Target.

If there are existing employment, severance, or golden parachute agreements, by and large the Buyer is stuck with them. The amounts payable under those agreements need to be factored into the true cost of the deal to the Buyer. As is discussed in Chapter 4, an analysis must be undertaken at the outset as to whether any special payments or benefits that will accrue to management as a result of the change of control will constitute "excess parachute payments." These provisions, which cover the most highly paid employees, result in substantial tax penalties. Management may be entitled to, or insist upon, being *grossed up* for the tax impact, meaning that they will get extra compensation so that their payment will be made on an after-tax basis. In acquisitions of private companies, these problems can usually be cured with a shareholder *cleansing vote*.

Types of Benefit Plans

Generally speaking, in an asset sale, the Buyer does not assume the Target's benefit plan liabilities. The plans are then frozen and the financial burdens of that process remain with the Target. If the Buyer purchases the stock of the Target or there is a merger, the Buyer assumes as a matter of law the Target's liabilities under the Target's benefit plans.

The essential issue is for the Buyer to determine what liabilities exist under the Target's benefit plans and what liabilities will result if the benefit plans are continued or terminated. The Buyer must determine whether the Target's plans have been maintained in accordance with legal requirements, whether they are solvent, and whether there is flexibility to change the plans if that is what the Buyer wants to do. In older businesses, one particular area of concern is accrued retiree health benefits, which can be extremely costly.

Benefit plans can be divided into two basic categories, as used in the federal statute that governs benefits, ERISA. There are pension plans and welfare plans. Pension plans can be defined benefit plans that provide for a payout on retirement and that have funding requirements to ensure that there will be funds available to pay out the accrued benefits. These are extraordinarily complicated and must be examined by a benefits expert to determine the financial implications if the Buyer assumes the plan or folds it into its own defined benefit plan. Fortunately, this type of pension plan has become fairly uncommon.

The other type of pension plan is the defined contribution plan, where the employee and/or the employer is required to make defined contributions. For example, 401(k) plans, which are now extremely common, are defined contribution plans. Since the Buyer is likely to have a 401(k) plan, the usual course is for the Target's existing 401(k) plan to be terminated, and for retained employees to participate in the Buyer's plan, with or without prior service credit for eligibility and vesting purposes. The individual employees of the Target would roll over their prior plan amounts to another plan, in some cases to the Buyer's plan and in others to one set up by the employee's financial advisers or broker. Care must be taken to analyze any potential liabilities resulting from employer match requirements.

In rare cases involving unionized employees, the Target may be a participant in a multiemployer pension plan. Specialists are required in this situation since there may be withdrawal liabilities and penalties in connection with such plans.

With respect to COBRA benefits, in a stock sale the Buyer effectively assumes those obligations; in an asset sale, the Buyer may have secondary liability.

ACQUISITION ACCOUNTING

In the not-too-distant past, accounting considerations were frequently as important as tax considerations in structuring acquisitions. That is because there were two forms of accounting for acquisitions by the Buyer with drastically different consequences. In so-called *acquisition accounting* (formerly referred to as purchase accounting), the Buyer reset the carrying value of the acquired assets to fair market value, and any related goodwill had to be amortized, sometimes over a relatively short period, particularly in technology deals. In the other form, a *pooling-of-interests*, there was no change in the carrying value of the acquired assets and no amortization of goodwill. This treatment was considered highly desirable, since it was difficult to do accretive acquisitions with goodwill amortization creating significant book expense going forward. The requirements for qualifying for a pooling were strict (e.g., the acquisition consideration had to be solely for voting stock). There were multiple other requirements as well.

This all changed a number of years ago, and now there is only one form of accounting treatment generally applicable to acquisitions of all of the Target's assets, regardless of the form of the transaction: Post-acquisition assets have a new carrying value tied to fair market value, and goodwill is not written off unless it is, or becomes, impaired.[3] There are alternative treatments for situations where not all assets are acquired or there is a specified residual minority interest, which we will also discuss briefly.

The accounting for acquisitions is relevant for several reasons. For a public company for which accounting net income and accounting earnings per share (EPS) are a principal driver for its stock price, minimizing the book earnings charges (expenses) resulting from an acquisition is important. Generally speaking, the principal reason for acquisitions is to create shareholder value by increasing EPS, either in the short or long term. Private company Buyers may be concerned because they must comply with debt covenants (e.g., the ratio of earnings to fixed charges) to avoid a default on their debt. Higher earnings per share are also desirable for purposes of the eventual acquisition of the company or for an IPO. In an IPO, the company, having become a public company, has the same earnings concerns. In an acquisition, maximizing accounting earnings per share of the to-be-acquired company should increase the earnings per share of the acquirer, all things being equal, and should result in a higher purchase price.

There are two different schools of thought relating to so-called *noncash charges*. Noncash charges are items of expense that create a book expense for accounting purposes but that do not require any cash outlay—like the previously mentioned amortization of goodwill. As a general proposition, all companies want to maximize their cash flow and their cash flow per share. It is hard to argue against higher cash flow per share being a good thing. But some companies, both public and private, are discounting to a greater or lesser extent the importance of EPS under generally accepted accounting principles (GAAP) that includes noncash charges. The reason is that, although the basic premises of accounting remain solid—matching revenue to the expense incurred in the applicable accounting period to create that revenue—noncash charges are increasingly becoming less important to analysts who follow the stock. Somewhat different is depreciation, because once the asset is fully depreciated or otherwise needs to be replaced, it will require cash to replace it. That is the whole basis of the GAAP concept of matching expense to revenue in the proper accounting period.

What if there are noncash charges attributable to stock options? Stock options generate cash on exercise. In other words, a company can have noncash expenses that may never negatively affect its cash flow. As we discuss elsewhere, traditional accounting for stock options granted at the fair

---

[3]Starting in 2013, non-public companies could elect to amortize goodwill over its useful life, not to exceed 10 years.

market value of the stock did not result in a book earnings charge. Under accounting rules, the value of the options themselves must be determined and expensed over the vesting period of the option. These noncash expenses will never affect directly the net cash flow of the business, although more shares outstanding will affect net cash flow per share. But expensing the options themselves is double counting, in a sense. Wall Street analysts, to a greater or lesser extent, are *backing out* (or disregarding) noncash expense charges because they will never affect cash flow. Instead, they just estimate the expected short- and long-term effect on cash flow per share.

Accounting for goodwill is another example, as noted earlier. Traditionally, in an acquisition accounted for as a purchase, where the purchase price exceeded the fair value of the assets purchased, which was usually the case given conservative historical cost accounting for assets, this goodwill had to be amortized over the expected useful life of the goodwill. For a company in the rapidly changing technology area, sometimes the amortization period could be quite short.

The current treatment is for the purchase price to be allocated to the acquired assets at their current fair market value; the excess is allocated to goodwill. Goodwill is *not* amortized after the transaction (subject to nonpublic companies' option to amortize as noted above), but is examined at that time and periodically thereafter as to whether the goodwill is no longer worth what it is carried for on the books, and is therefore impaired. This impairment charge, like option expense, is a noncash charge. Its relevance to financial performance, however, makes more sense because if the goodwill is no longer worth its book value, then that diminution probably results, directly or indirectly, from the diminished inability of that asset to generate earnings.

Accounting rules look to the substance of a transaction much more than do the tax rules. Transactions with similar economics can have drastically different tax results based on the form of the transaction. Conversely, if the Buyer acquires 100 percent of the assets of the Target, either directly through an asset purchase, or indirectly through a purchase of all of the stock or a merger that results in a purchase of all of the stock, acquisition accounting rules apply in the same manner.

It also is not necessarily obvious which entity is the acquiring entity, to the extent it makes a difference. There are guidelines relating to extent of ownership, management control, and the like that dictate who is the Buyer and who is the Target for accounting purposes.

The essence of the acquisition accounting approach is that the financials of the acquiring entity should reflect the total cost to the Buyer of the acquisition by the Buyer, direct or through a subsidiary, of the Target's assets. The *cost to the Buyer* in this context means the amount of cash and the fair value of equity issued (including an estimate of contingent payments) plus liabilities assumed.

It should also be noted that if the cost is less than the fair market value of the Target's assets, negative goodwill is created and, under current accounting rules, recorded in income at the date of acquisition. All of the Target's assets must be identified and valued, including intangible assets such as patents, customer lists, favorable leases, and the like. Intangibles are separately accounted for (i.e., outside of goodwill) where the assets arise from contractual rights or are transferable separately from the other assets of the business.

One point is worth emphasizing since it is another of those contrary-to-common-sense results dictated by Wall Street's analysis of companies, or at least the perception of it. Note that under current rules, in-process research and development (R&D) may not be written off at the time of the acquisition, but must be treated as an asset purchased in the acquisition (in which case it can be written off as impaired if applicable). The prior common practice had been to attempt to write off as much in-process R&D as possible, sometimes creating a large one-time hit to earnings and EPS. One would think that Wall Street would severely penalize the company for the one-time expense. Companies used to do this to write off as much as possible that would otherwise have to be taken into expense over the period of the research, thus dragging down earnings for years to come. Plus, the write-off was sometimes a noncash expense, making it particularly attractive. Wall Street usually rewarded companies for this shrewdness.

This same rationale applies to the treatment of goodwill. As previously noted, the past practice required companies to first allocate purchase price to tangible and intangible assets based on fair value and then allocate the balance to goodwill. Goodwill was then written off over the predicted future useful life of the goodwill asset. For companies in industries with rapidly changing technologies, like software, the period could be quite short. So, as was the case with purchased R&D, companies took the first opportunity to write off goodwill in one lump sum to attempt to eliminate the future drag on earnings.

Under the rules, as we have said, goodwill does not have to be amortized, but only written off if it becomes impaired. This is normally done at the annual audit, but also must be done if there are significant changes in the business. If goodwill has to be written off in part, companies try to take as large a write-off as they can in order to get the bad news behind them.

The situation gets more complicated if the Buyer purchases 20 percent or more, and less than a majority, of the Target's shares. The foregoing discussion assumes the usual case where the Buyer has purchased 100 percent of the Target or close to it. In the case of a complete acquisition, the Buyer would prepare consolidated financial statements, which are financial statements of the Buyer, including its consolidated subsidiaries. Normally, the Buyer would only publish consolidated financial statements, but may be required to prepare the Target-only financial statements for banks and others who are interested in the Target-only financial condition, such as banks with loans to the Target (which has the assets) that are not guaranteed by the Buyer. Note that where the Buyer purchases the Target's assets directly, then there is only one remaining entity, the Buyer (which includes the Target's assets), and therefore generally only one financial statement is published.

Where the Buyer buys between 20 percent and 50 percent of the Target's stock, the Buyer generally does not prepare consolidated financial statements with the Target (assuming variable interest entity consolidation rules do not apply). It accounts for its interest in the Target under the *equity method* of accounting, also called *one-line consolidation*. There the Buyer reports in a line item on its income statement its share of the net income of the Target (i.e., the Target's GAAP net income multiplied by the percentage of the Target owned by the Buyer).

Another question is whether the *Target's* financial statements must be modified going forward to reflect acquisition accounting charges. This is not a simple issue. Generally, the Target continues to prepare its own separate financial statements without reference to the acquisition transaction. Where the Target's financials have to be filed with the SEC, with certain exceptions, the SEC requires the Buyer to apply acquisition accounting principles to the Target's financial statements. This is called *push-down* accounting. The Target may also elect to apply push-down accounting absent SEC requirements.

Push-down accounting may appear to be a rather technical subject. But it is critically important to understand its possible application where the acquisition transaction has post-closing adjustments or there is an earnout. In these cases, care must be taken in the acquisition agreement to require the preparation of the Target's financial statements without the application of push-down accounting so that the added expense does not reduce the earnout or other amounts payable to the Target's former shareholders based on the future GAAP earnings of the Target.

RECAPITALIZATION ACCOUNTING

In cases where an acquisition, like most LBOs, does not result in a complete change in ownership of the Target (i.e., where some or all of the Target's shareholders own equity in the post-acquisition business), another form of accounting, called recapitalization accounting, may be applicable, rather than acquisition accounting. To take a typical example, the Buyer purchases directly from the Target new Target shares, the Target borrows money based on the equity infusion, and the Target then redeems part but not all of the shares held by the old Target shareholders such that the old Target shareholders continue to own a significant stake in the Target. In a transaction where there is no change of control of the Target, or where there is a change of control of the Target, the Target survives as an entity and the Target's old shareholders own more than 20 percent of the resulting business, recapitalization accounting should apply. Recapitalization accounting can apply in other situations as well. Oddly, in this area form seems to have some impact on the accounting for the acquisition.

The advantage of recapitalization accounting is that assets do not have to be written up for book (not tax), which increases depreciation, thereby reducing net income. Also, no goodwill is created, and the specter of a future write-off of goodwill is eliminated. So, in the case where the Target is to go public after the transaction, it will thereby be able to present better income statement prospects to potential IPO investors, which will enhance its IPO valuation. Recapitalization accounting applies to the financial statements of the Target in this case; where there is a change of control and Target's financial statements are consolidated with the Buyer's financial statements, acquisition accounting will continue to apply to the Buyer's consolidated financial statements. A variant of acquisition accounting will apply if the Buyer accounts for its investment on the equity method.

CROSS-BORDER ACQUISITIONS

Acquisitions can have international implications, which in some cases are not obvious. International considerations are discussed in Chapter 8.

APPENDIXES

The following appendixes are located on the website that accompanies this book. For information on the website, see the "About the Website" section at the back of this book.

Appendix 3A, Convertible Preferred Stock Term Sheet

Appendix 3B, Stock Option and Incentive Plan

Appendix 3C, Employment Agreement

CHAPTER 4

Tax Considerations

TAXABLE VERSUS TAX-FREE TRANSACTIONS: OVERVIEW OF RELEVANT SITUATIONS

Usually it is possible to structure an acquisition as either taxable or tax-free if both the Buyer and the Target are taxed as corporations (whether C or S corporations). Similarly, if both the Buyer and the Target are taxable as partnerships (i.e., flow-through treatment, which is true of most limited liability companies), an acquisition transaction could be structured as taxable or tax-free.[1] However, a corporation generally cannot acquire a partnership or its assets in a tax-free transaction, only in a taxable one.

Before examining in greater detail the ways in which an acquisition can be structured, let us summarize some of the considerations bearing on whether the parties will want the transaction to be taxable or tax-free:

- *Basis step-up.* In a taxable transaction treated as an asset sale by the Target,[2] although the Target will recognize taxable income on the sale of appreciated assets, the Buyer will take a tax basis in the assets equivalent in total to the purchase price, which includes liabilities that the Buyer assumes. This stepped-up basis will generate depreciation and amortization deductions for the Buyer in future years that may save it substantial taxes.
- *Type of consideration.* A tax-free transaction implies that owners of the Target receive equity in the Buyer rather than cash. If the Buyer is a publicly traded corporation, that may be acceptable, but if the Buyer is

---

[1]Unless it has elected to be taxed as a corporation, a multimember LLC is taxed as a partnership. All references in this chapter to "partnerships" refer to any business entity that is so taxed.
[2]The types of transactions so treated for tax purposes are explained below.

private, the Target's shareholders are likely to have a strong preference for cash (even though taxable) rather than illiquid private equity.

- *Capital gain tax rates at time of transaction.* As of 2016, the maximum federal capital gain rate for individuals is 15 percent. So long as this remains true, the tax cost of a taxable transaction is modest. If equity is received in a tax-free transaction, there is a risk that its eventual disposition will be taxed at a higher capital gain rate.

- *Existence of Target corporation net operating loss carryovers.* If the Target has substantial net operating loss (NOL) carryovers, a taxable transaction could be structured in which gain on its assets is realized but no tax is paid at the corporate level on such gain because it is offset by the NOL. This would give a stepped-up tax basis to the Buyer, and this may well be more tax efficient than a tax-free transaction in which the lower basis of the Target's assets carries over to the Buyer.

- *Ability to depreciate goodwill.* Recent changes in federal tax law allow the Buyer to write off purchased goodwill and other purchased intangibles on a straight-line basis over 15 years. This reduces the true tax cost of a taxable transaction in which gain is recognized on the disposition of the Target's assets because the entire purchase price can be depreciated/amortized against the Buyer's ordinary income. For C corporations that are taxpayers, this means each dollar in depreciation can save 35 cents in federal tax. In fact, if the Target is an S corporation (so that the tax rate on the disposition of its assets other than inventory and receivables generally is only 20 percent federally), the value of the depreciation deductions in the hands of the Buyer may essentially offset the tax cost of recognizing gain at the corporate level, once the transaction is analyzed in present-value terms.

- *Possible advantages of a tax-free transaction.* If some of the preceding assumptions are reversed, a tax-free transaction may be more attractive than a taxable one. For example, if for one reason or another the Buyer is unlikely to benefit from the extra depreciation deductions generated by a stepped-up tax basis in the Target's assets, recognizing gain that triggers tax at the Target corporation level is less attractive. Similarly, if the Buyer is a public corporation whose shares the Target's shareholders are reasonably content to hold, a tax-free transaction opens the possibility of the shareholders deferring payment of federal income tax related to their gain on their shares or eliminating it entirely if they die holding Buyer's shares and the shares receive a basis step-up at the holder's death.

- *Hybrid transactions.* As explored in greater detail later, the choice is not necessarily all or nothing. In some transactions, the shareholders of the Target receive both cash (which is currently taxable) and Buyer equity, which qualifies for tax-free (i.e., deferred) treatment.

DETAILED ANALYSIS OF THE POSITIONS OF THE TARGET AND ITS OWNERS AND OF THE BUYER

Nature of the Target's Business Organization

The tax treatment of an acquisition depends in part on whether the business is conducted in a C corporation (a regular taxable corporation) or in some other form (such as an S corporation or a partnership). If the entity is a C corporation, the taxable disposition of its assets will give rise to tax at the corporate level. Federally, such gain is taxed at rates of up to 35 percent (C corporations do not benefit from the low individual capital gain tax rates). However, if the C corporation has substantial NOL carryovers, the NOLs would shelter, in whole or in part, the gain on an asset sale, with the result that the transaction will have overall tax effects more like those of a transaction involving an S corporation or partnership.

S corporations and partnerships are flow-through entities not subject to tax at the entity level, so that an acquisition of their business will give rise to only a single tax, imposed at the owner level. An important exception involves S corporations that formerly were Subchapter C corporations and elected S corporation tax status within the preceding five years: To the extent of asset appreciation as of the time of the switch, such entities are subject to an entity-level tax on a sale of their assets.

Nature of Equity Owners

Most acquisitions involve a distribution of the transaction proceeds to the equity owners, which generally will cause them to recognize capital gain or loss unless the transaction is conducted under one of the tax-free reorganization provisions.[3] An exception would occur in the case of a corporate asset sale after which the selling corporation retains the proceeds (i.e., remains in existence) rather than distributing them to its owners. (Alternatively, the corporation could both distribute the proceeds and remain in existence, in which case the distribution would first be taxed as a dividend, to the extent of the distributing corporation's earnings and profits; next, as a tax-free return of shareholder basis; and any remainder as capital gain. Shareholders that are themselves C corporations pay a substantially lower tax on dividends than on capital gains, while individual shareholders, at current rates, are likely to be indifferent between the two.)

---

[3]Capital gain is measured by the difference between the proceeds received by the equity owner and the owner's tax basis in its shares in the distributing entity.

The optimal form of a transaction is usually dependent in part on the federal tax situation of the selling entity's owners. The tax rate faced by such owners will vary greatly. Federally, individuals currently are taxed at capital gain rates of no more than 20 percent. However, C corporations pay the same tax rate (up to 35 percent) on capital gains as on other income. In both cases, however, capital gain can be offset by capital losses and capital loss carryovers. (However, the *dividends received deduction,* which excludes a portion of dividends received by a C corporation from taxation, means that C corporations are taxed lightly on dividend income.) Certain shareholders—for example, qualified pension plans, exempt charitable organizations, and certain foreigners—pay no U.S. tax on capital gains.

Tax Position of the Buyer

Regardless of the Buyer's tax classification (C corporation, S corporation, partnership, etc.), the Buyer generally will desire a stepped-up basis in the assets of the acquired business. For example, if the Target's tax basis in its assets is $2 million, and the Buyer is buying the business for $10 million, the Buyer will want a $10 million basis in the assets rather than a carryover $2 million basis. Of course, there is no way the asset basis can be stepped up without gain being recognized on the transfer of the assets (no tax will be payable, however, if there are sufficient NOLs); in this example, the Target would need to recognize $8 million of taxable gain in any transaction that results in a stepped-up basis.

Thus, a transaction's optimal form will depend on the taxes, if any, that would be imposed on the Target and its owners in order to yield a stepped-up tax basis, and the expected tax advantage on the Buyer's side from such a step up. For example, if the Target has sufficient NOLs to shield $8 million of gain, a transaction designed to yield a stepped-up basis will make sense. However, if the Target would be fully taxable on the $8 million of gain, while the Buyer is not likely to owe any taxes for several years (e.g., because the Buyer operates at a tax loss), a stepped-up basis transaction likely would not be desirable.

The value to a Buyer of a stepped-up basis has been enhanced in recent years by the enactment of Internal Revenue Code (IRC) Section 197. That section permits amortization (i.e., depreciation deductions) straight-line over a 15-year period. Section 197 "intangibles" must be acquired in connection with the taxable acquisition of assets. Eligible intangibles include goodwill, going-concern value, workforce in place, information base, patents, copyrights, licenses, franchises, trademarks, and so forth. While the provision is basically taxpayer-friendly and reverses the prior rule that goodwill and going-concern value are nondepreciable for tax purposes, one restrictive feature of Section 197 is that amounts paid for a covenant not to compete in connection with the taxable purchase of a business are amortizable over only a 15-year period regardless of the length of the covenant or when they are paid. Prior to Section 197, purchasers tried to convert part of the purchase price into amounts that would be deductible over a short period by paying for a covenant not to compete that would last, say, three years, and deducting the amount paid for such a covenant over the three years; now the amounts must be amortized over 15 years regardless of the length of the covenant not to compete.

TAXABLE TRANSACTIONS AND THEIR TAX EFFECTS

Taxable Transactions Treated as Stock Purchases

These are easy to understand. The Buyer—whether a corporation, a partnership, an individual, or any other type of buyer—simply purchases some or all of the outstanding equity of a target corporation. (A way to accomplish this that provides the Buyer with isolation from the Target's liabilities would be for the Buyer to create a special-purpose corporate or limited liability company (LLC) shell subsidiary that buys the equity of or that merges into the Target, with the Target surviving;[4] the stock purchase or merger consideration will be cash or other taxable property.) In such a transaction, the Target's shareholders will recognize capital gain or loss on their sale of the Target's shares, and the Buyer will take a tax basis in the acquired Target shares equal to the purchase price.

If the Target had NOLs and tax credit carryovers, the use of such tax attributes after the purchase will be severely restricted. Under IRC Section 382, after a 50 percent ownership change, the use of the Target's NOLs is restricted each year to an amount equal to the value of the target corporation at the acquisition date multiplied by a federal interest rate that is adjusted annually. For example, if the target's value is $10 million and the interest rate is 3 percent, only $30,000 of NOL can be used annually after the acquisition. However, NOLs can be used without restriction to shelter gain realized on the disposition of assets that had "built-in" gain at the time of the ownership change.

A taxable stock purchase can involve further complications, such as the installment sales rules, contingent purchase price, and original issue discount, which are discussed later.

---

[4]Most states permit statutory mergers between a corporation and an LLC.

Transactions Treated as Asset Purchases

Plainly, the most straightforward such transaction is simply a purchase of some or all of the assets of the Target in a transaction that does not qualify as a tax-free C reorganization (described later in this chapter). The Target can distribute some or all of the proceeds and remain in existence, or it can distribute all the proceeds and liquidate. If the Target is an S corporation that has sold all of its assets, there is little reason for the Target to remain in existence. However, if the Target is a C corporation and liquidates, its shareholders will recognize capital gain or loss to the extent the proceeds they receive differ from their tax basis in their shares. If the Target remains in existence, the shareholders will treat any pro rata distribution as a dividend to the extent of the Target's earnings and profits.

Alternatively, there are ways in which the Buyer can acquire 100 percent of the Target's shares while the transaction is treated as an asset sale for tax purposes. One such device would be for the Buyer to create a shell subsidiary (corporate or LLC) into which the Target merges in exchange for cash consideration distributed to the Target's shareholders. This will be treated as an asset sale for tax purposes, followed by a liquidation of the Target with the consequences described earlier.

Alternatively, if the Buyer is a corporation and acquires 80 percent or more of the equity of a target corporation within a 12-month period, an election can be made under Section 338(g) to treat the transaction as an asset purchase rather than a stock purchase. Similarly, with an election under Section 338(h)(10), a corporate buyer can buy stock of an S corporation or can purchase a subsidiary out of a consolidated group with an election to treat the transaction as an asset purchase from the perspective of both buyer and seller. In such a case, the consolidated group or the S corporation shareholders will not be treated as having sold stock, but rather, the owning corporation will be treated as having sold its underlying assets; tax will be paid only once, on the gain from the asset sale.[5]

Such a Section 338 election (or, for that matter, an asset sale in general) makes particular sense where there is little gain to be recognized on the sale, or where the selling corporate group has NOLs to shield such gain. In the case of an S corporation Target, the Target's shareholders may be relatively indifferent as to whether they sell stock or make a Section 338 election to have the transaction treated as an asset sale; in many cases, their basis in

---

[5] Acquisitions from an affiliated group within a two-year period must be treated consistently; Buyer cannot treat its purchase of subsidiary X as an asset acquisition under Section 338 and treat its contemporaneous purchase of sister corporation Y as a stock acquisition.

the shares will be essentially the same as the basis in the assets that the S corporation has. In such case, since only one level of tax will be recognized, it clearly makes sense to have the transaction treated as an asset sale so that the Buyer can get a stepped-up basis. In fact, even if inside and outside basis differ, if the plan is to liquidate the S corporation after its assets are sold, the net tax effect to the selling S corporation shareholders may well be identical to a sale of their shares.

In an asset transaction, the Buyer's basis in the acquired assets will (cumulatively) equal the consideration paid plus the amount of liabilities assumed. That amount will also be the measure of the amount of gain (or loss) realized by the Target.

As mandated by IRC Section 1060, the Buyer and the Target will allocate the consideration among the transferred assets using the methods specified in IRC Section 1060 and the regulations thereunder. Generally speaking, they will also be required to file Form 8594 setting forth such allocation. Those rules allocate consideration first to cash and cash equivalents; next, to certain traded property, certificates of deposit, and foreign currency; next, to accounts receivable and similar items; next, to inventory; next, to other hard assets; and finally, to two classes of intangible assets. Although not required, it is almost always advisable for the parties to the transaction to agree on the allocation of the purchase price among assets and that they will report consistently for tax purposes. The agreement generally should be more detailed than the breakdown required under IRC Section 1060, so that there is no uncertainty or discrepancy as to the allocation to any asset that may have significance for tax purposes.

If the Target is a partnership for tax purposes, whether the Buyer purchases interests in the Target or purchases its assets, from the Buyer's perspective the transaction will be essentially like an asset purchase as previously described. The Target's owners will have income generally measured by the difference between the basis in their interest in the entity and the amount they receive; whether all of the income will be capital gain or whether some will be ordinary income will depend on the nature of the entity's assets in light of IRC Section 751. Thus, if the Target has a significant amount of inventory, accounts receivable, and certain other ordinary income-type assets, even if the Target's owners sell their equity interests, they will be compelled under IRC Section 751 to recognize substantial ordinary income on the sale (unlike the case with sales of corporate stock).

Installment Sale Treatment and Contingent Purchase Prices

Regardless of whether the transaction is taxed as a stock sale or an asset acquisition, a portion of the purchase price may be paid in a year subsequent to the year of closing, in which case the rules concerning installment sales and contingent purchase prices become relevant. (However, sales of stock of a publicly traded company and of inventory are not eligible to be reported as installment sales.) A qualifying installment note may not be readily tradable nor secured by cash equivalents.

Generally speaking, where installment sale treatment applies, the Target's tax basis is allocated pro rata in proportion to the different payments to be received, and gain is calculated and tax paid as the payments are received under the agreed schedule. Certain transactions will cause acceleration of the income on the unpaid installments, such as the disposition of the note, a borrowing secured by the installment note, or certain transactions involving related parties.

The economic value of installment sale treatment has been abridged by a rule that requires taxpayers who hold $5 million or more of installment notes at the end of a tax year to pay the IRS an interest-type charge based on the value of tax deferral that is inherent in the use of the installment method. Not only is much of the prior tax advantage in using installment sales removed by this interest charge for large installment notes, but a noteholder should also consider the possibility that the federal capital gains rate may be higher in a future year when the installment note is collected.

Either an S or C corporation could sell its assets for installment notes. If the notes are distributed to the shareholders within 12 months after adoption of a corporate plan of liquidation, the shareholders can report gain on their shares using the installment method. (This technique will not, however, prevent gain recognition at the C corporation level as well, or in the case of S corporations that elected S status within five years before the installment sale.)

It is typical for both stock and asset deals to include contingent payment amounts. Frequently, part of the purchase price will be reserved as security for the accuracy of the seller's representations and warranties. The purchase price may also be purely contingent in amount in an earnout. In either case, income will generally be recognized to the seller to the extent the contingency is resolved and further payments are received, and there are rules for allocating the seller's basis between the fixed and contingent amounts, which influences when gain is recognized (and taxed).

In any case of payments received substantially after the closing, whether fixed installment payments or contingent purchase price, a portion of any such later payment must be treated as interest for tax purposes. If sufficient interest is not stated in the agreement between the parties, the original issue discount (OID) rules will treat part of the payment as interest for tax purposes. Generally speaking, such interest will be deductible by the payer (the Buyer) and treated as ordinary income in the hands of the recipients. If an escrow is created to secure contingent payment amounts, earnings on the escrow will be subject to current taxation. As part of their agreement, the parties should agree on the tax treatment and reporting of the escrow fund.

TAX-FREE TRANSACTIONS

Tax-Free Transactions Where the Target and the Buyer Are Both Corporations

The Internal Revenue Code permits the tax-free acquisition of a corporate business by another corporation provided the transaction follows one of the prescribed forms found in the Code generally in IRC Section 368. Precise adherence to the requirements of the selected form is essential; here is an area of the tax law where a purely formal lapse can have disastrous tax consequences.

Generally speaking, all of these techniques involve the Buyer's transfer of its stock or other securities to the Target's shareholders in exchange for either the stock or assets of the Target. The Target's shareholders will receive the Buyer's stock tax-free, no gain will be recognized at the corporate level, and the Target's assets will not be stepped up in the hands of the Buyer. The selection of a particular technique can depend on a variety of factors, including the following: whether the Buyer insists on acquiring assets rather than stock; whether the Buyer wants to maintain the Target as a separate corporate entity after the transaction; whether the Target's shareholders are to receive cash or other property as well as the Buyer stock; whether the Buyer has a significant preexisting ownership interest in the Target; and local law and regulatory constraints that may affect the use of some of the techniques otherwise available under the Code.

A summary of the available techniques is provided next.

Type A Reorganization An A reorganization under IRC Section 368(a)(1)(A) simply involves the merger of the Target into the Buyer corporation pursuant to applicable state or foreign law. It can also include the merger of the Target into an LLC wholly owned by the Buyer (which, for tax purposes, is treated as a disregarded entity, causing the merger to be viewed identically to a merger of the Target into the Buyer). Use of a wholly owned LLC can obviate the need for a premerger Buyer shareholder vote and can isolate the Target liabilities in a separate limited liability entity with no tax impact. In either case, the Target's shareholders receive the Buyer stock, but they may also receive along with such stock a significant amount of cash or other consideration (which will be taxable under the "boot" rules discussed later).

Type B Reorganization A type B reorganization under IRC Section 368(a)(1)(B) involves the Buyer's acquisition of control of the Target solely in exchange for voting stock of the Buyer or its parent corporation. Control for this purpose and other purposes of the reorganization provisions means ownership of at least 80 percent of the total combined voting power of all classes of stock entitled to vote and at least 80 percent of the total number of shares of all other classes of stock.

An attempt at a B reorganization will turn into a costly taxable transaction if any consideration other than voting stock of the Buyer is found to have been used. While a B reorganization may complete a process in which the Buyer earlier acquired the Target shares, it cannot be combined with transactions in which the Target's shareholders received any consideration other than the Buyer voting stock. Also, post-acquisition dispositions of the Target stock by the Buyer or new issuances of stock by the Target may destroy control. Similarly, if the Target is immediately liquidated into the Buyer, the transaction is collapsed into an asset acquisition, but if the liquidation is by merger, then the collapsed transaction may qualify as an "A" reorganization.

Type C Reorganization A reorganization under IRC Section 368(a)(1)(C) involves the Buyer's acquisition of substantially all of the assets of the Target principally for voting stock of the Buyer. Twenty percent of the consideration can be cash, but this 20 percent figure is reduced to the extent that the Buyer assumes Target liabilities (liabilities may be assumed without limit, but will reduce the margin for nonstock consideration). For purposes of this and other provisions discussed here, the guideline for IRS rulings is that "substantially all of the assets" means the acquisition of assets equal to 90 percent of the net value and 70 percent of the gross value of the assets of the Target immediately before the transaction. This is the one type of tax-free reorganization that can be used where the Buyer is unwilling to assume undisclosed liabilities of the Target, as would happen with a stock acquisition.

Subsidiary Mergers For a variety of reasons, including the possible existence of undisclosed liabilities, the Buyer may wish to hold the Target as a separate subsidiary. A B reorganization accomplishes this, but because the B reorganization rules require the use solely of voting stock, it is often easier to get to the desired end by using one of the subsidiary merger techniques. In a forward subsidiary merger under Section 368(a)(2)(D), the Buyer creates a special-purpose shell subsidiary into which the Target is merged, with the Target's shareholders receiving not stock of the subsidiary but, rather, Buyer shares. (As a technical matter, the surviving subsidiary need not have been a shell, and could own substantial assets of its own, although this rarely is the case.) No subsidiary stock may be used as consideration, but other consideration may be issued to the Buyer shareholders. After the reorganization is completed, the surviving company must own "substantially all of the assets" of the Buyer (see preceding discussion).

In a reverse subsidiary merger under Section 368(a)(2)(E), it is the Target that survives. Again, the merger is conducted with a subsidiary of the Buyer, typically a specially created shell, which in this case merges into the Target. Again, the Buyer stock is issued to the Target's shareholders, although other consideration may be used as well. At least 80 percent of the Target's voting stock and at least 80 percent of the shares of all other classes of the Target stock must be acquired in exchange for voting stock of the Buyer. After the reorganization, the survivor (the Target) must own "substantially all of the assets" of each participating corporation. This type of transaction can be used to squeeze out the Target's shareholders and may also avoid the need for a Buyer shareholder vote.

Section 351 Transactions IRC Section 351 provides generally that property can be contributed tax-free to a corporation in exchange for stock of the transferee corporation (voting or nonvoting, common or preferred) if the persons making such contributions in an integrated transaction are in control of the transferee corporation after the transaction (the definition of *control,* as mentioned earlier, is basically an 80 percent test). This provision can sometimes be used to effectuate an acquisitive transaction, particularly in a private company context. For example, one or more target corporations could be contributed to the Buyer in exchange for Buyer stock—provided that the shareholders of those entities after the transaction own 80 percent or more of the Buyer. If the Buyer is an existing corporation, it may be possible to comply with this 80 percent requirement by having some meaningful property contributed by the Buyer's shareholders as part of the transaction in exchange for additional Buyer shares.

Nonstatutory Doctrines That Limit the Use of the Tax-Free Reorganization Provisions Several nonstatutory doctrines that limit the use of the tax-free reorganization provisions emerged over decades of case law and are now mostly reflected in the tax regulations. In brief, they are:

- *Business purpose doctrine.* A tax-free reorganization must have a legitimate business purpose and not be simply a tax-savings device.
- *Continuity of shareholder interest.* A tax-free reorganization must conclude with the Target's shareholders owning a substantial equity interest (through holding common or preferred stock) in the ongoing enterprise. Generally speaking, if 40 percent or more of the merger consideration is equity, this requirement should be satisfied (even if the

Target's shareholders later sell to a party unrelated to the Buyer some of the stock they have acquired). However, an A reorganization in which 25 percent of the consideration is stock and 75 percent is cash or debt would likely fail the continuity of shareholder interest requirement.

■ *Continuity of business enterprise.* The Buyer must continue a significant line of business of the Target or continue to use a significant part of the Target's historic business assets in the conduct of the Buyer's business. This requirement is intended to prevent the use of the reorganization provisions to enable the Target's shareholders to diversify tax-free from a historical business into a new portfolio of passive investments. There are also statutory provisions that prevent the tax-free reorganization of two investment companies. Under these provisions, tax-free treatment is denied to any investment company engaging in a putative tax-free reorganization with a second investment company if the first company has more than 25 percent of the value of its total assets invested in the securities of a single issuer or 50 percent or more of the value of its total assets invested in the securities of five or fewer issuers. These adverse provisions do not, however, apply to regulated investment companies and real estate investment trusts (REITs).

■ *Step transaction doctrine.* Under this judicial doctrine, a putative tax-free reorganization is analyzed in light of all of the integrated steps that are part of the plan to determine whether tax-free treatment should be afforded. For example (as discussed further in a later section of this chapter), a noncorporate entity like a partnership cannot be acquired tax-free using the corporate reorganization provisions of Section 368. If, as part of a single plan, a partnership were incorporated tax-free under Section 351 and then merged in a statutory merger into a corporation, tax-free treatment as an A reorganization would be denied because the incorporation and merger steps would be combined and the transaction would be recharacterized as a combination of a partnership with the Buyer corporation, triggering gain on the appreciation in either the partnership assets or the partnership interests. The parameters of the step transaction doctrine cannot be logically inferred; any proposed transaction that raises step transaction issues needs to be analyzed in light of the abundant case law concerning the types of prereorganization transactions that may be respected and those that are likely to be disregarded.

Tax Consequences to the Target Shareholders

In a tax-free reorganization, the Target's shareholders can exchange tax-free their stock or securities in the Target for stock or securities in the Buyer (or, as permitted by the relevant reorganization provision, a parent of the Buyer).

Obviously, securities cannot be used instead of stock to the extent a form of reorganization demands the use of stock (e.g., a solely-for-voting-stock B reorganization).

For purposes of these tax-free provisions, stock includes preferred stock, but does not include *nonqualified* preferred stock, the receipt of which generally will be taxable like cash or other *boot* (discussed in a moment) and will not qualify as good consideration for purposes of the reorganization rules requiring the use of stock. Generally speaking, nonqualified preferred stock is stock with a dividend rate that varies in whole or in part with reference to interest rates, commodity prices, or similar indexes, and which the holder can require the issuer to redeem, or which the issuer is required to or likely to redeem.

The definition of *securities* that can be received tax-free has been the subject of considerable litigation for over 60 years. Short-term instruments are not securities for this purpose, but long-term bonds and notes likely will qualify as securities that can be received (or surrendered) tax-free. Generally speaking, debt instruments with a maturity of five or more years will be treated as securities, but the nature of the instrument needs to be examined in light of the relevant case law.

Although securities may be received tax-free, gain will be recognized to the extent that the principal amount of debt securities received exceeds the principal amount of debt securities surrendered; securities received in retirement of claims for accrued interest will also give rise to tax (at ordinary income rates).

Finally, warrants and similar stock rights may now be received tax-free as part of a qualifying reorganization.

As indicated earlier, in the case of many tax-free reorganizations, it is possible that the Target's shareholders will receive nonqualifying property—which the tax law calls *boot*—in addition to qualifying stock and securities. The boot may be and typically is cash but could also be other property or, as mentioned before, nonqualified preferred stock. Generally speaking, the Target's shareholders will recognize gain on their Target shares to the extent of boot received, but they will not be allowed to recognize any losses. If a Target shareholder holds both high-basis and low-basis shares, with the former having a built-in loss, he will not be able to offset the loss in the high-basis shares if he receives boot; rather, to the extent apportionable to the low-basis shares, the receipt of boot will give rise to taxable gain.

Preferred Stock   Preferred stock has additional special rules:

- If the preferred stock bears an "unreasonable redemption premium" and carries a put right or a mandatory redemption provision, the effective discount is treated as a taxable dividend.

- If the preferred stock is paid-in-kind (PIK) preferred that pays a dividend in additional PIK preferred, the most likely tax treatment is one that resembles original issue discount (OID) in the debt context.
- Section 306 preferred stock, when sold, is treated as a dividend or ordinary income. Preferred stock acquires its Section 306 taint if it is received as a nontaxable dividend on common stock, or if it is nonparticipating preferred stock received in a reorganization or a Section 351 tax-free incorporation where cash would have been treated as a dividend.

Convertible or Exchangeable Instruments   Debt that is convertible into stock is treated for securities law purposes as an equity security. For tax purposes, convertibility does not affect OID calculations and similar issues. Convertible preferred stock is similarly treated. In both cases, conversion is not a taxable event, nor is exercise of a warrant. A change in a conversion ratio can result in a constructive distribution or dividend, but that is generally not the case with typical antidilution adjustments.

Exchangeable instruments are those that can be exchanged for instruments of another corporation, usually a parent corporation. The tax consequences of exchangeable instruments are beyond our scope.

Treatment of Corporations Party to a Reorganization

The general principle is that neither the Buyer nor the Target recognizes gain or loss in participating in a tax-free reorganization. The Buyer will take a carryover tax basis in the former Target assets and will succeed to various tax attributes of the Target, such as NOLs, tax credits, and other carryforwards. However, as noted earlier, severe limitations apply to the ability to use Target NOLs in the future.

The Target will not recognize gain or loss upon distributing Buyer stock or securities to its shareholders as part of the reorganization, but the distribution of boot-type appreciated assets by the Target to its shareholders will trigger taxable gain at the Target level.

SPECIAL SITUATIONS

Acquisitions from a Consolidated Group

Under the federal (but not always state) income tax scheme, a parent and its subsidiaries can file a consolidated income tax return. The rules for the most part treat a "consolidated group" as one tax-paying entity. This has some esoteric effects on acquisitions of a subsidiary or assets from a consolidated group.

Like any other seller, the group's basis in its assets, including the stock of subsidiaries, must be determined in order to establish the reference point for gain or loss. Because the group is effectively treated as one entity, there are a number of basis adjustments that are made annually to the parent's basis in the stock of its subsidiaries. If a subsidiary recognizes income, that income is taxed to the group. Somewhat like a Subchapter S corporation, the gain (or loss) adjusts the parent's basis in the stock of that subsidiary. Basis adjustments can create what is known as an *excess loss account,* which is essentially a negative basis.

This is largely irrelevant from the Buyer's point of view. One aspect of the consolidated return regulations that is highly relevant, however, is that each corporation in the consolidated group is jointly and severally liable for the taxes payable by the group. Thus, if the stock of even a small subsidiary is purchased from a consolidated group, the Buyer may acquire a large contingent tax liability along with the subsidiary. Consolidated group members also typically enter into a tax sharing agreement to assign responsibility for the group's taxes among themselves. Those agreements need to be examined closely as part of the due diligence process when purchasing a subsidiary from a group. In addition to the foregoing, there are extensive rules limiting the ability of a consolidated group to recognize a loss on the disposition of a member.

When a subsidiary leaves a consolidated group, it retains a share of certain tax attributes of the group, like NOLs. Due diligence is required to determine the amount and nature of these attributes. Since these attributes can be affected by post-transaction gains or losses of the group, that fact needs to be dealt with in the acquisition agreement.

ESOP Transactions

The sale of stock to an employee stock ownership plan (ESOP) is a tax-favored transaction outside the scope of the reorganization provisions we have been discussing. This is a device that may allow the owners of a business to dispose of some or all of their holdings on a tax-deferred (and potentially tax-free) basis and obtain a broad opportunity for investment diversification.

An ESOP is a type of tax-deferred qualified retirement plan, designed to invest primarily in stock of a corporation that employs the plan participants. The ESOP must comply with the Code's rules for widespread participation and nondiscrimination in benefits that apply generally to tax-qualified plans. Without elaborating on all of those rules and other ESOP restrictions and requirements, the sale of stock to an ESOP can qualify for tax-deferred treatment under Section 1042 if, after such sale, these conditions are met:

- The ESOP holds at least 30 percent of the stock of the corporation that was sold.
- The selling taxpayer has held the securities sold for at least three years.
- Within the period beginning 3 months before and ending 12 months after the date of sale to the ESOP, the selling taxpayer reinvests the proceeds in stock or securities of a domestic *active* corporation (i.e., one whose passive investment income is not excessive under a test set forth in the statute).

There is no specific restriction on the selling taxpayer borrowing against the replacement securities, which means that a sale to the ESOP can generate both investment diversification on a pretax basis and a source of ready cash.

So-called leveraged ESOP transactions are typically financed by having the ESOP borrow much or all of the purchase price for the securities from a financial institution, with a loan guaranteed by the corporation itself. The loan is paid off by tax-deductible corporate cash contributions or special tax-deductible dividends to the ESOP, freeing up shares that are then allocated to the accounts of plan participants over time as the loan is paid off.

An ESOP is an eligible shareholder for S corporation purposes; if the ESOP owns 100 percent of the S corporation, operating profits will not be subject to regular income taxes, subject to anti-abuse provisions.

Dispositions of Unwanted Assets and Spin-Offs

The Target frequently owns some assets that the Buyer is unwilling to acquire. A recurrent planning problem is how to deal with such unwanted assets on the eve of a reorganization transaction, whether taxable or not.

Generally speaking, it is not possible to distribute (spin off) such assets from the Target in a tax-free manner in connection with an acquisition, whether taxable or not. Under IRC Section 355, a corporation can distribute to its shareholders (whether pro rata or non–pro rata) stock consisting of a controlling interest in a subsidiary (whether historic or newly created) that includes assets that have been used for five or more years in the conduct of an active trade or business. The distributing corporation has to meet the same active trade or business requirement. Many other restrictions and requirements, too lengthy to explain here, must be met in order for such a spin-off to be tax-free; the most significant is a rigorous requirement that the spin-off have a business purpose other than federal tax savings. If all of the requirements are met, no gain or loss is recognized by either the distributing corporation on its transfer of appreciated assets or by the shareholders who have received the stock of the spun-off entity. However, if either the distributing or controlled corporation is to be acquired, whether in a taxable or tax-free transaction, the tax-free spin-off provisions are basically unavailable.

Therefore, a different solution needs to be found for the Target's unwanted assets. Either a sale or distribution of the unwanted assets will trigger corporate gain recognition on any appreciation in them. More intricate solutions can include a post-acquisition long-term lease of the unwanted assets from the Buyer to the Target's shareholders, or the transfer of the desired assets from the Target in a tax-free Section 351 incorporation (discussed earlier) or to an LLC or other entity in which the Buyer will have a controlling interest, leaving the unwanted assets behind.

Acquisitive Transactions Where Either the Buyer or Seller Is Not a Corporation

The tax-free reorganization provisions of Section 368 are not applicable unless both the Buyer and the Target are taxed as corporations (whether C corporations or S corporations). If the Target is a partnership for tax purposes or is an S corporation, a taxable transaction will often be in order. Except where the Target is an S corporation that holds assets that within the preceding five years were held by a C corporation and continue to have built-in gain dating from the C corporation period, a taxable acquisition can be structured so that there is only one level of tax on the Target side.

A Target shareholder's income in such a case generally will be a long-term capital gain, except to the extent that ordinary income assets such as inventory and unrealized receivables are being sold. With the stepped-up basis that the Buyer will benefit from, such a transaction is likely to be as tax efficient as a tax-free combination. If partnership interests are sold in their entirety, this is analyzed as an asset purchase on the Buyer side and a sale of equity on the Target side, but some ordinary income may nevertheless need to be recognized under IRC Section 751.

However, if a tax-free combination indeed is desired, there are various ways in which this can be accomplished even if one or both of the parties is not taxable as a corporation. As already mentioned, one method is a Section 351 transaction in which the Target's business is transferred to a corporation in exchange for stock of the transferee in a tax-free transaction (which may also include some boot, which will be taxable to the extent of the built-in gain in the transferred assets). The transferee corporation could either be a newly formed entity or could be the Buyer.

Another nonrecognition provision that may be available to combine businesses is Section 721, which permits the tax-free transfer of property to a partnership in exchange for partnership interests. For example, if both the Target and the Buyer are partnerships, either the partnership interests in the Target or the assets of the Target could be transferred to the Buyer in exchange for partnership interests in the Buyer, which then can be distributed tax-free to the Target's owners. If the Buyer is a corporation, a new partnership entity could be created to which the Target assets are contributed in exchange for the tax-free receipt of partnership interests. Presumably, the Buyer will contribute some or all of its business, or will contribute cash to such a partnership. Frequently, a transaction like this is utilized when owners of real estate wish to transfer their real estate to a REIT without immediate gain recognition; the assets in fact are transferred to a partnership in which the REIT has a controlling interest.

Any transaction under Section 721 has to be carefully analyzed in light of the disguised sale rules of IRC Section 707, which can trigger gain recognition where property is transferred to a partnership and there is an associated distribution of cash or property to any partner.

Management Tax-Free Rollovers in LBOs

Leveraged buyouts (LBOs) where significant continuing management participation is desired (in other words, a management buyout, or MBO) present unique problems because of the complex objectives of management in these situations. Leveraged buyouts cash out the Target's shareholders, and management typically will want to cash out to a degree. Management also will want to increase its equity percentage in Newco from its percentage in the Target and roll over part of its Target stock on a tax-free basis as part of its payment for Newco's equity.

Management buyouts put management in a somewhat awkward position. On the one hand, as shareholders and directors of the Target they owe a fiduciary duty to the Target's shareholders to get the best deal for the Target (and for themselves as sellers of the Target's stock). The irony is that they are also indirectly buyers of the Target's stock via their equity participation in Newco. The situation is exacerbated where management is unable to achieve favorable tax treatment. It is important that management (if it wants to) gets the same securities for its rolled-over stock as the investors who have paid cash instead of the Target stock for the securities.

In these transactions, management contributes a part of its Target stock to Newco and gets back Newco stock in return. Standing alone, this should be nontaxable if the stock received in return is not nonqualified preferred stock. Management then sells the rest of its Newco stock to the Buyer for cash. One would expect that management would recognize gain equal to the cash received minus the basis in the stock sold.

If the transactions are integrated, however, management would have contributed all of its stock to Newco in return for Newco stock and cash. In that instance, the cash is boot and the basis cannot offset the cash received. One technique that is used here is for management to sell its stock that it intends to cash out to a third party for cash, which then sells the stock to Newco for cash, thus preventing integration of the sale and the contribution. If the shares contributed to Newco by management were incentive stock option (ISO) shares acquired prior to the requisite holding period, the Section 351 transaction could be a disqualifying disposition and ordinary income would result; however, the appreciation from the date of exercise is protected under Section 351. Where management is a major shareholder in both the Target and Newco, there is risk of dividend treatment under some circumstances.

Leveraged buyouts are discussed in more detail in Chapter 7.

GOLDEN PARACHUTE TAX

Stiff tax penalties can apply to compensation payments made to the Target's top-paid employees in connection with a corporate (not a partnership) change of control. These penalties, which apply to *excess parachute payments,* include a 20 percent excise tax payable by the employee (in addition to income taxes) and the denial of any corporate tax deduction for the payments. The combined effect can make excess parachute payments very expensive to the parties. Thus, it is important for corporations that may be involved in acquisitions to consult with their advisers on how to avoid or minimize these penalties.

Background

Congress enacted these provisions to discourage corporations that are potential targets of an acquisition from offering golden parachutes to their executives. The argument was that the potential payments to the executives were so large that they would deter an acquirer or reduce what an acquirer would pay for the company, to the detriment of the corporation's shareholders. Regardless of whether the rules achieve the policy goals, they add considerable complexity to planning for executive compensation in the context of an acquisition.

Basic Provisions

The excise tax and disallowance apply to excess parachute payments, determined using the following formula:

> If the present value of the *parachute payments* made to a *disqualified individual* equals or exceeds three times the individual's base amount, then the parachute payments, to the extent they exceed such base amount, will constitute *excess parachute payments*.

An individual's *base amount* is the individual's average annual compensation from the company for the five years ending prior to the year of the acquisition. If the individual has not worked for the company for five years, the average is computed over the period of actual employment and certain other adjustments are made.

The *parachute payments* in the formula include any payment in the nature of compensation that is contingent on a change in ownership or control of the corporation or a change in ownership of a substantial portion of the assets of the corporation. It does not matter whether the payments are from the Target or from the Buyer. Payments of compensation not specifically made contingent on the change are presumed to be contingent on the change if contracted for within one year before the change.

Cash payments such as salary, bonuses, and severance can be parachute payments. Also included are certain noncash payments such as fringe benefits, grants of stock and stock options, and the value (computed under a complex formula in the regulations) of accelerating the vesting of existing options, restricted stock, or of other compensatory rights.

Payments will not be parachute payments unless they are compensatory payments made to a disqualified individual. A *disqualified individual* is an officer, a shareholder, or a highly compensated individual. Shareholders are covered only if they (or related persons or entities) own more than 1 percent of the fair market value of all classes of stock outstanding. Highly compensated individuals include employees or independent contractors who earn at least $120,000 and are among the highest-paid 1 percent of employees, counting certain independent contractors as employees for this purpose. The maximum number of highly compensated individuals in a corporation is 250.

No more than 50 employees (or if less, 3 or 10% of the employees) are disqualified individuals as a result of their status as an officer. An individual who is not otherwise treated as a disqualified individual in one category, may still be one if he or she falls within another category. Numerous special rules apply in making the disqualified individual determination.

Example: In connection with an acquisition, an individual executive with average annual compensation of $100,000 for the prior five years will receive $300,000 in present value of parachute payments. The consequences are as follows.

Base amount = $100,000

3 × Base amount = $300,000

Parachute payments = $300,000

Excess parachute payment = $200,000

20% excise tax = $40,000

Cost of lost compensation deduction = $70,000 (35% corporate rate)

Total additional tax cost = $110,000

This example illustrates the cliff effect of the formula. If the parachute payments in the example had been $299,999—just one dollar less—there would have been no excess parachute payments and thus no additional tax cost. Thus, the payment of the last dollar in the example cost $110,000 in additional taxes.

Exceptions

Reasonable compensation for services actually rendered either before or after the change in control will not be treated as an excess parachute payment, but there is a special burden of proof to demonstrate reasonability.

Small business corporations are not subject to the parachute payment rules. These are corporations that, immediately before the change in ownership or control, are eligible to elect to be S Corporations, regardless of whether they have actually made that election. Among other requirements, a corporation: must not have more than 100 shareholders; must have as shareholders only individuals, estates, and certain trusts (no corporations or partnerships); and must have only one class of stock. For purposes of this exception (and unlike the Subchapter S rule), a corporation may have a nonresident alien as a shareholder.

The adverse tax rules also do not apply to payments made by privately held corporations if they are contingent on shareholder approval. Approval must be by persons who own more than 75 percent of the voting power of the corporation's stock immediately before the change in ownership or control (excluding the affected executive) after adequate disclosure to all shareholders of all material facts concerning the payments. The shareholder vote must not be merely a ratification of the payments (that is, if more than 75 percent approval is not obtained, the employee may not receive the payments).

Planning Techniques

If the Target is public or a shareholder vote is not feasible, a different approach to the parachute problem is needed. One planning technique is to keep the payments below 300 percent of the disqualified individual's base amount. This sometimes can be done by carefully determining in advance the amount of payments that could be deemed parachute payments. However, accelerated vesting of options and other forms of equity compensation can sometimes trigger the tax, and it is impossible to know the precise value of the award until the transaction is about to close.

A different approach to achieve the same goal arises from including a provision in compensation agreements that will operate at the time of the acquisition to reduce the parachute payments to be made until they are below the 300 percent level. In many cases where the payments would be only slightly above the 300 percent threshold, the employee will come out ahead on an after-tax basis if the parachute payments are reduced to avoid the tax penalties. One could write the agreement to provide for an automatic reduction if the after-tax return to the employee from the reduction is higher than the after-tax return if no reduction occurs.

If it is clear that the payments will be well above the 300 percent level, the parties can agree that the corporation will gross up the employee for the effect of the 20 percent excise tax (and for the income and excise tax on the gross-up amount). Of course, the gross-up payments will be both taxable and also nondeductible parachute payments and will therefore increase the tax penalties, making a gross-up very expensive for the payer.

Other planning techniques include increasing compensatory payments that will be included in determining the base amount (but this must occur prior to the year in which the change-control occurs), modifying the timing of payments to be made after the acquisition to reduce their present value (although other tax loans may limit this technique, such as

IRC Section 409A), identifying and substantiating payments as reasonable compensation for services, and reorganizing the corporation to make it eligible for S corporation status.

Note that there may also be accounting consequences to using some of these techniques. For example, changing the terms of stock options at or near the time of an acquisition may result in a charge to earnings, or it may affect the accounting treatment of the acquisition itself. And as noted, complex rules also apply to a wide range of "deferred compensation" arrangements under IRC Section 409A. These rules are best left to specialists in the field of deferred compensation.

CHAPTER 5

The Definitive Acquisition Agreement

ECONOMIC TERMS

Acquisition agreements—stock purchase agreements, merger agreements, and asset purchase agreements—are usually lengthy and complicated. They are also very important documents because mergers and acquisitions (M&A) is a zero-sum game; if one side scores a point, the other party inevitably suffers an equivalent loss. Big money can turn on how a particular clause in the acquisition agreement is drafted.

Even though the different forms of acquisition agreements are all complex, they are similar in most respects. The mechanics are different, but the approach and the large majority of the provisions and language are identical. Asset purchase agreements present a different set of issues because there is substantial leeway in identifying which assets are being sold and which liabilities are being assumed, if any. Those aspects are discussed in detail in this chapter.

A full-blown annotated form of merger agreement appears in the appendixes. Here we show various section headings of that agreement and discuss some of the important structuring and negotiating considerations in selected sections. You might read the sample merger agreement side by side with the following discussion.

Introductory Paragraphs

The first paragraph of the agreement identifies the parties.

In a merger agreement, the parties include the merging corporations, and if one of them is an acquisition subsidiary, then the parent of the acquisition subsidiary also signs. The form of agreement in the appendixes provides for selected Target shareholders to sign as well. This serves several purposes:

If the Target's shareholders are to indemnify the Buyer beyond an escrow, then they must sign a document that creates the indemnification obligation; the signature by the requisite approval percentage of shareholders under applicable law, combined with an agreement to vote for the deal (or better, an actual vote for the deal), creates a lock-up device; and the agreement serves as a vehicle for the shareholders to make required representations about themselves (e.g., related to their stock ownership). As to the last point, the agreement provides for a representation letter to be signed by shareholders as a closing document; if there is to be a simultaneous signing and closing, then those representations must be incorporated into the acquisition agreement or a separate agreement that is contemporaneously signed.

In a stock purchase agreement, the selling shareholders are parties along with the Buyer; a separate question is whether the Target also should be a party. It is not essential since it is the shareholders who are selling the stock, not the Target. If there is a deferred closing, however, the Target needs to sign because there are covenants in the agreement that regulate how the Target will conduct its business between signing and closing, as well as a lock-up and other provisions.

In an asset purchase agreement, the party selling the assets and the Buyer are parties. If it is not clear what company in a corporate group holds the assets, the parent may also sign and agree to transfer the agreed assets on behalf of whichever subsidiary owns them. Where the assets being sold comprise all or a large portion of the entity selling them, it is critical for the parties receiving the proceeds, or another solvent entity, to sign the agreement. Otherwise, there will be no entity with any assets to provide indemnification.

The first substantive terms you see in an acquisition agreement are the provisions in the first or second section describing the economics of the deal: how much is being paid and the form of the consideration (cash, stock, both, other); whether there is an escrow; a listing of any ancillary contracts being executed in connection with the acquisition, such as employment agreements, registration rights agreements, non-compete agreements, shareholders agreements, and the like; and if promissory notes constitute a portion of the purchase price, then their terms—subordination, interest rate, maturity schedule, and so on. Sometimes there are post-closing purchase price adjustments, particularly if there is to be a deferred closing, based on changes in the Target's net worth or net working capital or other financial measures between signing and closing or between the latest available financial statements and closing. Purchase price adjustments can be extremely complicated and are discussed later in this chapter.

How the economics of the purchase price are handled is not necessarily a simple matter. As noted in Chapter 3, the Buyer will want to acquire all of the equity interests in the Target, meaning all outstanding stock. The Buyer will *also* want to make sure that *all rights to acquire* the Target's stock are terminated prior to or as part of the merger or are converted into the merger consideration. The purchase price complication arises because Buyers think that the end of the discussion is that they are going to pay $X million to acquire the Target—but $X million for what exactly? The Buyer's assumption is that it will acquire/terminate all of the Target's stock and equity equivalents for $X million.

The Target will (and should) argue that it thought that the $X million was only for outstanding shares, or more credibly, that the $X million certainly should not be for unvested options that survive the merger because the underlying shares may never be issued, and in any event the Buyer, not the Target, will receive the benefit of the incentives provided to employees by the continued vesting of options. The Target will also argue that the $X million should not be applied to options and warrants that are out-of-the-money or under water, meaning that the exercise price of the options and warrants is above the price being paid for the Target's stock. The argument is similar to that for unvested options—underwater options might never be exercised, so why should they be taken into account in allocating the purchase price among the Target's equity holders?

This debate between the Buyer and the Target ultimately must be reduced to actual merger agreement terms that work clearly. As simple as it sounds to throw out terms like "$X million for the fully diluted equity," the deal lawyers must convert the deal into actual exchange mechanics. The way this is done is to draft very precise language as to how you get from $X million to the *purchase price per share* of the Target's stock. That is how you figure out who gets what among the Target's shareholders. Put another way, each Target shareholder only cares what that particular Target shareholder is being paid, and the only way to do that is to arrive at a purchase price per share. In order to get to a purchase price per share, you have to divide the total merger consideration by the number of the Target's shares outstanding—on a fully diluted basis from the Buyer's perspective, and excluding unvested and underwater options from the Target's perspective. Once you have determined the price per share, the mechanics can be spelled out for each of the various kinds of stock and rights to acquire stock of the Target.

In acquisitions of companies with convertible preferred stock outstanding, the corporate charter of the Target has to be examined to see how the liquidation preferences of the various series of preferred stock operate. The preferred holders, at minimum, have the choice of receiving the greater of their liquidation preference or what they would receive upon conversion to common stock; or, in *participating preferred stock,* they first receive their liquidation preference and then share in the balance of the acquisition proceeds with the holders of common stock. Typically, the terms of the convertible preferred stock provide that a merger is considered a liquidation for purposes of calculating what the preferred holders are entitled to in an acquisition of the company.

One further complicating factor is a debate as to whether by buying all of the Target's stock options and warrants, the Buyer is entitled to the economic benefit of the exercise price of those same options and warrants. The Target will argue that the Buyer, in setting the price, probably did not even know the aggregate exercise price of the options and warrants, and so the exercise price belongs to the Target, not the Buyer. In other words, the aggregate exercise price must effectively be added to the purchase price. The Buyer will then respond that it always intended that the exercise price should belong to it since that is what "fully diluted" means. In other words, the Buyer is acquiring all of the Target's equity interests and all that goes along with them, like the exercise price of options and warrants. The Buyer will also turn the Target's arguments around, saying it makes no sense to add the exercise price of unvested options or underwater options to the purchase price because the Buyer may never receive that exercise price. The Target may respond that in such a case the Buyer will not suffer the dilution of the unexercised options or warrants, so the Buyer will be in no worse of a position if it does not receive the exercise price.

If the Target wins the argument, sometimes the way it is implemented is via the *treasury stock method*. That method is something of a misnomer since it really is an income statement accounting concept that has been adapted to the M&A context. In the income statement context, the treasury stock method is used to arrive at fully diluted earnings per share versus primary earnings per share (EPS). It is not considered valid corporate finance to simply divide earnings by the number of shares outstanding plus all shares underlying options and warrants. The reason is that EPS would not be affected to that degree if all options and warrants were exercised because the company would have the benefit of the option and warrant exercise price to make money with or buy back shares in the open market to reduce the number of outstanding shares. So the treasury stock method for public companies means that the number of shares on a fully diluted basis for purposes of computation of fully diluted EPS is *reduced* by the number of shares that the company could buy with the proceeds of exercise in the public trading market.

A similar concept is used in the M&A context where the Target has won the argument that it is not fair to simply put all common and common equivalent shares into the denominator of the purchase price per share calculation

Assume:

   Gross deal price is $100,000

   9,000 shares outstanding

   1,000 options outstanding with exercise price of $5 per share

Price per share on fully diluted basis: $100,000/10,000 = $10 per share.
   Price per share on the treasury stock method: $100,000/(10,000 − Number of shares that aggregate option exercise price of $5,000 can buy at the deal price, or approximately 500 shares) = $100,000/ (10,000 − 500) = $10.53.
   The more common way of looking at the treasury stock method is as follows:

Gross deal price of $100,000 + Option exercise proceeds = $105,000

Price per share is $105,000/10,000 shares = $10.50

without adjusting for the exercise price. In effect, you should buy some of those shares back with the expected proceeds of the option and warrant exercises, which would increase the price per share.
   The treasury stock method can be illustrated by the following example.
   Under the treasury stock method, the Buyer is effectively paying 50 cents more per share for the same number of shares plus options assumed.
   The Basic question is this: Is the Buyer or the Target to get the credit for the hypothetical option exercise proceeds of the Target if the Buyer is assuming the Target's options because it is buying the entire equity of the Target?
   Let us say, alternatively, that the Buyer wins the argument and it is paying $X million for all of the stock and stock equivalents of the Target and that it is entitled to the option exercise proceeds. Here is another complication: if the Buyer permits the Target to allow net issuances of stock options prior to closing, a result similar to the treasury stock method occurs. A "net issuance" means that upon exercise of a stock option, instead of the optionee paying money to the company and getting a specified amount of shares (or the cash into which those shares have been converted), the optionee upon exercise pays out no cash and gets a reduced number of shares, or cash in lieu thereof, on the built-in profits on his or her option. The effects of

net issuances can be illustrated by the following example where the Target's shares are to be converted to cash in the acquisition.

SCENARIO 1, NO NET ISSUANCE

Price is $100,000 fully diluted, as in the previous example. No options are exercised prior to closing.

Price per share of the Target is $10 based on there being 10,000 shares outstanding, fully diluted, at the closing with no application of the treasury stock method. The Buyer is assuming the Target's options, meaning that on exercise and receipt of $5 in exercise price for each share, the Buyer will pay out $10 per share. So, the Buyer pays $90,000 for 9,000 shares outstanding and assumes the outstanding options, meaning that the 1,000 outstanding options at the $5 per share exercise price convert, in the aggregate, into the right to receive $10,000 for an exercise price of $5,000. Assume that all options are exercised immediately after closing, with the Buyer paying out $10,000 but getting back $5,000—i.e., the Buyer pays out $5,000 net after the closing.

Result for no net issuance: The Buyer pays out $100,000 total but gets $5,000 back. It pays $95,000 net.

Article I: The Merger

1.1 *The Merger.* Which company is merging into which? In other words, which merging corporation will be the surviving corporation?

1.2 *Effects of the Merger.* Who will be the officers and directors of the surviving corporation, and which corporation's charter and bylaws will govern the surviving corporation? If there are to be any amendments to the charter or bylaws of the surviving corporation, they are referenced here and attached as an exhibit.

1.3 *Closing.* When and where is the closing to be held? This assumes that there is not a simultaneous signing of the acquisition agreement and closing. You need a deferred closing if all of the conditions to closing cannot be met at the time of signing (e.g., regulatory approvals, required third-party consents, shareholder approval). If there is a simultaneous signing and closing, the section dealing with preclosing covenants should be deleted. Technically, the section containing conditions to closing can be deleted as well, but it is often left in as a reminder of the various deliveries that have to be made at the closing. If there is a simultaneous closing, you would substitute language to the effect that the closing is taking place simultaneously with the execution of the agreement.

SCENARIO 2, PERMIT NET ISSUANCE

Seller has 9,000 shares outstanding and 1,000 options at $5 per share.

All options are exercised prior to the closing on a net issuance basis, meaning with no cash paid to the Target, the optionees get $5,000 in cancellation of their options based on the tentative purchase price per share of $10.

Purchase price per share becomes $100,000/9,000 shares outstanding at closing (there are no longer any options), or $11.1111 per each of 9,000 shares, or approximately $100,000 in the aggregate. Plus, Target at closing will have $5,000 less in cash to be added to Buyer's consolidated balance sheet, which may or may not be recouped by the Buyer depending on whether or not there is a post-closing purchase price adjustment based on net working capital or another financial measure.

1.4 *Approval by the Target's Shareholders.* This section is drafted for a public company issuing stock to the shareholders of a private company. If a private company is acquiring another private company for stock, then the provisions relating to the Buyer's stock price are not required since the Buyer's stock is not publicly traded. The form in the materials assumes that only common stock is being issued for common stock. The merger consideration could be cash, stock, or a mixture of cash and stock, and the Target may have outstanding more than one class of stock and/or outstanding warrants or convertible debt. If the Target has more than one class of stock outstanding, then the merger consideration payable to each class of stock must be specified.

Article II: Conversion and Exchange of Shares; Dissenting Shares

2.1 *Conversion of Shares of the Target Capital Stock.* This section sets forth the price to be paid by the Buyer. It may be in the form of cash, stock and/or notes. The total purchase price should be stated, with provisions to convert that into a purchase price per share based on the number of shares outstanding at closing. Normally, new shares cannot be issued unless pursuant to previous contractual commitments.

The price may be a simple statement of how much cash is being paid for each share of the Target stock, or it can be expressed as a conversion ratio of how many shares of the Buyer are issuable for one share of the Target. An evolving technique in acquisitions of private companies, particularly those with multiple classes of stock outstanding, is to substitute a spreadsheet showing who gets what in the acquisition for the verbiage showing how the purchase price per share is calculated.

Mergers involving public companies present unique problems because the market price of a public company varies from day to day. These problems are discussed later under "Special Issues for Articles I and II."

2.2 *Escrow Shares.* This agreement assumes that there is an escrow. The pros and cons of an escrow agreement are a hotly debated topic. One view is that, given that escrow agreements almost always provide that no money may be released until both parties agree on a resolution of any disputes, unless there is a concern regarding the creditworthiness of the Target (in an asset purchase) or there are numerous Target shareholders in a stock purchase or merger (making pursuit of the Target's shareholders for indemnification administratively difficult), an escrow agreement is not really necessary and adds an unnecessary complication to the transaction. In merger transactions where not all shareholders sign, an escrow is normally essential to providing a mechanism for the nonsigning shareholders to pay their pro rata share of any damages. In this case, the escrow agreement is made an integral part of the merger transaction, and the escrow funds are placed in escrow pursuant to the merger agreement that has received the necessary board and shareholder approvals. It is commonly accepted that these escrow provisions are binding on nonconsenting shareholders.

2.3 *Dissenting Shares.* There is a statement of the right of holders of shares who do not vote for the merger to seek an appraisal of their shares in court. As noted earlier, transaction planners worry a lot about trying to avoid appraisal rights, but they are exercised infrequently in reality since the process is extremely costly for all concerned, and generally an individual shareholder doesn't have enough at stake to bother to initiate the procedures. Provisions related to appraisal rights are necessary since those shares are not technically converted into the merger consideration.

2.4 *Delivery of Evidence of Ownership.* This section sets out the mechanics of the delivery of the existing stock certificates in exchange for certificates representing the securities of the surviving corporation.

2.5 *No Further Ownership Rights in Target's Capital Stock.* This section contains additional boilerplate to the effect that the separate existence of the disappearing corporation will cease, that there can be no further transfers of the Target capital stock, and the like.

2.6 *No Fractional Shares.* The exchange ratio may result in fractional shares required to be issued to holders of the Target stock. This provision states that there will be no fractional share issuances and that fractional share interests resulting from the exchange ratio will be cashed out at fair market value based on the merger consideration.

2.7 *Assumption of Stock Options.* The Target's equity compensation plans need to be closely examined before drafting these provisions. (The same is true for any outstanding warrants.) Poorly drafted stock option plans may not provide that outstanding options are converted into the right to receive the merger consideration automatically; in theory, that would mean that the Buyer could not acquire all of the equity interests in the Target. In that case, the safe route is to require that all option holders consent to the merger. If they won't, the merger agreement simply says that the options are converted into the right to receive the merger consideration as part of the merger terms on the theory that the common stock of the Target is itself converted into something else pursuant to the merger. Opinions differ as to whether that works. The Target's stock option plan may provide that all options terminate to the extent not exercised before the merger, and this section would need to be modified accordingly.

The Buyer's management also needs to be advised as to whether any Target options accelerate vesting in connection with the transaction at hand. That is an important economic point; if the options do not accelerate, they provide the Buyer with free incentive compensation to the employees of the Target who remain with the Buyer after the closing. That is incentive compensation that otherwise would have to be paid by the Buyer. The Buyer may also fear that acceleration may make the option holders/key employees so rich that they have no real desire to work and contribute to the business after the closing. Some Buyers insist that as an integral part of the deal, option holders waive their acceleration rights. As we have discussed, investors in the Target have their own point of view—if options do not accelerate, then there may be more merger consideration for them.

Other: Deposits. On occasion, acquisition agreements will call for a deposit. Adding such a clause would appear to be simple and the purpose obvious, but it is actually somewhat complicated. Sometimes closings do not take place for a variety of reasons. Only some of them should result in the Buyer losing its deposit. For example, what happens if the deal doesn't close because *both* parties allege that the other breached? What if one is primarily at fault but the other is at fault as well?

Special Issues for Articles I and II

Special Provisions in Asset Purchase Agreements The Buyer wants the description of the assets being purchased to be as broad as possible. If an entire business is being purchased, there is typically a long laundry list of the assets being purchased, along with a catchall phrase to the effect that the Buyer is purchasing all assets used in the business, or all assets used primarily in the business. The Target would prefer to use the word "exclusively" rather than "primarily" or no qualification at all because if only part of its business is being sold, the Target wants to keep those assets that it uses in its other businesses. In most negotiations, the compromise is to use "primarily." In terms of identifying the assets being purchased ("Purchased Assets") and the business in which the assets are used ("Business"), it is common to use precise definitions to describe each.

If the Buyer is purchasing substantially all of the Target's assets, rather than assets of a discrete business of the Target, it may be preferable to revise sections relating to assets "of the Business" to provide that the Target agrees to transfer all of the assets it owns and remove any ambiguity about whether an asset is used in the business.

A typical laundry list of assets is as follows:

- All leases and subleases of, and other right, title, and interest in real property (and all related buildings, fixtures, and improvements thereon and all appurtenances, easements, and other rights benefiting or appurtenant thereto) used by the Target or held by the Target for use in connection with the Business, including without limitation those properties listed in the Target Disclosure Schedule.
- All personal property and interests therein, including machinery, equipment, furniture, office equipment, communications equipment, vehicles, spare and replacement parts, and other tangible property, including without limitation the items listed in the Target Disclosure Schedule.
- All raw materials, work-in-process, finished goods, supplies, and other inventories, wherever situated, a listing of which as of a recent date is set forth in the Target Disclosure Schedule.
- All rights under all contracts, agreements, leases, licenses, commitments, sales and purchase orders, and other instruments, including without limitation the items listed in the Target Disclosure Schedule.
- All accounts, notes, and other receivables.
- All prepaid expenses and deposits including without limitation ad valorem taxes, leases, and rentals.
- All petty cash located at operating facilities of the Business.
- All of the Target's rights, claims, credits, causes of action, or rights of setoff against third parties relating to the Purchased Assets, including, without limitation, unliquidated rights under manufacturers' and vendors' warranties.
- All of the Target's Intellectual Property Rights, including without limitation the items listed in the Target Disclosure Schedule.
- All transferable licenses, permits, or other governmental authorizations affecting, or relating in any way to, the Business, including without limitation the items listed in the Target Disclosure Schedule.

- All books, records, files, and papers, whether in hard copy or computer format, including, without limitation, engineering information, sales and promotional literature, manuals and data, sales and purchase correspondence, lists of present and former suppliers, lists of present and former customers, personnel and employment records, and any information relating to tax imposed on or with respect to the Purchased Assets (including copies of tax returns).
- All goodwill associated with the Business or the Purchased Assets, together with the right to represent to third parties that the Buyer is the successor to the Business.

Sometimes the Buyer will not purchase the Target's accounts receivable for the principal reason that the Buyer does not want to have to raise the extra funds required to purchase the receivables. If the Buyer is not purchasing the Target's accounts receivable, there is often a covenant pursuant to which the Buyer will attempt to collect the Target's receivables (as the Buyer may be in the best position to do so and may want to control relationships with ongoing customers). If, after the closing, both the Buyer and the Target have receivables from the same customer, an allocation mechanism must be specified.

You should discuss whether any assets otherwise included in the definition of Purchased Assets should be excluded. For example, a plant used in the business may be excluded because the Buyer already has unused capacity or the plant has environmental liabilities.

Transactions vary as to the liabilities to be assumed by the Buyer. In certain deals, it is the intention of the parties that the Buyer is to assume all the liabilities of the Business. In this case, the Target may want the definition to be broad and may prefer to use the following language:

Assumption of Liabilities. Upon the terms and subject to the conditions of this Agreement, the Buyer agrees, effective at the time of Closing, to assume all debts, obligations, contracts, and liabilities of the Target arising primarily out of the conduct of the Business of any kind, character, or description whether known or unknown, accrued, absolute, contingent, or otherwise, except for the Excluded Liabilities, including without limitation, the following ...

From the Buyer's perspective, even where the parties intend that the Buyer assume all of the liabilities of the Business, the Buyer wants the maximum protection from undisclosed liabilities and wants the definition of *assumed liabilities* to be as narrow and specific as possible. One way to do this is for the Buyer to assume only liabilities accrued on the Target's most recent balance sheet (note that this does not include certain contingent liabilities) plus liabilities incurred in the ordinary course of business since the date of that balance sheet, as well as those listed on a schedule delivered at signing.

Other assumed liabilities could include:

- All obligations and liabilities arising from any action, suit, investigation, or proceeding relating to or arising out of the Business or the Purchased Assets that are pending on the closing date against the Target or any Purchased Asset before any court or arbitrator or any governmental body, agency, or official, including but not limited to all litigation listed on Schedule.
- All liabilities and obligations relating to any products manufactured or sold by the Business on or prior to the closing date, including, without limitation, warranty obligations and product liability claims.
- All payroll, sales, use, and property taxes of the Target incurred in the conduct of the Business on or prior to the closing date to the extent accrued on the "closing balance sheet."

Where the Buyer is not assuming certain pre-closing liabilities, a mechanism must be set up to cover adjustments of liabilities that cover pre- and post-closing periods. Typical language might be:

> *The parties will estimate and settle at the Closing, to the extent practicable, the amount of all routine operating expenses that relate to periods before and after the Closing, such as [personal property taxes,] lease payments, utilities, and rent, with the Target being responsible for amounts relating to the period prior to the Closing and the Buyer being responsible for amounts relating to periods after the Closing. Bills for such items received prior to the Closing will be paid by the Target; and bills for such items received after the Closing will be paid by the Buyer, but the Target will promptly reimburse the Buyer for its allocable share of such items.*

Under certain circumstances, a Buyer of all or substantially all the assets of a business may, by operation of law, be at least secondarily liable for liabilities of a business the Buyer has expressly excluded in the purchase agreement. This area, known as *successor liability*, is complicated and is discussed elsewhere.

Article 6 of the Uniform Commercial Code (UCC) requires prior notice to creditors of all bulk transfers subject to the Article. Some states have adopted that provision, although most have repealed it. See UCC Section 6-105 (requiring at least 10 days notice prior to the earlier of payment and transfer). The central purpose of Article 6 is to address commercial fraud, where, for example, a merchant, owing debts, sells his stock in trade to a Buyer, pockets the proceeds, and disappears, leaving his creditors unpaid. Advance notice to the creditors is the primary protection that bulk sale statutes give. The penalty for noncompliance is that creditors of the transferor may seize the relevant goods from the Buyer to satisfy the Target's debts. See UCC Section 6-104.

Because compliance with the notice provisions of Article 6 is burdensome, expensive, and time-consuming, most sophisticated Buyers and Targets waive compliance with the provisions of Article 6 and the Target agrees to indemnify the Buyer should creditors of the Target seek to enforce any judgments against the Target without compliance with Article 6. Obviously, the Buyer should not agree to such a waiver if the Target's ability or willingness to satisfy the claims of its creditors is in doubt. A Buyer may agree to indemnify the Target in those instances where the Buyer is buying substantially all of the assets of the Target and assuming all the Target's liabilities, since the Buyer (not the Target) will be paying all of the Target's trade creditors.

A bulk transfer is any transfer in bulk and not in the ordinary course of the transferor's business of the materials, supplies, merchandise, and other inventory of a business subject to the Article. Businesses subject to the Article are all those whose principal business is the sale or rental of merchandise from stock, including those that manufacture what they sell. See UCC Section 6-102. On the theory that unsecured credit is not commonly extended to such businesses on the basis of a stock of merchandise, businesses such as farms, contractors, professional services, airlines, hotels, cleaning shops, barber shops, and so forth are not covered by the Article (although this may vary by state).

Purchase Price Adjustments   Acquisition agreements often contain *purchase price adjustment* provisions. These provisions appear more frequently in deals with a deferred closing, but do appear in others because of the gap between the signing/closing and the date of the most recent financial statements. Essentially, the purpose of these provisions is to keep the pre-closing economic risks and rewards of the business with the Target by retroactively adjusting the purchase price after the closing to reflect financial results after the date of the latest Target financial statements.

Most commonly, a purchase price adjustment says that the purchase price is adjusted up or down retroactively based on the increase or decrease in the Target's net worth (assets minus liabilities) or net working capital (current assets minus current liabilities) in the applicable measurement period. Again, the base measurement date is the date of the most recent balance sheet prior to signing. Therefore, if the Target has lost money, the purchase price will go down, and if the Target has made money and not distributed it to its shareholders, the purchase price will go up. This is because, as an accounting matter, the profit or loss is reflected in the Target's net worth, assuming that there are no adjustments to net worth outside the income statement. In addition to the *bona fide* purpose of risk transfer, some aggressive Buyers seek purchase price adjustments because the post-closing financial analysis used to determine closing net worth gives them an opportunity to pick at the balance sheet the Target supplied. If there are any problems in that balance sheet, then the Buyer is entitled to an adjustment that is not subject to the basket for immaterial claims.

Note that in a stock purchase, the business is effectively run for the account of the Buyer if the Target is not allowed to pay dividends between signing and closing. If the business deal is that the business is to be run for the Target's account, however, then a purchase price adjustment is required.

Purchase price adjustment provisions are often quite complicated, and there are a number of common pitfalls. The most common mistake is to allow the purchase price adjustment to be based on only selected balance sheet items, as opposed to net worth, which takes into account all assets and liabilities. The parties may say that they do not really care if there is any change, for example, in the value of fixed assets, but do care if there is a change in working capital. The logical conclusion is that the purchase price adjustment provisions only need to relate to working capital items. This might work, but the risk to this piecemeal approach to the balance sheet is that the Target will manipulate the balance sheet by, for example, selling some capital equipment to increase working capital by the amount of cash received. That said, working capital adjustments are now more commonly used, and when they are combined with strict covenants to run the business in the ordinary course, they simplify the calculation and are often implemented successfully.

Another purchase price adjustment may be for an increase or decrease in long-term debt, but it does not make sense for the purchase price to change if the Target merely pays down some debt with cash or incurs debt and adds an equivalent amount of cash to its balance sheet. For that reason, debt adjustments should be for net debt or debt minus cash.

In an asset purchase, the risk of the piecemeal approach is exacerbated because in an asset deal where the Buyer pays cash, cash is an asset that typically is excluded from the assets the Buyer is buying—in other words, there is no point to the Buyer buying the Target's cash with the Buyer's cash. Therefore, cash is an excluded asset. Where cash is an excluded asset, you have to have a purchase price adjustment to take into account increases or decreases in the cash that the Target keeps because that differential is effectively an increase or decrease in the purchase price.

Cash can change even if there is no change in the business (e.g., accounts receivable are collected and no new ones are generated). This would produce an anomalous result.

Some examples of how purchase price adjustments work are provided in the following example.

March 31 Balance Sheet

Cash	$ 1,000	Trade payables	$ 1,000
Accounts receivable	1,000	No other liabilities	
Inventory	1,000		
Fixed assets	7,000	Net worth	9,000
Total	$10,000	Total	$10,000

Assume:

- The business operates at a 50% gross margin and sells $500 worth of inventory in April—that is, it sells $500 of inventory for $1,000, creating a $1,000 receivable and reducing inventory by $500.
- The business collects $750 of accounts receivable in April, adding that to cash and reducing accounts receivable by a like amount. The only other expenses in the period are general and administrative expenses of $250/month, which reduce cash by a like amount.
- Closing takes place on April 30.

April 30 Balance Sheet

Cash	$ 1,500	Trade payables	$ 1,000
Accounts receivable	1,250		
Inventory	500		
Fixed assets	7,000	Net worth	9,250
Total	$10,250	Total	$10,250

Purchase Price Adjustment Examples

Stock deal: If there is no purchase price adjustment, the business is effectively "run for the account of" the Buyer (i.e., the Buyer gets the

(*Continued*)

benefit of $250 in net profit in the month ($500 in profit from the sale of inventory minus $250 in general and administrative expenses) and the equivalent increase in net worth).

- If you change the example slightly, and general and administrative expenses are $750 rather than $250 as in our example, then there would be a decrease in net worth of $250 that the Buyer would absorb.

Asset deal: Assume that the Buyer is buying all assets but cash, and is assuming all liabilities of the business, all for a fixed price. Assume that the business deal is that the Target keeps interim income/loss. If the business did nothing but collect the accounts receivable (i.e., there were no revenues or expenses), then you would still need a purchase price adjustment to avoid an anomaly resulting from the increase in the excluded asset. The purchase price should be reduced for the increase in cash that the Target keeps and the decrease in accounts receivable that the Buyer purchases. If the business is run for the account of the Buyer, then you would need to have a purchase price adjustment to reflect the increase in cash that the Target keeps and the decrease in accounts receivable that the Buyer purchases.

The take-away point here is that mistakes are common in purchase price adjustment provisions, and the businesspeople and investment bankers involved in the deal, and not just the lawyers, should be strongly encouraged to think through the details of these provisions.

REPRESENTATIONS AND WARRANTIES

The next major sections of the agreement contain the representations and warranties of both the Target and the Buyer. The Target will make representations about its business, anywhere from 10 to 30 pages long, covering such things as capitalization, no litigation, required consents, no adverse change, no undisclosed material liabilities, environmental compliance, taxes, and on and on. The draftsperson should take care to add to the boilerplate representations that are appropriate to the particular situation, like additional representations that are appropriate for Targets in particular industries. For example, there would be more comprehensive intellectual property representations for a technology company.

Generally, representations serve three functions:

1. They create a basis for due diligence by confirming that various elements of the business are sound and that the business does not have undisclosed material contingent liabilities (such as litigation or environmental claims). It is therefore important to adapt, reduce, or add to these representations and warranties in order to reflect the nature of, and risks inherent in, the business being acquired. In some industries, particularly regulated industries, such as banking, securities, and insurance, specialized representations and certain related conditions should be included.

2. In transactions with a delay between signing and closing, the continuing truth as of the closing date of the representations and warranties given on the date of the agreement is generally a closing condition, giving the Buyer an additional opportunity to investigate the business and a right not to close if it determines the representations were not true as of the signing or are no longer true at closing. Consequently, the representations should be drafted and reviewed with great care.

3. Representations are the foundation of the Buyer's indemnification rights because indemnification is generally not available to the Buyer unless it can prove certain representations and warranties are untrue. Indemnification provisions provide that if there are any breaches of any representations or agreements by a party, that party must indemnify the other and pay the damages and expenses caused by the misrepresentation or breach.

Usually, the Target will be unable to make some of the representations set forth in this article and may accordingly request various exceptions. The generally accepted format for exceptions is to allow the Target to prepare disclosure schedules setting forth the information constituting the basis for these exceptions. Disclosure schedules are prepared in advance of the execution of the agreement and attached as exhibits. The representations will make reference to the disclosure schedules, where the representing party's exceptions to the representations and warranties are disclosed and where various detailed information about the business is required to be listed.

It is essential that the Buyer and its counsel review carefully each item listed in the disclosure schedules because the effect of including an item in the disclosure schedules is to deprive the Buyer of the right to refuse to close the purchase or make a claim under the indemnity provisions based on the adverse effects, if any, of the disclosed event or condition. That is not to say that the Buyer will not extract a reduction in the purchase price or a separate indemnity with respect to the requested exceptions when it learns of them.

The Buyer will also make representations. If the deal is for cash, then the representations are minimal—just that the deal has been properly authorized and is valid and binding on the Buyer. If, however, the Buyer is issuing stock to the selling shareholders, the representations and warranties of the Buyer frequently are as extensive, or nearly as extensive, as those of the Target.

One Buyer trick that usually fails is to circulate a draft of the merger agreement in a stock deal that requires the Target to make extensive representations and the Buyer to make only minimal representations. Don't bother. It is usually a good argument that the Buyer should make the same representations as the Target because the Target is in effect investing in the Buyer's business by taking the Buyer's stock. But bear in mind that if the Buyer is a public company issuing stock, its representations are usually somewhat abbreviated because reference is usually made to the accuracy of the Buyer's reports filed with the Securities and Exchange Commission (SEC), which contain comprehensive information about the Buyer.

Some agreements are drafted in such a way that there is a reference to a numbered schedule each time an exception is needed for a particular representation or warranty. In this style, the representations call for various information to be separately listed and disclosed in a separately numbered schedule. The introductory paragraph in the standard agreement we have supplied contemplates a single disclosure schedule, meaning all representations are made subject to exceptions set forth in the disclosure schedule in a numbered section that corresponds to the place where the representation is made.

Targets sometimes ask that a disclosure in one section be sufficient disclosure of that particular matter wherever an exception is relevant. For example, a Target could state in one section that there is a breach of a material contract but forget to list that contract in a schedule of material contracts. Conversely, the Target could list the contract among material contracts but not mention the breach. Because the Target may subsequently argue that the Buyer has no remedy because the contract was disclosed in at least one section, Buyers resist the inclusion of the one-for-all language. One common compromise is to introduce the concept of deemed cross references to other sections, but only where the implications of the particular disclosure are obvious or "clearly apparent" with regard to the other sections.

These issues should be battled out in the agreement itself; if you represent the Buyer, you should not accept contrary introductory language to the Target's disclosure schedule. The introduction in the sample agreement also contains the language "whether or not the Target Disclosure Schedule is referred to in a specific section or subsection." This means that you do not have to repeatedly include words to the effect of "except as set forth in the Disclosure Schedule."

When representing a Target, it is helpful to have the lead-in to Article III state "except as previously disclosed to the Buyer in writing," although you should still exercise care in making disclosures and consider preparing a formal schedule to avoid disputes down the road. Buyers strongly resist this language since it later may result in a "he said, she said" debate.

In rare cases, the Target may request that it be permitted to deliver disclosure schedules (or freely amend previously delivered disclosure schedules) after the execution of the agreement. If the Buyer agrees to this type of arrangement, the agreement should include a fairly broad right on the part of the Buyer to terminate its obligations under the agreement if the subsequent disclosure reveals information that is adverse from the Buyer's point of view. A Buyer that agrees to this type of arrangement should be warned that litigation is likely to arise if the Buyer seeks to exercise its right to terminate the agreement, and that the subsequently disclosed information would have to be very significant in order for the Buyer to avoid legal exposure in exercising such right. The implied covenant of good faith and fair dealing will limit the Buyer's rights even if the provision grants it absolute discretion.

Targets frequently attempt to qualify certain representations by providing that such representations are made "to their knowledge." The effect of a knowledge limitation is generally to limit the Target's responsibility to actual fraud (i.e., where it knew a representation was false and failed to disclose it). This raises a deeper question: What risks should a Buyer assume, or not assume, in an acquisition transaction? In other words, should the Buyer assume the risk of a problem that the Target did not know about? Targets will argue that they are selling the business in order not to have to worry about these kinds of problems. Buyers will argue that the price they are paying is based on there not being any exceptions to the representations, even if the Target did not know about the problem. One way to look at this is that knowledge representations are only allowed, if at all, where a Target would not be in a position to determine if there were exceptions regardless of the effort to find them.

Where the Buyer chooses to accept a knowledge qualification, its effect can be limited by specifying the procedures used by the Target to confirm the accuracy of the representations. The following is an example:

> *Knowledge of the Target. Where any representation or warranty contained in this Agreement is expressly qualified by reference to the knowledge or the best knowledge of the Target, the Target confirms that [(i) the Target has in effect procedures that are reasonably designed to inform the Target fully as to the matters that are the subject of such representation and warranty and that the Target has observed such procedures and (ii)] the Target has made due and diligent inquiry as to the matters that are the subject of such representation and warranty.*

The other major battle that is fought in the representation section is the extent to which the Target is permitted to make representations that are qualified by "materiality." The debate here is somewhat similar to the knowledge qualifier debate. Targets will argue that there are certain representations where it is almost certain that there are exceptions for any business, and therefore the Target should only be required to represent that there are no *material* exceptions. For example, it is likely that no business complies in all respects with every law and regulation that applies to it. Laws and regulations are simply too complex. The Target's logic here is that the Target should only be responsible for those legal violations that are material and that the Buyer should be willing to take the business subject to those nonmaterial exceptions.

These issues are important, as stated earlier, because the Target will have to give back part of the purchase price via the indemnification section if there are any violations of the representations. It makes a significant difference to the potential economics if there are materiality and knowledge exceptions. We discuss later the interplay between the representations section and the indemnification section.

Now, let us turn to the typical representations in an acquisition agreement, with more extensive attention to the ones that most often provoke debate between the Buyer's and the Target's lawyers.

Article III: Representations and Warranties of the Target and the Shareholders

3.1 *Organization, Standing, and Power; Subsidiaries.* The Target represents that it was validly organized and that it currently exists and is in good standing. It also represents that it is qualified to do business where it is supposed to be; this may seem trivial, but if it isn't so qualified, there may be a significant state tax problem.

3.2 *Capital Structure.* All equity interests are required to be disclosed. It is important, obviously, for the Buyer to know exactly who owns what equity interests in the Target. For example, if the employees of the Target have not received an industry-standard amount of equity in the Target, the Buyer will effectively have to assume the cost of bringing the incentive equity up to the appropriate amount.

3.3 *Authority.* The Target represents that it has the power and authority to conduct its Business as currently conducted and as proposed to be conducted and to own, operate, and lease its properties and assets. The Target also represents that all action required to be taken by it, its board of directors, and its stockholders in connection with the acquisition agreement and the transactions contemplated by the acquisition agreement has been duly and properly taken, and that the acquisition agreement is valid and binding and is enforceable in accordance with its terms.

3.4 *Compliance with Laws and Other Instruments; Non-Contravention.* The Target represents that it is in compliance, in all material respects, with all laws and regulations in general and that the acquisition will not result in its violating any laws or contravening any of the provisions of the agreements that it is a party to or otherwise bound by.

3.5 *Technology and Intellectual Property Rights.* The Target is required to list all of its intellectual property that is able to be listed—patents, trademarks, and the like. The Target states that it has all intellectual property rights necessary to conduct its business; that its licenses in and licenses out are valid, binding, and not in default; that it owns its intellectual property; that no one is infringing its intellectual property; and that its business does not infringe anyone else's intellectual property. The infringement representations are often qualified to knowledge because it is effectively impossible to tell with certainty whether there are patents that are being violated, particularly in the case where a patent application has been filed and has not yet been made public. However, the Buyer may insist that potential infringement claims are a risk appropriately borne by the Target's shareholders, and therefore knowledge qualifiers for these representations are not acceptable.

3.6 *Financial Statements; Business Information.* This is perhaps the most important representation. When asked if they could only have one representation, most M&A lawyers would say the financial statements representation. Here, the Target represents that its financial statements are prepared in accordance with generally accepted accounting principles (GAAP), which in theory should give the Buyer a pretty good snapshot of the financial aspects of the business—assets, liabilities, income, and cash flow. Regarding unaudited interim financial statements, exceptions are taken for the absence of footnotes and for customary year-end nonmaterial audit adjustments; it is customary for unaudited financial statements not to contain footnotes, although they are technically required by GAAP.

In fact, preparation of GAAP financial statements does not tell the Buyer all that it needs to know about the Target's liabilities. There are very specific accounting rules related to what liabilities must appear on the balance sheet, what liabilities must appear in the footnotes, and what liabilities do not have to be disclosed at all, either on the face of the financials or in the footnotes. The Target can have all sorts of different liabilities—liabilities that are known and quantifiable, liabilities that are known but not quantifiable, liabilities that are contingent and likely, and liabilities that are contingent and only remotely likely. Generally, the first group appears on the balance sheet, the second and third groups appear in the footnotes, and the fourth group doesn't appear anywhere. But the Buyer wants to know about all of them.

Because GAAP financials do not tell the Buyer all that it needs to know about all actual and contingent liabilities of the Target, acquisition agreements typically include a representation to the effect that as of the date of the last balance sheet, the Target did not have any (material) liabilities or obligations, whether actual, contingent, quantifiable, or nonquantifiable, that are not disclosed in the financial statements. To complete the picture, to this is added that there are no such (material) liabilities or obligations that have accrued since the date of the balance sheet other than in the ordinary course of business.

Without a materiality qualifier, this representation can never be true, nor would it be reasonably possible to prepare a complete list of liabilities for the disclosure schedule. So there is usually a materiality qualifier of some sort. Even then, this representation draws a lot of resistance from the Target because realistically, you probably can't do a complete disclosure schedule relating to all liabilities and obligations even with the materiality qualifier. There then begins a debate about risk allocation. Who is to bear those risks? Another more reasonable variation is to say that there are no undisclosed liabilities that, individually or in the aggregate, would have a material adverse effect on the Target.

Targets will often try to water down the "no material liabilities" representation to say only that there are no liabilities required to be shown on the balance sheet in accordance with GAAP that are not shown. Adding this provision will virtually eliminate any protection this representation would add to the financial statement representation, because it then boils down to a repetition of the representation about the financial statements and does not pick up liabilities that are not required in the financial statements by GAAP.

This representation may need to be modified for asset acquisitions. As a general matter, the "no undisclosed liabilities" representation is appropriate in some form where the asset acquisition is of an entire business but in the form of an asset purchase and assumption of liabilities. Where the Buyer is only assuming specified liabilities, however, an argument can be made that it is not necessary to require a representation about there being no undisclosed liabilities since the Buyer is not assuming them. The counterargument is that the Buyer would nevertheless like to know about them for what they reveal about the economics of the business and its solvency. If the parties agree to limit the representation, one way to do it is to say there are no other liabilities that would become obligations of the Buyer or would otherwise adversely affect the Buyer. This approach does not work in significant part if one of the assets that the Buyer is purchasing is the stock of certain subsidiaries of the Target.

3.7 *Taxes.* This representation, sometimes in a separate section, states that the Target has filed all tax returns required to be filed by it and has paid all taxes it owes, as well as more technical representations, such as that there are no tax disputes and the like.

3.8 *Absence of Certain Changes and Events.* This is another very important representation not only because of its substance but because it can affect the mechanics of the deal. Here the Target represents that since the date of the latest audited or unaudited balance sheet, a laundry list of items has not happened. In addition to the laundry list, this is where the so-called material adverse change (MAC) representation appears. This representation says that since the specified date there has been no MAC in the business or in the financial condition or prospects of the Target. Because all representations have to be reaffirmed ("brought down") as of the closing as a closing condition, this representation protects the Buyer from adverse events at the Target before the closing.

Key points of debate here usually turn around the use of the word *prospects.* Buyers argue that the Target's prospects are exactly what they are buying. Targets virtually always take exception to the use of the term prospects in the definitions of *material adverse change* and *material adverse effect.* They may argue that the terms are too speculative, or that an adverse change in prospects should be the Buyer's risk. The phrase "would reasonably be expected to have a material adverse effect" can offer some comfort regarding impending developments not yet reflected in the business's performance. Some Targets feel somewhat more secure with this type of language than with the term *prospects,* on the theory that a development would have to have a greater nexus with the business to reach this standard. Occasionally, the parties make an effort to distinguish among various types of developments where it may be more appropriate for the Buyer to assume risks, like those relating to the economy generally or the Target's industry or arising from the announcement of the transaction.

The list of adverse events and prospects that the Buyer wants to include sometimes contains its own laundry list of items that have not been materially adversely affected, like assets, liabilities, results of operations, personnel, and so on. Technically, all of the accounting/financial elements are contained in the accounting definition of *financial condition,* including results of operations. *Financial position* is the accounting term used to describe a balance sheet condition.

3.9 *Leases in Effect* and 3.10 *Owned Personal Property; Real Estate.*
The Target is asked to list all of its leases and owned real and personal property and to represent that there are no defaults under its leases and that there are no title problems with its owned property.

3.11 *Certain Transactions.* This representation captures so-called insider transactions or transactions between the Target and its management and/or owners. The Buyer needs to know about these because these transactions are frequently not at arm's length, and the Buyer's normalization of them may have a significant effect on the income of the Business. The Buyer may also require termination of these arrangements at closing.

3.12 *Litigation and Other Proceedings.* The Target represents that there is no litigation or similar proceedings to which it is a party and that, to its knowledge, none have been threatened. Sometimes the Target is asked to represent that there is no basis for it being sued; this one is always debated.

3.13 *No Defaults.* The Target represents that it is not in default on any of its obligations, including its material contracts, and is unaware of defaults by its counterparties.

3.14 *Major Contracts.* The Target is asked to list all of its material contracts. There is usually a very long list of the categories of contracts that are required to be listed. Contracts below a specified dollar amount are exempted from being listed. The dollar amount depends on the specifics of the Business and what is material to it. Targets will attempt to set higher thresholds so as to minimize the work required to prepare its disclosure schedule.

3.15 *Material Reductions.* The Target represents that there have been no losses of significant customers or material reductions in orders.

3.16 *Insurance and Banking Facilities.* These are required to be listed so that the Buyer can hit the ground running and make the necessary changes in these items after the closing. An insurance claims history is also sometimes required to be disclosed.

3.17 *Employees* and 3.18 *Employee Benefit Plans.* The employees of the Target, or a subset thereof, are required to be listed, along with their salaries and other compensation data. Extensive disclosure relating to the Target's benefit plans is also required, as well as a representation that they have been maintained in accordance with applicable law.

The Target may also be asked to represent that it does not have any information that any of its key employees intend to quit after the closing. This type of representation in some form may be appropriate in connection with acquisitions of businesses where people are the principal assets of the business (such as service businesses) or where the Buyer has no ability to manage the acquired business profitably without the support of incumbent management. In these situations, the parties should consider getting signed employment agreements contemporaneously with the signing of the definitive acquisition agreement, rather than making them a condition to closing. That should flush out any problems that the key employees have with the deal or the Buyer, and will also decrease their negotiating leverage if the key employees know that their not signing employment agreements could blow up a deal that is about to close.

3.20 *Guarantees and Suretyships.* This representation asks the Target to disclose material powers of attorney that have been issued to others, as well as material obligations under guaranties.

3.21 *Brokers and Finders.* The Target represents as to whether it has retained any brokers or finders in connection with the deal. The Buyer wants to avoid claims that it owes these fees because the Target didn't pay its debts in this regard.

3.22 *Environmental Matters.* This representation, which can range from a simple paragraph to several pages in length, asks for disclosure of environmental liabilities and other environmental problems. As the environment increasingly caught the public's attention over the years, it became fashionable to make this representation as long as conceivably possible. In most businesses, that approach is likely overkill—like for a software company—but in others it is extremely important, such as a manufacturing business that uses hazardous chemicals.

3.23 *Enforceability of Contracts, etc.* The Target represents that it knows of no reason why its contracts are not enforceable.

3.24 *Products.* In a business that sells products, the Target is asked to represent that its products comply with applicable legal requirements and that there have been no material, out of the ordinary course of business, problems with its products since a specified date.

3.25 *Information Statement.* If the transaction requires the Target to send out a formal information statement (i.e., a proxy statement) to its shareholders, this representation states that it contains all material information about the Target and is not misleading.

3.26 *HSR Act.* Information relating to the Hart-Scott-Rodino Act (HSR) requirements as applicable to the Target are required to be set forth.

3.27 *Disclosure.* This is the catchall so-called 10b-5 representation that nothing in the representations and nothing that the Target has told the Buyer is untrue in any material respect or omits any material information. The Target will vigorously oppose this with a vagueness argument and argue that it has just made 20 pages of representations and suffered through exhaustive due diligence—so that should be sufficient. The Buyer will argue that no set of representations can ever be complete, and wants to hedge its bets via a 10b-5 representation.

3.28 *Inventories and Receivables.* Depending on the transaction, specific representations on inventories and receivables may or may not be appropriate or necessary. Where inventory or receivables are not particularly important to the transaction, one can rely on the financial statement representation, because GAAP requires stale inventory and receivables to be written off. More specific representations may be appropriate where inventory and receivables are key components of the business being acquired.

Other. If the transaction is conditioned on approval by the Target's shareholders and the Target's shares are registered under the Securities Exchange Act of 1934, it will probably be appropriate for the Buyer to seek 10b-5 type representations from the Target with respect to the Target's proxy statement and for the Target to obtain similar representations from the Buyer with respect to information about the Buyer included in that proxy statement.

Article IV: Representations and Warranties of the Shareholders

4.1 *Title to Shares;* 4.2 *Authority;* 4.3 *Non-Contravention;* 4.4 *Acquisition for Investment.* Where the Target's shareholders are signing the agreement, these sections are where they are asked to make separate representations about their title to their shares and that they are legally able to sign the agreement. If securities of the Buyer are being issued as deal consideration in a private placement, this is where the shareholders' SEC "investment representations" are made. If the shareholders do not sign the agreement, a mechanism needs to be set up for the shareholders to sign a separate document with these representations.

Article V: Representations and Warranties of Parent [Buyer] and Merger Sub

The scope of these representations will depend on whether the consideration consists, in whole or in part, of the Buyer's securities. Representations and warranties relating to capitalization, financials, and adverse change need to be included only where stock of the Buyer is to be issued. The representations and warranties of the acquiring company are somewhat limited in this document, and assume a publicly traded Buyer that files periodic reports with the SEC. As discussed earlier, if the Buyer is a private company and is issuing stock, expect the Target's counsel to request representations from the Buyer that are parallel to those of the Target. If the consideration is cash, the Buyer's representations should be even more limited.

Representations given by a public company acquiring a private company for stock are typically significantly less extensive than those of the Target.

For one, there is extensive information about the public Buyer in its SEC filings, which in theory should tell the Target's shareholders all they need to know about the Buyer; there is simply added a representation that these filings are complete and not misleading. In addition, it is often impractical for a public company of any size to prepare the information that would be required in a disclosure schedule tied to extensive representations and warranties. For a public company, give some thought to not volunteering the 10b-5 representation; it is dangerous because if the Buyer's stock price drops, allegations of fraud, often unsubstantiated, may be alleged, and the representation can be used to tag along on lawsuits initiated by unhappy public stockholders.

If the Buyer's ability to finance the purchase of the Business is a concern, the Target may ask the Buyer to make an appropriate representation regarding financing. The appropriate representation will depend on the facts. The following is an example of a financing representation that would be appropriate where the Buyer's obligations are subject to financing, and the Target is proceeding on the basis of bank commitments or bridge or equity commitments received by the Buyer.

> *Financing. The Buyer has received and furnished copies to the Target of commitment letters (the "Commitment Letters") from (i) [name of bank] dated as of [date], pursuant to which [name of bank] has committed, subject to the terms and conditions thereof, to enter into a credit agreement with the Buyer and a syndicate of banks for which [name of bank] will act as agent and will provide financing and (ii) [name of equity investor] dated as of [date], pursuant to which [name of equity investor] has committed, subject to the terms and conditions stated therein, to enter into a stock subscription agreement with the Buyer to contribute to the equity capital of the Buyer. The bank credit agreement referred to in clause (i) above and the stock subscription agreement referred to in clause (ii) above are referred to herein as the "Financing Agreements," and the financing to be provided thereunder or under any alternative arrangements made by the Buyer is referred to herein as the "Financing." The aggregate proceeds of the Financing will be in an amount sufficient to acquire the Purchased Assets, [to effect all necessary refinancing and to pay all related fees and expenses]. As of the date hereof, the Buyer knows of no facts or circumstances that are reasonably likely to result in any of the conditions set forth in the Financing Agreements not being satisfied.*

COVENANTS

Article VI: Covenants of the Target

If there is to be a deferred closing, this section deals with preclosing and post-closing covenants. Preclosing covenants limit what the Target (and perhaps the Buyer) can do between the signing and the closing. This section is relatively uncontroversial. Post-closing covenants deal with such issues as how the Target's employees and benefit plans are to be treated. Sometimes post-closing non-competition covenants are included here as well.

As for preclosing covenants, the Buyer does not want the Target to be taking cash out of the business or taking strategic actions that it might disagree with. So this section requires that the business be run in the ordinary course, that there be no dividends declared or paid or securities issued (other than the exercise of stock options where the Target has a preexisting commitment), no change in the charter or bylaws, no material acquisitions of another business or capital equipment, no sales of assets other than inventory and the like in the ordinary course, no unusual incurrence of bank debt, no raises in compensation, and no filing of lawsuits. A description of other typical covenants follows.

6.9 *Access to Properties and Records* and 6.10 *Breach of Representations and Warranties*. The Buyer will want to continue its due diligence after the signing of the agreement and keep current on the Target's business developments. A clause is included in the agreement permitting the Buyer's representatives to have continued access to the Target's management and records. Because of the time and expense of due diligence, regulatory filings, transition planning, and preparation for the closing, the Buyer would like to find out about new problems as soon as they occur. One mechanism is a Target covenant that it will promptly apprise the Buyer of any developments that would have had to appear on the Target's disclosure schedule.

6.11 *Consents*. As you will recall from our discussion of non–tax-structuring issues, often the acquisition transaction will require consents from the counterparties on the Target's material agreements. Because the receipt of these consents, or at least the ones that are important, will be a closing condition, the Target will be required to use its best efforts (or at least commercially reasonable efforts) to obtain these consents as soon as possible to avoid a delay in the closing.

6.12 *Tax Returns*. The Target must continue to keep itself in tax good standing by filing all required tax returns and paying all taxes due and owing.

6.13 *Shareholder Approval* and 6.14 *Preparation of Disclosure and Solicitation Materials*. If shareholder approval is required, the Target agrees to use its best efforts to get it and to properly prepare and send any required disclosure documents.

6.15 *Exclusivity; Acquisition Proposals.* Because of the time and expense that the Buyer has already incurred and will incur on the transaction and because it likes the deal and wants to keep it, deal-protection devices are almost always included in the agreement or in a separate agreement that key shareholders sign. The limits to these deal-protection devices are the subject of the famous Delaware takeover cases—Revlon, Unocal, and the like, which are discussed in detail in Chapter 6.

Although these limitations in theory apply equally to the acquisition of both public and private companies, private company acquisition practice has historically largely ignored these limitations. Therefore, very strong (*preclusive*, in Delaware parlance) deal-protection measures have normally been included in private company acquisition documents. Partly because of the *Omnicare* case discussed later, this practice is changing, and deal-protection devices typically used for public companies are being used in private company acquisition agreements. The sample agreement we have included uses the old approach. The latest, greatest deal-protection device variants can be found on the SEC's website, where public-to-public merger agreements have to be filed.

If a Target shareholder vote is required, the Buyer may require that the vote be completed before entering into the agreement. That approach is impractical when the Target is a public company. Alternatively, the Buyer may wish to obtain a commitment of the Target (via the board) to recommend the transaction to its shareholders and/or a commitment from one or more major Target shareholders to vote in favor of the sale at the Target's shareholder meeting. An example of a commitment of a major shareholder of the Target to vote in favor of the transaction is as follows:

> *From the date hereof until the termination of this Agreement, neither [shareholder] nor any of its affiliates will vote any shares of the Target Stock in favor of the approval of any other sale of assets, reorganization, liquidation, or winding up of the Business or any other extraordinary transaction involving the Business or any matters in connection therewith, or any corporate action the consummation of which would either frustrate the purposes of, or prevent or delay the consummation of, the transactions contemplated by this Agreement.*

6.16 *Notice of Events.* This is another requirement to keep the Buyer promptly notified of selected significant events that may happen and affect the deal.

6.17 *Reasonable Best Efforts.* The parties generally agree to do all that is necessary and reasonable to get the deal done. In certain cases, consideration should be given to whether exceptions to this best-efforts covenant are appropriate. In transactions requiring regulatory approvals, the obtaining of which is uncertain, the parties may wish to define the limits to which the parties must go in seeking such approvals. For example, the Buyer may wish to clarify that it is not required to appeal in the courts any denial of regulatory approval or agree to conditions (such as significant divestitures of assets or requirements that certain businesses not be integrated) that may be burdensome to the Buyer in order to obtain any such approval.

6.18 *Insurance.* The Target is required to keep its insurance in force. In addition, the Target wants to be sure that its officers and directors have insurance coverage after the closing for their actions prior to the closing. The Buyer is usually obligated to maintain such insurance in place after the closing.

6.19 *Resignations.* The Buyer will want to replace all (or most) of the Target's officers and directors. This covenant requires the Target to get resignations that are effective at the closing.

6.20 *Noncompetition.* The Buyer does not want to buy the business and then have the Target's principals compete against it after the closing. The agreement typically includes a requirement for a noncompetition agreement from key managers and shareholders. Where the Target is selling only part of its Business, the appropriateness of a noncompete clause from the Target will depend on the transaction and should be closely examined to determine the effect on the Target's remaining businesses and on future acquisitions. The clause is principally designed to protect the Buyer from renewed competition by the Target but may also have tax consequences.

A noncompete clause is generally required to be reasonable both in geographic scope and duration and may be invalid if it does not meet those criteria. Accordingly, where a noncompete clause is included, it may be appropriate for a law firm opining on the legality of the agreement to qualify its opinion. In the context of a sale of a business, three years is usually enforceable. Noncompete agreements typically also include a nonsolicitation provision that says that one party may not solicit the employment of the other party's employees. The stricter form of this provision includes as well that one party may not hire employees of the other for a specified period of time. The reason to add the no-hire clause is that breach of a nonsolicitation clause is difficult to prove. If employees are paid for noncompetes, it is ordinary income to them versus capital gain on stock.

6.21 *Section 338(h)(10) Election.* This is a technical tax election discussed in Chapter 4.

6.22 *Approval of Parachute Payments.* As discussed in Chapter 4, acquisitions can trigger penalty taxes if the deal is too rich for the Target's management. For private companies, this problem can be cured with shareholder approval. This section in the sample agreement requires such approval.

Article VII: Covenants of Buyer

This article contains covenants of the Buyer that are appropriate to the deal. These will vary depending on the form of the acquisition consideration and the relative size of the parties.

ADDITIONAL AGREEMENTS

Article VIII: Additional Agreements

The "Additional Agreements" section captures more general covenants that mostly apply to both parties.

- In a stock purchase, there are covenants supporting the private placement status of the issuance of stock by the Buyer signed by the signatory Target shareholders.
- The parties will agree to use their best efforts to fulfill the conditions to closing.
- The Target's board will frequently try to look out for the Target's employees after the acquisition. There may be a covenant specifying how many of the Target's employees will be given job offers by the Buyer. As for those employees who are hired, provision will be made to allow them to apply their years of service with the Target as a credit for participation and vesting purposes in the Buyer's benefit plans.
- Who will pay expenses? In a merger or a stock purchase, if nothing is said, the Buyer will effectively be paying for the legal fees of the Target and also the Target's shareholders. Generally, the Target's regular law firm will handle the acquisition, and its bills will be sent to the Target and become obligations of the Target that the Buyer assumes. Astute Buyers will try to insert a provision that the Target's and the Target's shareholders' legal expenses in connection with the acquisition will be borne by the Target's shareholders, often by a deduction from the purchase price. Sometimes the Buyer will pick up some of the expenses up to a limit that will encourage the Target's counsel to be reasonable and not run up the bill.
- The Buyer and the Target will usually agree to coordinate any announcement of the deal. There is often a conflict here since the Target wants to keep things quiet until the deal is done, and the Buyer, if it is a public company, has disclosure obligations if the deal is material.
- Usually, there will be a confidentiality agreement in effect between the Buyer and the Target while the merger agreement is being negotiated, and frequently one party or the other will prefer to retain the existing

arrangement rather than replace it. You should review any such agreement carefully to ascertain whether it should be amended or superseded. If it is retained, the integration clause should reflect that fact.

8.8 *Affiliate Agreements.* These agreements were universal in public/public acquisitions that were accounted for as a pooling of interests. Poolings have been abolished. These agreements are still often used, even though there is no technical requirement for them under the securities laws. They are also used if there are to be imposed on affiliates restrictions on transfer of Buyer stock to be received in the acquisition as a business term.

8.9 *Hart-Scott-Rodino Filing.* If an HSR filing is required, the parties agree to make the filings. This section also deals with what the parties are obligated to do if the antitrust filings do not go smoothly.

CONDITIONS TO CLOSING

Article IX: Conditions Precedent

One big issue that arises is whether there is, or has to be, a deferred closing—that is, the parties sign the agreement but understand that they cannot close until certain external contingencies are resolved. For example, the contingencies could include the need to get antitrust regulatory clearance under HSR or approval of a disclosure document by the SEC, each of which requires filings with government agencies and a waiting period. Also, shareholder approval may be needed but cannot be obtained immediately, particularly where there are a large number of shareholders of the Target, as there always are in public companies. It's a lot simpler to do a simultaneous signing and closing, if possible, both in terms of the complexity of the agreement and in economic terms as well.

If there is to be a deferred closing, then the agreement must contain conditions to both parties' obligations to close. Typical conditions are the regulatory and shareholder conditions just discussed. But Buyers also almost always insist that there be representations that ensure that Targets retain the risk of owning the business until the closing. Therefore, typical closing conditions include a *bring-down* of the Target's representations and warranties, meaning that the Target has to reaffirm those representations as of the closing date, including that there has been no material adverse change in the Target's business. Sometimes Target has enough bargaining leverage to shift the risks of the business to the Buyer upon signing, not closing. In that case, the bring-down of certain or all representations is not a condition to closing.

Other conditions are the completion of various ancillary actions that are a part of the deal, like the signing of the agreed-upon employment agreements, noncompete agreements, and the like.

Targets will often object to some of these conditions, particularly the requirement that the representations be brought down at the closing and that there be no pending proceedings. Where a long delay between signing and closing is expected, it may be acceptable in some cases to limit the scope of the bring-down to key representations or representations within the control of the Target. It may also be acceptable to establish a different standard for the litigation and other conditions. Perhaps more appropriate is a bring-down that says that the representations and warranties are true and correct as of the closing, with only such exceptions that, individually or in the aggregate, would not have a material adverse effect on the Buyer. In any case, a careful analysis of the business and legal risks between signing and closing is important.

Note that the knowing waiver of a closing condition will ordinarily compromise the opportunity for indemnification based on the facts giving rise to the failure to satisfy the condition. A waiving party seeking to preserve its rights should negotiate a separate indemnification or other arrangement prior to closing.

SURVIVAL OF REPRESENTATIONS AND INDEMNIFICATION

Article X: Survival; Indemnification

As previously discussed, Buyers require contractual protection in the event of a misrepresentation in the acquisition agreement by the Target or if the Target breaches any other provision of the agreement. The Target's shareholders also require indemnification if there is a breach by the Buyer where the acquisition consideration is Buyer stock; in that case, as we have said before, the Target's shareholders are in effect buying the Buyer's stock.

The acquisition agreement will therefore say that the representations and warranties *survive* the closing (i.e., that breaches can be asserted after the closing) and provide for indemnification for breach. The only exception to this pattern is acquisitions of public company Targets. Except rarely and only in troubled situations, as a matter of commercial practice the representations and warranties do not survive the closing in acquisitions of public companies, and there is no post-closing indemnification.

The language of indemnification provisions is basically the same in all forms of transactions: The *indemnitors* indemnify the *indemnitees* for all losses, expenses, damages, and liabilities arising out of a breach of a representation, warranty, agreement, or covenant by the other party in the acquisition agreement. That part is not controversial. Other related issues are usually hotly contested.

Although the inclusion of indemnification provisions in an agreement does not automatically require the creation of an escrow, Buyers want to segregate funds so they are easier to reach if they have a valid claim and can be assured that there will be a ready source of indemnification. In a merger with multiple shareholders, the only practical source of protection is an escrow because of the difficulties of suing multiple parties. One exception is where there is a particularly large shareholder, and the Buyer extracts joint and several indemnification from that shareholder. But even then, that shareholder will object to covering all of the damages where it has received only part of the acquisition consideration.

Most acquisition agreements, at least where there are multiple sellers, provide for an escrow. Escrows sometimes are favorable from the point of view of the larger Target shareholders because that is the only practical way to get all the Target's shareholders to come up with their fair share of the damages. Escrows are released for the pro rata account of the contributing Target shareholders.

Once it is determined that an escrow will be part of the deal, additional questions arise, such as what percentage of the purchase price the escrow should be and how long it should last. Generally, the percentage ranges from 5 to 15 percent, and the warranties survive for one to three years, with certain representations like capitalization and title to shares, tax and environmental representations, and sometimes intellectual property (IP) representations, surviving longer on occasion. The Target's shareholders obviously would like to get their money sooner, and probably have the better of the argument that new claims are highly unlikely to arise after a year or so.

In addition to the size and length of the escrow, the negotiations will also revolve around whether there will be exceptions and limits to the indemnification provisions.

Targets in a strong bargaining position try to limit the indemnification to the escrow, meaning that there can be no claims against the acquisition consideration paid up front directly to the Target's shareholders and not put into escrow (with exceptions for fraud and perhaps the longer-surviving representations mentioned earlier). Buyers are well advised to seek a larger escrow if indemnification is limited to the escrow. For example, if there is a $10 million escrow and a $15 million problem, the Buyer is out the $5 million. Targets argue, in support of limiting the indemnification to the escrow, that they are selling the business and don't want to have to worry about it anymore and want the assurance that they can keep the money already received. Institutional investors, like venture capital funds, will argue that they have to distribute to their own partners/investors the proceeds that they receive in the sale and so the money is gone as soon as they get it (notwithstanding that they may have access to additional funds from their investors). Furthermore, Targets will argue that the Buyer should not be too worried because it did extensive due diligence on the business before signing the acquisition agreement and should know that the Target is a clean company. Conversely, Buyers will argue that the problems they are most worried about are the big ones, and that limiting the indemnification to a relatively small escrow will not cover them in any really big, career-ending mess. Targets will counter that if there is to be indemnification above the escrow, then there must be some limit short of all proceeds.

Another provision that is almost always present is the so-called *basket*. A basket means that the Buyer will not be entitled to indemnification unless a certain dollar threshold of claims is reached and sometimes that each individual claim has to exceed a certain threshold before it can be asserted. The rationale for baskets is that small mistakes are likely, and the parties should agree in advance that neither side need be bothered with the time and expense required to resolve small claims. The underlying assumption is that minor problems are an assumed part of the economics of the deal to the Buyer.

The dollar amount of the basket varies with the size of the deal, and a figure of 1 percent is frequently mentioned, although 1 percent can be a large number to cover small mistakes, particularly in large deals. There is also a distinction between a *true basket* or *deductible,* on the one hand, and a *threshold* or *disappearing basket* on the other hand. In the latter case, once the threshold of claims is reached, damages are to be reimbursed beginning at the first dollar. In the former, only the damages above the threshold are reimbursable. There are multiple arguments for each approach.

One argument asserted by some Buyers is to say that because the basket is meant to cover immaterial mistakes, then, for purposes of indemnification only (and not the conditions to closing), all materiality qualifiers in the representations are to be ignored. Targets will argue that the materiality qualifications in the representations are necessary, or otherwise they could not make them truthfully. In effect, with no materiality qualifiers in the representations, the preparation of the disclosure schedule exceptions to the representations would be extremely onerous and difficult to get right. Buyers will then argue that acquisitions are not a morality play, and that what is really going on is risk allocation between the Buyer and the Target (or actually, the Target's shareholders). Buyers will say that they should be indemnified for immaterial breaches if they get above the basket.

Buyers will also raise the so-called double materiality problem: First they have to prove that the particular problem rises to an unspecified level of materiality in representations that contain materiality qualifiers; then, on top of that, Targets will argue that the only damages that Buyers are entitled to are the amounts by which the troublesome facts exceeded the unspecified materiality level; and then, on top of that, Targets are entitled to the basket exclusion.

To solve that problem, Buyers argue that for purposes of indemnification only (and not the conditions to closing), all materiality qualifiers in the representations should be ignored. A better view on this particular issue is that once it is determined that a material misrepresentation was made (with the materiality qualifier left in), the damage calculation in connection with the misrepresentation should ignore any materiality threshold. Another variation would be to ignore the materiality qualifiers only for the purpose of determining whether the basket is exceeded; if it is exceeded, the basket is eliminated but the materiality qualifiers are still included to determine whether there has been a breach and presumably excluded for purposes of damage calculation. This gets a bit mind numbing.

To see the implications of these variations, consider the following example: $100,000 aggregate basket; a representation that there are no material undisclosed liabilities and no threatened material litigation; after closing, the Buyer determines that there are 20 undisclosed nonmaterial $10,000 liabilities and 1 undisclosed threatened material $200,000 lawsuit.

- *Threshold versus deductible.* There is a total of $200,000 in potentially reimbursable damages (from the lawsuit) since each of the $10,000 claims is not material and therefore not reimbursable. If the basket is a deductible, then the Buyer would get reimbursed for the $100,000 above the basket. If there is a threshold that resets to zero, then the Buyer gets the full $200,000 because the $100,000 basket is exceeded.
- *Materiality qualifications ignored for indemnification purposes.* If there is a $100,000 aggregate basket and there is a clause that the materiality qualifications are ignored for purposes of indemnification, there is $400,000 in damages. If there is a deductible, the Buyer gets the $300,000 over the basket. If there is a resetting threshold, then the Buyer gets the full $400,000.

Assume now that there is a $100,000 aggregate basket; a representation that there are no material undisclosed liabilities and no undisclosed threatened litigation of any type; after closing, the Buyer determines that there are

20 undisclosed nonmaterial $10,000 liabilities and one undisclosed threatened $50,000 lawsuit.

- *Threshold versus deductible.* Each of the $10,000 claims is not material and therefore not reimbursable. With either a threshold or a deductible, the Buyer would get back none of the $250,000 in aggregate damages because the $100,000 basket has not been reached since the only misrepresentation that counts is the $50,000 lawsuit.
- *Material qualifications ignored for indemnification purposes.* If there is a clause that the materiality qualifications are ignored for purposes of indemnification, there is $250,000 in reimbursable damages because all of the small claims and the litigation are reimbursable. If there is a deductible, the Buyer gets the $150,000 over the basket. If there is a resetting threshold, then the Buyer gets the full $250,000 because the basket has been exceeded.

Buyers should be careful to limit the operation of the basket solely to misrepresentations and not to other breaches of the agreement or to liabilities that are specifically indemnifiable. For example, if it is agreed that damages relating to a preexisting lawsuit are reimbursable from the escrow, the basket is not meant to be a deductible or threshold for that liability.

Another issue to be aware of is how indemnification mechanics work in an asset purchase. Where you are buying selected assets from an established well-financed seller, there is no issue—you are adequately protected by indemnification from the Target. But if you are buying all assets and there is no escrow, and all of the proceeds are distributed to shareholders who did not sign the asset purchase agreement, there is no practical source of reimbursement. The solution here, obviously, is to get the Target's shareholders to sign the asset purchase agreement or separate indemnification agreements, or get an escrow—or both.

Finally, well-advised Targets will insist on a *sole remedy* clause to the effect that the Buyer's sole remedy for a breach of the representations is to proceed under the elaborate compromises reached in the acquisition agreement. Otherwise, the Buyer may sue under a common-law breach-of-contract damages claim outside of the provisions of the agreement.

One brief note on procedures: As is typically the case with indemnification provisions in other contexts, usually the indemnitor is able to control the defense of third-party claims that give rise to indemnification claims. The argument is a good one—if the indemnitor is financially responsible, it does not want the indemnitee to be playing with its money and doing a lousy job on the defense. One area where there are exceptions is where there is a potential for a much broader impact on the business now in the hands of the Buyer than a mere damage claim. An example would be a patent infringement claim that may destroy the business if the case were lost. This latter problem is exacerbated where damages are limited to a relatively small escrow.

TERMINATION

Article XI: Termination

This section provides for the termination of the merger agreement under defined circumstances. Those include that a party may terminate if the conditions to its obligation to close are not met and it does not desire to waive those conditions, or it can terminate if there is a material breach of the merger agreement by the other party. It also may deal with the situation where, in advance of the closing, it is clear that a condition to closing cannot be met, such as the occurrence of a material adverse change in the other party's business. Certain conditions, like a financing commitment, may have a separate deadline; if that condition fails, the other party may terminate. In addition, certain termination provisions might include cure provisions or requirements that the party seeking termination has used its reasonable or best efforts to remedy the problem.

Also, typically there are termination provisions if the transaction becomes illegal for some reason. There may be circumstances that justify a narrower illegality clause in the termination provision. For example, if there are foreign or local laws that might be broken by closing the transaction, one might not want the other party to have a broad termination right in order to keep pressure on that party to modify the deal in some way that can accommodate the problem.

There is usually also a drop-dead date, meaning that if all of the conditions to closing have not happened by a specified date, even though the parties have been proceeding in good faith, either party may terminate because the transaction has been in limbo for too long.

MISCELLANEOUS

Article XII: Miscellaneous

These are the typical miscellaneous provisions in the sample agreement relating to notice, waivers, and the like. One interesting twist is in the "Consent to

Jurisdiction" clause. This provides that if one party wants to sue another, it must do so in the other party's home state. This is provided as a disincentive to lawsuits. Bargaining power may dictate otherwise.

The Buyer may want the ability to assign its rights to indemnification to a successor. In a leveraged buyout, care must be taken to allow the Buyer's rights to be assigned as security for financing sources.

A newer provision often seen in acquisition agreements borne out of recent case law provides for the Buyer's consent to the Target's attorneys' continued representation of the Target's shareholders after the closing, in connection with any disputes or other matters between the Buyer and Target's shareholders that may arise post-closing. Generally, one of the assets of the Target that remains with the Target absent agreement to the contrary is the attorney-client relationship that the Target has with its law firms, at least one of which is usually the same law firm that represents the Target's Board and shareholders in connection with a sale. Without this consent, the Buyer could try to assert a conflict of interest or attorney-client privilege with respect to the pre-closing relationship in order to prohibit the law firm from continuing to represent the selling shareholders after the deal closes, which could put the shareholders at a disadvantage in the event of a post-closing dispute.

REPRESENTING TARGETS: A SUMMARY

Representing the Buyer is the easier task at the outset of the agreement preparation process. The lawyer representing the Buyer presents his firm's standard buyer-oriented merger agreement. Different firms and lawyers have different philosophies about exactly how onerous the Buyer's first draft should be. Some Buyers and their counsel serve up a highly Buyer-favorable agreement and force the Target and its counsel to fight for every point—even ones that the Buyer feels it will have to agree to change. Others serve up a relatively middle-of-the-road agreement that is still Buyer favorable but is intended not to waste everyone's time with obnoxious clauses that will have to be conceded in any event.

Regardless of the approach, the Buyer's first draft will need at least some tweaking by the Target and its counsel. That task is always more difficult because what the Target should ask for may not be in the four corners of the agreement and can be overlooked. The following is a checklist of issues that Targets and their counsel should consider in negotiating the detailed terms of acquisitions. Some of these points are redundant with the preceding material, but may prove to be useful in one place. Whether some or all of these issues should be brought up at the letter of intent stage is discussed in Chapter 2.

- *Purchase price adjustments.* Purchase price adjustments that tie to changes in net worth or balance sheet items may seem innocuous, but they invite claims that the Target's books were not maintained in accordance with GAAP, and they also can be an end run around the basket. These clauses are very tricky and should be reviewed by Targets and their advisers carefully to make sure they work.
- *Liquidity issues.* Worry about liquidity. If it is a stock deal, is the market for the Buyer's stock thinly traded? If the selling shareholders are getting restricted stock in a public company, insist on a registration rights agreement with shelf registration rights. This means that the Buyer automatically has to file a resale registration statement for the shares issued in the acquisition within a specified (short) period after the closing.
- *Ancillary agreements.* If there are to be noncompete agreements or employment agreements, at the outset have at least a term sheet describing what is to be in them.
- *Representations and warranties.* Add materiality and knowledge qualifiers wherever possible. If stock is part of the consideration, try to get Buyer's representations as broad as the Target's.
- *Conditions to closing.* Try to shift the risk of the business to the Buyer by limiting the representations that have to be "brought down" or at least trying to avoid a bring-down of the material adverse change representation.
- *Indemnification:*
  - Try to limit the amount of time that the representations survive to one year or less.
  - Try to limit the indemnification to the escrow, even at the price of a larger escrow—this may be the most important seller provision of all.
  - If indemnification is not limited to the escrow, then try to obtain a dollar or percentage limit to indemnification claims.
  - If there is liability beyond the escrow, try to get a provision that the Buyer can sue an individual seller only for its percentage of the overall damages. Even in that case, there should be a contribution agreement among the selling shareholders to reimburse each other if any shareholder pays more than its percentage share relative to the other shareholders (e.g., where only a few shareholders are sued).
  - Try to get a true basket or deductible, rather than a disappearing basket or threshold.

- Try to get a provision that the Buyer is not entitled to indemnification if it had actual knowledge of the condition or event that gave rise to the breach, even though it was not disclosed in the Target's disclosure schedules. What if the Target, in a deferred-closing transaction, discovers that it had inadvertently left out a particular claim in the disclosure schedules delivered at signing? Try to get a provision that the Target is permitted to supplement the disclosure schedules before closing and that the Buyer takes subject to the revised disclosure schedules. The Buyer can still walk away if there was a material breach, but it cannot close and then sue the Target a moment later.
- If the acquisition consideration is wholly or partly Buyer stock, consider providing that indemnification claims can be paid back in Buyer stock valued at the time of the closing. Even better, insist that the Target can at any time substitute cash for the shares in escrow valued at that fixed price, or pay valid claims in cash. That way, Targets have the best of both worlds: If the Buyer's stock goes up, they can keep it and pay the indemnification claim in cash; if the Buyer's stock goes down, they can pay the indemnification claim in overvalued (for indemnification purposes) Buyer stock. If, instead of a fixed price, the value of the Buyer's stock is allowed to float for indemnification purposes, try to get a floor on how low the stock can go for purposes of valuing it for reimbursement purposes.
- Make sure the agreement states that the negotiated terms of indemnification are the Buyer's sole remedy for a breach of the agreement (i.e., that the Buyer cannot sue outside the agreement under contract law).
- Try to limit the type of reimbursable damages (i.e., try to exclude incidental, special, consequential, and punitive damages).
- Try to include a provision that the Buyer's damages are measured net of tax benefits from the loss and net of insurance recoveries. Try to exclude from the damages any that result from a change in the Target's tax allocations and positions prior to closing. Try to require the Buyer to maintain insurance that will cover damages that are otherwise reimbursable.
- Try to require the Buyer to use its best efforts to mitigate damages and to measure damages net of any recoveries that the Buyer is entitled to (insurance, other indemnification sources, etc.), but the Buyer shall not be required to consider or exercise any remedy against any director, officer, or employee (whether current or former) of the Target.

APPENDIXES

The following appendixes are located on the website that accompanies this book. For information on the website, see the "About the Website" section at the back of this book.

Appendix 5A, Annotated Long-Form Merger Agreement

Appendix 5B, Annotated Long-Form Asset Purchase Agreement (economic sections only)

CHAPTER 6

Acquisitions of Public Companies

PUBLIC-TO-PUBLIC MERGERS: WHAT IS DIFFERENT?

All of the tax, corporate, and other structural parameters for acquisitions of private companies apply with equal force to acquisitions of public companies. Public companies are those that are traded on the New York Stock Exchange, Nasdaq, one of the other stock exchanges, or another trading market, and that have registered their stock with the Securities and Exchange Commission (SEC) under the Securities Exchange Act of 1934 (Exchange Act). SEC registration can be accomplished by a traditional initial public offering (IPO), or by direct registration under the Exchange Act without a simultaneous offering of stock.

Even though the structuring fundamentals are the same, the process of one public company acquiring another public company is enormously different from the acquisition of a private company. An acquisition of a private company by a public company for cash is not much different from the acquisition of a private company by another private company for cash. The same holds true for an acquisition of a private company for public company stock, but only if the acquisition can be structured as a private placement under the federal securities laws. If such an acquisition cannot be structured as a private placement, then that acquisition will more closely resemble a public company acquisition—something to be avoided. It would be highly unlikely for a private company to acquire another private company for stock with a concomitant SEC registration since that, in effect, would be a simultaneous IPO and acquisition.

So what is different about a public-to-public acquisition?

First, because public companies have a large number of shareholders, the only feasible ways to acquire a public company are: (1) a merger or (2) a public tender offer. As discussed previously, a merger is a transaction that combines two or more companies into a single entity. A tender offer is an offer by a company to purchase directly from shareholders, often at a premium price, a substantial percentage of another company's shares for a limited period of time, usually followed by a merger after the acquiring company gains control.

A private stock purchase is impractical, except as a first step in the acquisition. Solicitations of public company shareholders (for anything, including a merger vote) are heavily regulated by the SEC's proxy rules under the Exchange Act and require an elaborate proxy statement. State rules may also apply. Tender offers are regulated by the SEC's tender offer rules under the Exchange Act. If the Buyer's equity securities are part of the acquisition consideration, then the merger or the tender offer (in this case, called an exchange offer) is considered a sale of the Buyer's securities, subjecting the transaction to registration under the Securities Act of 1933 (Securities Act). The registration requirement is satisfied by the Buyer filing a Form S-4 registration statement, which also involves compliance with the proxy rules in connection with a merger or the tender offer rules for a tender offer.

The proxy rules impose minimal substantive regulation on the terms of the transaction. Similar to the SEC's registration rules under the Securities Act, the proxy rules are primarily designed to ensure full disclosure to the persons whose votes are being solicited—in our case, generally the Target shareholders but also the Buyer's shareholders where Buyer stockholder approval is required. The SEC's tender offer rules do regulate the substance of the transaction and require that certain procedural requirements be followed, such as the length of time that the tender offer has to remain open.

Second, given that the merger consideration generally will reflect a premium to the prior trading price of the Target and will often significantly affect the price of the Buyer's stock, disclosure or nondisclosure of merger negotiations becomes extremely sensitive. In a sense, it's a no-win situation. If you do not disclose and shareholders sell in that period, they will be angry because they sold at too cheap of a price. If, however, the merger negotiations are disclosed prematurely—meaning there is no solid deal yet—and the transaction never happens, Buyers in the period will be angry because the price of the Target's stock most likely traded up on the announcement and then went back down when it was disclosed that there really was no deal. There is enormous pressure on all of the participants in this situation.

The Buyer and the Target abhor premature disclosure. If the deal does not happen, there is egg on everyone's face, and, as discussed in Chapter 2, damage may have been done to employee, supplier, and customer relationships. The thinking around when disclosure is required, including the leading case of *Basic Inc. v. Levinson,* is discussed in the next section.

Third, public company acquisitions usually involve big money, and big money brings out the business and legal vultures in our society. They are ready to pounce on the slightest mistake. In addition to case law, there are a number of time-critical SEC rules on the timing and filing of information relating to a proposed merger or tender offer. Many involve difficult judgments that the vultures are ready to attack.

Fourth, as discussed later in this chapter, a broad and entirely confusing body of Delaware case law has evolved dealing with board fiduciary duties in the acquisition context. No one really knows where the next Delaware case will come out in the area of lock-ups, no-shops, fiduciary outs, and the like. The Delaware courts seem to have developed an appetite for eroding the scope of a board's business judgment and have invalidated many agreements that boards thought were in the Target's best interest. The problem, in part, derives from the old adage that bad cases make bad law. Just as honest public companies get dragged into class action securities suits along with the crooks, so too do good boards of directors get stuck with Delaware judges second-guessing them because of what bad boards have done. Imperfect business judgment should not equate to a breach of fiduciary duty.

These differences result in intense time pressure to sign the definitive agreement as soon as a deal is reached in principle in order to prevent premature leaks of the deal and the ensuing stock market turmoil. There is also pressure to close the deal as quickly as possible to minimize the possibility of an upset offer from another bidder. Many merger agreements are drafted, negotiated, and signed within a few days of an agreement in principle being reached. Due diligence is rushed and, to compound matters, there is almost always no survival of the representations and warranties because there is no practical way to enforce them where there are thousands of Target shareholders. These considerations limit, to a degree, the games that acquisition lawyers can play with one another, as there is no time to posture and overnegotiate.

One other complication in public deals worth discussing here is how to deal with the fact that the stock of one or both companies is publicly traded and floats on the market between the signing of the definitive agreement and the closing. If a Target agrees to be acquired by a Buyer for a fixed number of shares of the Buyer's stock, the value paid by the Buyer at closing may be a lot less than what the value was at the time the deal was signed; or, from the Buyer's viewpoint, the Buyer may be overpaying if its stock price rises significantly. Conversely, if the Buyer agrees to pay the Target a fixed dollar amount and lets the number of shares float, then the Buyer could wind up issuing too many shares if its stock price drops significantly, resulting in excessive dilution. From the Target's perspective, its shareholders may receive too few shares if the Buyer's stock price rises significantly (and perhaps temporarily).

The contractual solution to these problems is to have *caps* and *collars* on the price or number of shares. More specifically, one alternative is to vary the number of shares to achieve a specified aggregate dollar purchase price. The aggregate number of shares locks when the Buyer's stock price rises or falls to the top or bottom of a range called a *collar*. The Target's shareholders do not participate in the upside and downside when the stock price rises or falls inside the collar, but do participate from market fluctuations outside the collar once the number of shares locks.

Another alternative is to fix the number of shares within a Buyer's stock price collar. The specified number of shares is issued as long as the share price stays within the collar. The aggregate dollar value of the deal locks when the Buyer's stock price gets to the stock price collar. Above or below the collar, the number of shares changes to achieve the locked dollar value. The Target's shareholders participate in the upside and downside as the stock price fluctuates inside the collar, but are insulated from market fluctuations outside the collar.

These clauses can be extremely complicated, but the essence is that if the price or dollar amount rises or falls above or below a collar, the adjustment stops at a certain point. If the deal value then continues to rise or fall up to a further point, or cap, then the "aggrieved" party may have a right to get out of the deal in that circumstance—unless the other party agrees to waive the cap. And so on.

CASE LAW–DEVELOPED FIDUCIARY DUTIES AND STANDARDS OF REVIEW

Introduction

This section discusses some of the landmark Delaware acquisition cases. It is not meant to be a complete or scholarly treatment, but only a discussion of some of the business issues that the existence of these cases introduces into merger discussions.

Before some of the principal Delaware takeover cases are summarized, it is useful first to examine the common aspects of the business transactions to which all of these cases relate. The public company merger process can start in a number of ways. There are two general categories: (1) friendly acquisitions and (2) hostile acquisitions. The distinction is not necessarily helpful because in certain cases friendly acquisitions can be interrupted by hostile takeover attempts, and hostile takeover attempts often wind up with a negotiated merger agreement that in a sense becomes a friendly acquisition at that point.

Generally speaking, a friendly acquisition means a negotiated acquisition where the parties perform due diligence and negotiate price and other deal terms. A friendly acquisition can start off with an unsolicited approach by the potential suitor. *Hostile* indicates unsolicited, but it really means more than that. The classic hostile takeover is where the bidder does not negotiate with the Target board (or stops at a certain point), but rather makes a tender offer directly to the shareholders at a price set by the bidder in the absence of negotiation. A hostile bid can start with a *bear-hug* letter where the bidder names a price and offers to negotiate, but signals that it is prepared to go directly to the Target's shareholders.

Sometimes, as with private companies, a public company will receive an unsolicited inquiry where there is no implied threat of a hostile takeover. Officers and directors of public companies, like those of private companies, can be curious about what the Target could be sold for—particularly where the officer or director holds a large equity stake.

Another route is for the Target's board to decide that it is time to put the Target up for sale. The possibilities here range from approaching a particularly likely bidder, to approaching a limited number of bidders that are potentially interested, to an auction where the company invites anybody and everybody to make a bid.

In a friendly deal, the usual acquisition process we have been discussing is followed, but typically in a more abbreviated form. One or more bidders does due diligence on the Target, and a merger agreement is negotiated and signed.

Bidders do not do this for sport. Where a deal is struck, the Buyer has decided to buy the Target at the specified price, and the Buyer does not want to spend a lot of time and money that ultimately might be wasted by an embarrassing loss of the deal to another bidder. Bidders therefore build in *lock-up* provisions that have ranged from preclusive lock-ups structured to make it impossible, as a practical matter, for anyone else to upset the deal, to provisions that discourage but do not preclude another bid.

These provisions are included because there necessarily is a delay between signing and closing due to the need to hold a shareholders meeting, among other things. In that interim period, an upset bid can emerge.

More specifically, the history of common lock-up devices has included:

- *No-shop agreements.* A no-shop agreement says generally that the Target will not seek other bids, and may also say that the Target may not negotiate with, or furnish confidential information to, new prospective bidders. These clauses come in multiple strengths—from an absolute lock-up where there can be no discussions with another bidder or furnishing of due diligence materials under any circumstances, to a window-shop clause where unsolicited bids may be entertained, sometimes only under certain circumstances (such as higher bids that, in addition, are not subject to financing contingencies), to a go-shop clause where the Buyer is permitted to solicit bids for a limited time.

In the definitive agreement, the Target is also required to use its best efforts to secure shareholder approval, and the board is required to recommend the deal to the Target's shareholders. No-shop agreements, however, typically have *fiduciary out* clauses that allow the Target to negotiate with and furnish information to a prospective bidder if the Target board concludes after receiving legal advice to the effect that the board's fiduciary duty requires it to do so.

The fiduciary out is conceptually confusing because it begs the question as to when the duty is measured. The board has agreed, in the definitive merger agreement, to be bound not to shop or negotiate with another bidder—how then can it be a breach of fiduciary duty to comply with a binding agreement that the Target signed after board authorization? The courts have essentially determined, in a variety of cases, that the board breached its fiduciary duties by too quickly authorizing an agreement with a lock-up provision, or authorizing an agreement with a lock-up provision that is too strict under the circumstances. In other words, courts have found certain types of "preclusive" lock-ups to be *per se* a breach of fiduciary duty, and have found others to be a breach of duty where the board had not tried hard enough or well enough to sell the Target before authorizing the agreement. In effect, in order for the board to take advantage of a fiduciary out in an agreement, counsel must advise that, after a new bid has emerged, it would now be a breach of fiduciary duty for the board not to talk to a new bidder. But that was exactly what it had agreed to in the definitive agreement it had authorized, presumably validly after good investment banking and legal advice. So the Target's counsel in effect would be required to advise the board of the Target that the process and agreement that the same counsel had previously advised the board were proper are now, in retrospect, improper.

Allowing boards to get out of their agreement to recommend the deal to the Target's shareholders is easier to understand. Boards can't irrevocably bind themselves to recommend a deal if a better deal is offered before the shareholder vote. It has been determined that the board has to be free to withdraw its recommendation in those circumstances. To do otherwise would be a breach of duty. In order to make getting out of the deal harder for the Target, some agreements require that the deal be submitted to the shareholders even if the board has withdrawn its recommendation. That introduces delay and confusion into the process for the new bidder.

Other conundrums posed by the different variations of these clauses include whether the Target has to first receive a *superior proposal* before it is allowed to negotiate with another bidder. That raises the question of whether the Target is allowed to furnish confidential information only after the receipt of the bid—but how does another bidder, as a practical matter, make such a bid if it doesn't have the full picture of the financial and business condition of the Target?

■ *Breakup fee.* So what happens if these hurdles are crossed and the Target wants to take a better deal? The no-shop is typically combined with a provision that the Target can terminate the acquisition agreement if it gets a superior proposal but only if it pays the original suitor a *breakup fee* and/or a *topping fee.* This means that the Target, in order to terminate the agreement, must pay the original suitor's expenses (sometimes unaccountable and sometimes actual out-of-pocket expenses, possibly with a cap) plus a fixed fee and/or a fee equal to a percentage of the amount that the new bid exceeds the original deal.

A key question here is when the fee has to be paid. These fees are usually very substantial, even so high that the Target may not have the cash to pay it. This issue is particularly acute if the fee is payable upon termination of the original agreement rather than only payable if the superior deal closes. These fees can be combined with a stock option where the first bidder is given an option that survives termination to purchase a number of shares of the Target's common stock at the then-current market price or the original bid price. This effectively increases the upset price because the next bidder will have to pay for more shares, and so the option acts like a topping fee. These options are for less than 20 percent of the Target's stock because of limitations imposed by the stock exchanges on private sales of a listed company's securities.

■ *Crown jewels option.* The original varieties of lock-up devices included a *crown jewels option* that gave the Buyer the option to buy a critical piece of the Target's business, or the "crown jewels," if the deal didn't close for any reason other than the Buyer's breach (e.g., in the event the Target's shareholders did not vote for the deal, particularly if they did not approve the deal after another bidder announced that it would pay more). These lock-up devices often effectively precluded another bidder from coming in and trying to scoop the deal, even if it offered a significantly better price for the Target. These preclusive lock-ups were invalidated by the courts on a number of occasions as a breach of fiduciary duty on the part of the board of directors of the Target, which rendered the merger agreement unenforceable.

■ *Voting agreements.* Here, the bidder gets agreements from key share-holders that they will vote for the bidder's deal and will not tender their shares into a tender offer made by a rival bidder. They may be required to vote for the original deal *come hell or high water,* or they may be required to vote for it only if the merger agreement is not terminated. Given that the original deal needs majority shareholder approval and that bidders have threshold requirements as to how much stock they have to acquire—they do not want to become minority owners in a ten-der offer or not have enough shares to do a later squeeze-out merger in order to acquire 100 percent of the Target—these agreements make it harder (and maybe impossible) for an upset bid to emerge. To take an extreme case, if a majority of the Target's shareholders agree to vote for the original deal come hell or high water, then another bid is ren-dered impractical; this arrangement was addressed (and invalidated) in the *Omnicare* case discussed later.

In addition to lock-up devices in negotiated deals, potential Targets have implemented defensive measures that are meant to make difficult (or perhaps impossible) the completion of a hostile bid. These devices include the *poison pill,* staggered terms for directors, and other devices. Anti-takeover devices are discussed later in this chapter.

The other procedural aspect that must be kept in mind in public com-pany deals is that mergers are subject to shareholder approval that can only take place well after signing. If the board agrees to a particular deal with a bidder and includes the most stringent of lock-up provisions or anti-takeover devices, the shareholders still may not vote for that deal. That can happen, particularly in a locked-up deal, if an upset bidder announces publicly that it is prepared to pay more for the stock of the Target than the deal to which it has agreed. So even if some of these clauses and devices can discourage another deal, they cannot ensure that the negotiated deal will be completed (other than if a majority of the shareholders are locked up and execute voting agreements). One possibility, then, is that the Target does not have to termi-nate the signed merger agreement and pay a breakup fee—it can simply wait for the shareholders to veto the deal. What happens to the original bidder under those circumstances—does it get a breakup fee? The answer is usually yes, but that is a tough one for the Target, particularly if the breakup fee is payable in cash, since another deep-pocketed new bidder has not emerged that can pay the breakup fee for the Target.

The essence of the Delaware takeover cases is to determine which of these devices are valid and enforceable and under what circumstances, if any. If these devices are held to violate the directors' fiduciary duties, they are considered unenforceable by the Delaware courts. This brings us to the duties that the courts examine in takeover cases.

There are two fundamental fiduciary duties owed by directors to shareholders that apply in all situations, acquisition or otherwise:

1. *Duty of loyalty.* The duty of loyalty requires that directors make decisions in good faith based on the best interests of the corporation and its shareholders, and not based on their own self-interest. A director who is either on both sides of a proposed transaction or who can be expected to derive material personal financial benefit from it (other than as a shareholder of the corporation, like any other) is not *disinterested*—and an action of a board that relies on the votes of directors who are not disinterested may be subject to attack for violating the duty of loyalty.
2. *Duty of care.* The duty of care requires that directors exercise reasonable care in making decisions on behalf of the corporation. This means that directors must inform themselves regarding a matter before them, and must act in a deliberate and careful manner after taking into account all relevant information reasonably available to them. In the acquisition context, the Target board's duty of care requires that the board use reasonable diligence to secure the best available transaction on behalf of the Target's shareholders.

The principles just summarized are analyzed in hindsight, where the Target, acting through its board of directors, has taken an action (such as agreeing to a strategic stock-for-stock merger) and a shareholder has sued to overturn that action, ordinarily on the grounds that the directors have failed to live up to their duties to the shareholders. The *business judgment rule* provides that generally the court hearing such a lawsuit will not second-guess a board of directors or substitute the judgment of the court (or the complaining shareholder) for the business judgment of the board, if that business judgment has been exercised in a careful and disinterested manner. As the Delaware courts have phrased it in *Smith v. Van Gorkom*, the rule itself "is a presumption that in making a business decision, the directors of a corporation acted on an informed basis, in good faith and in the honest belief that the action taken was in the best interests of the company."

What started with the simple and straightforward business judgment rule has become a menu that includes more stringent standards that courts use to measure whether the board has fulfilled its fiduciary duties. The reason for this is that the courts have had to deal with a wide variety of transactions with different factual patterns, changing market conditions, and acquisition techniques that put limits on the appropriateness of the simple business judgment rule.

In theory, all of the duties and standards for directors elaborated upon by the Delaware takeover cases are equally applicable to private companies. But provisions in acquisition agreements that are designed around the case law historically have been very different in public and private mergers, partly because public mergers, or at least the big ones, are a natural target for other public company Buyers, both predatory and benign. From the sell side, the shareholder base in a private company is small and therefore there are fewer Target shareholders to complain and/or initiate litigation. Plus, in most private company situations, the shareholder group is harmonious, and the shareholders are the ones who have appointed director representatives who have approved the deal—so they would in essence be suing themselves.

Additionally, private company mergers are done quickly and often without public disclosure prior to closing, and so other bidders are much less likely to upset the deal because they do not even know that the Target is for sale. Private company boards pay lip service to the Delaware takeover cases (and their counsel should instruct them as to their duties), but the procedures, in reality, are still much different. For one thing, until fairly recently, the full panoply of fiduciary outs, breakup fees, and the like did not make it into private company merger agreements. Those clauses can now be found in private deals, but given the typically short time to shareholder approval or closing, disputes rarely arise.

EVOLUTION OF FIDUCIARY DUTY CASE LAW AND JUDICIAL REVIEW

Standards: Historical Perspective

Following is a brief discussion of the landmark Delaware cases that have significantly changed the acquisition process.

Smith v. Van Gorkom   *Van Gorkom* is a leading case in the evolution of the standards by which boards are measured. This decision drew extremely sharp criticism from the acquisition bar. The "good ol' boys" days were over.

In *Van Gorkom*, the directors were found to be liable for a decision to merge with a third party, despite the fact that the merger price was at a 48 percent premium over the Target's market price, where, in connection with the approval process, (1) the directors were uninformed as to the role of the chairman in arranging for the merger and in establishing the merger price; (2) the directors were uninformed as to the "intrinsic value" of the Target; (3) the proposed merger was discussed at a board meeting for only two hours and there had been neither advance notice to the directors of the subject of the meeting nor any prior consideration by them of a sale of the Target; (4) there was no crisis or emergency that required the directors to act in the short time frame in which they did; (5) the proposed merger was described only in a 20-minute oral presentation and no documents were presented to the board reflecting the terms of the transaction or supporting the merger price; (6) the merger agreement had not been read by any of the directors; (7) no investment banker was retained for an opinion on the fairness of the valuation; and (8) the directors failed to make reasonable inquiry concerning the adequacy of the merger price. Due to these factors, the Delaware Supreme Court held that the presumption that the directors had properly informed themselves was rebutted, and that generally directors do not receive protection from the business judgment rule when they have not properly informed themselves.

Commentators argued at the time that if there is anything close to a perfect market, then the substantial premium offered over the market price was evidence itself as to the adequacy of the offer, and that there was exigency in fact because the Buyer had imposed a strict short time limit on when the offer had to be accepted.

There is some debate as to whether *Van Gorkom* is a business judgment case. The question is whether it merely interpreted the business judgment rule or limited the applicability of the business judgment rule in acquisition transactions. Given current legal practices in the acquisition arena, the Van Gorkom board seems to have been extraordinarily sloppy and cavalier about the offer. What is clear is that the case changed significantly the dance that lawyers and bankers go through with boards in acquisition situations.

Subsequent cases clearly held that there are significant limitations on the applicability of the business judgment rule in takeover situations. They may simply be saying that sound business judgment in these situations requires extra care and prudence and special procedures, or they may be saying that the business judgment rule doesn't apply in certain situations. Some seem to take the former position and others the latter.

Weinberger v. UOP *Weinberger* was a case where the business judgment rule was found to be inadequate to protect the shareholders. The court adopted the very strict "entire fairness" standard to certain insider transactions in the acquisition context.

The case involved two public companies, one of which was a subsidiary of the other. The parent wanted to acquire the minority interest in the subsidiary held by the public shareholders. Two of its officers, who were also members of the subsidiary's board, prepared a report based on data obtained from the subsidiary that at a price of $24 the acquisition would be desirable for the parent. The parent proposed a price of $20 to $21, which was an approximately 50 percent premium over market. The independent directors of the subsidiary approved the merger and received a fairness opinion from an investment banking firm. The transaction was submitted to the shareholders of the subsidiary, and it was made a condition of the merger that a majority of the minority shares vote in favor of the merger. The vote was obtained, and the merger was completed.

The court found that this process was inadequate. For transactions where insiders are on both sides of the matter, it required that the transaction be subjected to an "entire fairness" standard rather than the business judgment rule. Entire fairness was defined to mean both *procedural* and *substantive* fairness.

Procedural fairness meant that procedures needed to be established that ensured fair bargaining on behalf of both parties. It also meant that the majority shareholder in this case was required to make available to the independent subsidiary directors and to the minority shareholders the results of its own internal study that justified a $24 price. This would appear to be entirely unfair to the majority—basically asking it to negotiate against itself—but the court placed significant weight on the fact that the data was compiled using internal, presumably nonpublic, data from the subsidiary. Suggested internal procedures were the establishment of disinterested committees of the board to negotiate the deal. The "majority of the minority" voting standard for shareholders also was viewed as desirable. The fact that this level of vote was obtained here was found to be inadequate by the court since full disclosure of the internal report was not made to the minority shareholders.

Substantive fairness means that the price has to be fair based on the application of modern accepted valuation methodologies. So, apparently, even if all of the procedural safeguards are properly implemented, the courts can second-guess the result.

The court stated the entire fairness standard as follows:

> *The concept of fairness has two basic aspects: fair dealing and fair price. The former embraces questions of when the transaction was timed, how it was initiated, structured, negotiated, and disclosed to the directors, and how the approvals of the directors and the shareholders were obtained. The latter aspect of fairness relates to the economic and financial considerations of the proposed merger, including all relevant factors: assets, market value, earnings, future prospects, and any other elements that affect the intrinsic or inherent value of a company's stock ... However, the test for fairness is not a bifurcated one as between fair dealing and price. All aspects of the issue must be examined as a whole since the question is one of entire fairness. However, in a non-fraudulent transaction we recognize that price may be the preponderant consideration outweighing other features of the merger. Here, we address the two basic aspects of fairness separately because we find reversible error as to both.*

One wonders about the reach of this case. It would not be surprising to find it being increasingly applied to situations like *down round* financings of venture capital-backed companies where the venture investors sit on the company's board.

Revlon v. MacAndrews & Forbes   *Revlon* is perhaps the most famous of the Delaware takeover cases. At issue was the enforceability of an acquisition agreement where the Buyer was granted an option to purchase certain Target assets, an exclusive dealing provision, and a breakup fee of $25 million. The case arose from a hostile bid by Pantry Pride for Revlon. The Revlon board implemented certain defensive actions, including a form of rights plan and an exchange offer of notes for a portion of Revlon's stock. The defensive measures did not deter Pantry Pride, which successively increased its bid. Forstmann Little, a leveraged buyout (LBO) firm, became involved in the fray as a *white knight* and made successively higher offers for Revlon. At a certain point in the process, Revlon agreed to a no-shop with Forstmann and a breakup fee and granted Forstmann a crown jewels option at a below-market price. Forstmann also agreed to certain provisions protecting the noteholders who had acquired their notes in connection with Revlon's defensive measures.

The court invalidated the agreements with Forstmann because

> . . . *in reality, the Revlon board ended the auction in return for very little actual improvement in the final bid. The principal benefit went to the directors, who avoided personal liability to a class of creditors to whom the board owed no further duty under the circumstances. Thus, when a board ends an intense bidding contest on an insubstantial basis, and where a significant by-product of that action is to protect the directors against a perceived threat of personal liability for consequences stemming from the adoption of previous defensive measures, the action cannot withstand the enhanced scrutiny which* Unocal *requires of director conduct.*

The court effectively ruled that where the breakup of the company is certain, the directors' duty was solely to maximize the price to be paid to the shareholders. The court concluded that the concessions granted to Forstmann effectively ended the auction without a concomitant gain to Revlon's shareholders. Part of the rationale for the court's decision was that the directors feared personal liability with respect to recent price declines in the notes that had been issued as a defensive maneuver. The court inferred that the directors' actions were not entirely disinterested and were motivated in part by the desire to protect the board from liability to the noteholders.

The court implied that a strict lock-up in exchange for a significant price increase might be enforceable. The *key question* left open was whether there are circumstances where a board could rationally end the auction process with preclusive lock-ups and other devices in exchange for sufficiently increased consideration that would justify the extreme deal-protection measures.

Another question is whether and when auctions are required. *Revlon* stated that the board becomes an auctioneer when there has been a decision to sell the business. But subsequent cases have held that *Revlon* does not really mean that. Under appropriate circumstances, the board can sell to one selected bidder. But that does not mean it can do so and enter into a preclusive lock-up with that bidder.

What about a decision to merge with another company in a strategic, stock-for-stock exchange? That is a *sale* in ordinary parlance, but does *Revlon* apply?

Subsequent to *Revlon*, in the case *Paramount v. Time*, the court drew a distinction between a situation where there is a change in control and a merger where there was no change in control. In *Paramount*, the court found that because both companies involved in the takeover were widely held, they would continue to be widely held after the merger, and therefore there was no change in control.

Paramount is a very peculiar case. It would appear that the court implicitly thought that applying *Revlon* in cases like this would not make sense, and therefore constructed this rather fine distinction between transactions involving a change in control and ones that do not. Why should there be a distinction in public-to-public stock mergers based on the identity of the shareholder base of the two companies?

It would be relatively easy to apply a different standard to cash acquisitions. Cash is cash. The Target's shareholders are cashed out and couldn't care less about what subsequently happens. Even in that case, an auction does not necessarily make sense. In advising companies that want to put themselves up for sale, investment bankers will advise that there are a variety of ways to proceed, only one of which is a real auction. A real auction may not be the best way to maximize price because bidders may not want to bother with a deal that they have low odds of winning.

But why should *Revlon* duties not apply to stock-for-stock exchanges regardless of the makeup of the public shareholders? Why should those deals be treated differently than cash deals? True, strategic decisions are complex, and the merger of two giants requires very sophisticated analysis of synergies going forward. But the ultimate goal is still maximizing shareholder value. So if in *Paramount* the board decided that the shares would reach a certain level sometime after the synergies took effect, why should the board not be forced to consider a cash offer that exceeded that value in present value terms?

But if you go down that path, what do you do in a situation where the board projects, based on internal projections of future earnings, that the corporation's stock will reach $100 per share in five years based on current multiples? What happens if a bidder comes along and offers $125 per share in present value terms? Does the board have to take the deal and initiate a sale, or can it just say no? But why should it be able to do so? Why is that different from a situation where the company has decided to sell and has to consider all offers and have an auction? Maybe, in some circumstances, it's simply that the board doesn't know what the company is worth and only knows that it will be worth a lot more later.

Notwithstanding all of the foregoing factors, if the board has decided to sell, selling to the first person that comes along, whether for cash or stock, is inherently dangerous, even if the offer appears to be a great price. How does the board know that someone will not offer a better price?

The way the process usually works is that the bankers will approach a select group of potential bidders, narrow them down to those that are most interested, and then try to play them off against one another. Some would argue that a sealed final bid round would maximize value in that situation. It might, and then again, many potential bidders might not want to bother with the deal if a sealed bid is the method of sale—essentially the same argument against a true auction.

In a friendly situation, one might argue that the best approach is to narrow the field and then tell the bidders to make one last offer in exchange for a preclusive lock-up, or, even more radically, make a preclusive lock-up a possibility for a truly preemptive bid in the first round. In a private deal, bidders often will try to preempt the process by making a great first offer in return for an end to the sale process. That way you may have the best of both worlds: More than one bidder is invited so that you are not just taking the first deal that comes along; the number is limited to make it more interesting to the likely bidders; and the prospect of a quick lock-up deal via a preclusive lock-up is offered to elicit the maximum possible bid. But is that approach valid under the Delaware takeover decisions, which seem to want to preserve all options to the bitter end? Why should structuring the process that way upon the advice of investment bankers in order to maximize value be a breach of fiduciary duty?

Unocal v. Mesa Petroleum *Unocal* was an important decision because it opened the door to a slightly different standard of review. Many of the critical Delaware cases have arisen in the context of hostile takeovers where boards searched for a means to defeat hostile offers. *Unocal* adopted the so-called enhanced scrutiny review standard in those situations. At the same time, it seemed to affirm the business judgment rule. As the court put it:

> *When a board addresses a pending takeover bid, it has an obliga-*
> *tion to determine whether the offer is in the best interests of the*
> *corporation and its shareholders. In that respect a board's duty is no*
> *different from any other responsibility it shoulders, and its decisions*
> *should be no less entitled to the respect they otherwise would be*
> *accorded in the realm of business judgment... There are, however,*
> *certain caveats to a proper exercise of this function. Because of the*
> *omnipresent specter that a board may be acting primarily in its own*
> *interests, rather than those of the corporation and its shareholders,*
> *there is an enhanced duty which calls for judicial examination at the*
> *threshold before the protections of the business judgment rule may*
> *be conferred.*

A hostile raider had made a tender offer for a majority of Unocal's shares, and had proposed a back-end squeeze-out merger where the remaining securities would be converted into junk bonds. The Unocal board, after significant deliberation and based on extensive presentations from its investment bankers, concluded that the offer was "inadequate" and "coercive." In response, it proposed a conditional exchange offer whereby Unocal would itself offer to exchange senior debt securities valued substantially in excess of the bidder's offer, for approximately 50 percent of the outstanding shares. The bidder would not be allowed to participate in the exchange offer. The purpose of the exchange offer was either to make it impractical for the original bid to proceed because the issuance of the debt would interfere with the bidder's financing, or to ensure that the share-holders received a fair price when the bidder's or the corporation's offers were accepted.

The bidder challenged the decision of the board as being influenced by self-interest and argued that it could not be excluded from the company's exchange offer because the corporation owed a duty to *all* shareholders.

The court found that the board acted deliberately and rationally and made reasonable decisions in the circumstances. The court agreed that the front-end-loaded tender offer was coercive and that it had to be parried. The court found that the measures adopted by the directors were a reasonable response. In concluding its discussion, the court said:

> *A further aspect is the element of balance. If a defensive measure is*
> *to come within the ambit of the business judgment rule, it must be*
> *reasonable in relation to the threat posed. This entails an analysis*

by the directors of the nature of the takeover bid and its effect on the corporate enterprise. Examples of such concerns may include: inadequacy of the price offered, nature and timing of the offer, questions of illegality, the impact on "constituencies" other than shareholders (i.e., creditors, customers, employees, and perhaps even the community generally), the risk of nonconsummation, and the quality of securities being offered in the exchange ... While not a controlling factor, it also seems to us that a board may reasonably consider the basic shareholder interests at stake, including those of short term speculators, whose actions may have fueled the coercive aspect of the offer at the expense of the long term investors. Here, the threat posed was viewed by the Unocal board as a grossly inadequate two-tier coercive tender offer coupled with the threat of greenmail ...

In conclusion, there was directorial power to oppose the [bidder's] tender offer, and to undertake a selective stock exchange made in good faith and upon a reasonable investigation pursuant to a clear duty to protect the corporate enterprise. Further, the selective stock repurchase plan chosen by Unocal is reasonable in relation to the threat that the board rationally and reasonably believed was posed by [the bidder's] inadequate and coercive two-tier tender offer. Under those circumstances the board's action is entitled to be measured by the standards of the business judgment rule. Thus, unless it is shown by a preponderance of the evidence that the directors' decisions were primarily based on perpetuating themselves in office, or some other breach of fiduciary duty such as fraud, overreaching, lack of good faith, or being uninformed, a Court will not substitute its judgment for that of the board.

So, was the business judgment rule departed from in *Unocal* or affirmed? The decision seems contradictory. The court essentially said that in any hostile takeover, board members have an inherent conflict of interest—they like where they are seated and don't want to get thrown out by a raider. The decision then goes on to affirm the business judgment rule. But before it got there, it reviewed in detail the process and rationale of the board's decisions and concluded that they did a good job and were entitled to the benefit of the business judgment rule. But the business judgment rule says that the courts won't second-guess the directors' judgments if they were disinterested, acted in good faith, and the like. *Unocal* simply seems to say that in a hostile takeover situation, the court will take a harder look to see if the directors did a thorough and unbiased job. But aren't the courts supposed to take a good, hard look in *all* cases?

Mills Acquisition. v. MacMillan *MacMillan* was another famous Delaware takeover case that attempted to further clarify the extent of *Revlon* duties and the *Unocal* enhanced scrutiny and enhanced board duties standards.

As the court put it:

> *When Revlon duties devolve upon directors, this Court will continue to exact an enhanced judicial scrutiny at the threshold, as in Unocal, before the normal presumptions of the business judgment rule will apply. However, the two-part threshold test [is that] at the outset, the plaintiff must know...that the directors of the Target company treated one or more of the respective bidders on unequal terms...In the face of disparate treatment, the trial court must first examine whether the directors properly perceived that shareholder interests are enhanced. In any event the board's action must be reasonable in relation to the advantage sought to be achieved, or conversely, to the threat which a particular bid allegedly poses to shareholder interests...If...the test has been met, the directors' actions necessarily are entitled to the protections of the business judgment rule.*

This decision seems to say that if the board has behaved well and diligently and structured the transaction to the court's liking, then the business judgment rule will be applicable. But what is there to judge at that point?

Subsequent cases examined the applicability of these duties and standards of review to more traditional transactions.

In *Paramount v. Time*, the lower court determined that a change of control was needed in order to implicate the potential application of *Revlon* and the like. It concluded, however, that because the shareholder base of both companies was broadly held, after the merger the public would continue to hold the stock, without any significant control block, and so there really wasn't a change of control. That seems to be an odd point of differentiation. The ostensible rationale was whether the transaction would deprive the existing shareholders of the Target of ever getting, or substantially reduce their chances of getting, a control premium for their shares.

On review in the Delaware Supreme Court, the Court agreed with the change of control analysis, but stated that broader considerations should dictate how to apply *Revlon*. It stated that the emphasis should not be on determining when it was appropriate to force a board to attempt to maximize the current return to shareholders, but it never really said what the determinant should be.

Ironically, Paramount, the loser in *Paramount v. Time,* tried what it thought was the same strategy successfully used against it by Time in connection with a proposed merger with Viacom. In the proposed transaction, the Paramount shareholders would get cash and Viacom securities. The parties signed a merger agreement with fairly strict and onerous deal-protection devices.

QVC Network had expressed an interest previously in acquiring Paramount and sued to invalidate the deal-protection devices in *Paramount v. QVC.* There the court pinned its analysis on the fact that Sumner Redstone, the controlling shareholder of Viacom, would be the controlling shareholder of the combined company after the merger. The court found that because there was a clear change of control of Paramount, the Paramount board's duty was to maximize value, and that its actions including the harsh deal-protection devices were a violation of the board's duty. The court invalidated the deal-protection devices. One of the rationales for the court's decision was its skepticism of the Paramount board's alleged desire to engage in a strategic transaction for the long-term benefit of the Paramount shareholders. Because of the change of control, the court was not impressed due to the possibility that the controlling shareholder could depart unchecked from the purported strategic direction after the merger was finalized.

The case almost seems to suggest that where there is more than one interested Buyer, deal-protection devices are inappropriate. But in the real world, these devices are *demanded* by the successful bidder. For the Target's board to just say no to deal-protection devices is unrealistic. Just saying no is not without cost. It risks losing what the board perhaps in good faith and with good information thinks is a desirable transaction. *Unocal* and subsequent cases appear to stand for the proposition that in order to prefer a bidder with a lock-up or similar device, there has to be received in exchange for the device some consideration that relates to a benefit to the shareholders. But cannot that benefit simply be getting an attractive deal for the shareholders?

What happens in reality is that the parties agree to deal-protection devices. They are standard. The real task from the Target's viewpoint is to try to make them as weak as possible, or alternatively negotiate some real concessions from the bidder in question in exchange for increasingly strict deal-protection devices.

In summary, it is very difficult to make sense out of the array of Delaware takeover cases. All have different factual patterns, and it is therefore hard to generalize what the true meaning and reach of the cases are. But it is fair to say that the ultimate objective of all of the cases is to try to ensure that the value of the Target is maximized for its shareholders. The board of the Target is obligated to do everything possible to maximize its value, or at least that should be the primary focus.

The Delaware cases have never said that lock-ups are impermissible, but have rejected preclusive lock-ups on a number of occasions. *Revlon* does not necessarily require that an auction cannot end with a lock-up. All auctions must end. The real mistake there was likely that the hostile bidder wasn't offered the same opportunity for a lock-up as the friendly bidder.

The other implicit theme is trying to decide who should make the decision. If there is going to be a sale of the company, or if there is going to be some big terrain-altering transaction, should that decision be up to the board alone, or should the shareholders have a say? The Delaware statute seems to vest the board with such a power, and the shareholders have the right to vote only on certain limited matters. Of course, the shareholders get to vote for directors and, therefore, have an indirect say in these matters. In reality, though, shareholder proxy contests are rare, and the slate approved by the board is almost always elected.

Clearly, any change in control is not a transaction that needs to involve shareholder choice under the statute. The board could just issue new stock to an investor that will constitute a majority of the outstanding shares. But, as we have seen, courts are suspicious of the conduct of boards in the takeover context because it is the natural tendency not to want to get thrown out of office. So, even if we posit a hypothetical sale of the company for a blockbuster price that the board has reasonably concluded is the absolute maximum value after thorough investigation, an auction or quasi-auction, and an investment banker's opinion, *all in exchange* for a preclusive lock-up, one that in effect forces the shareholders to approve the transaction—should the board alone be allowed to make that decision or should the shareholders be allowed to make their own determination? The general tendency of the Delaware courts, correctly or incorrectly, seems to be to preserve decisions and opportunities for the shareholders, perhaps because boards cannot be fully trusted in these situations. The end result of that approach may be that shareholder value in reality is not maximized.

So what does an M&A lawyer advise in these situations?

First, what should be the advice to a board if a potential acquirer approaches the Target and states that it is interested in starting merger negotiations? Can the board just say no? Apparently, it can under the case law. Presumably, the board cannot be charged with responding to all such inquiries, and the courts have been supportive of boards in that situation. The board is busy and has a company to run.

But is it really so simple? One thing that the Delaware Supreme Court seemed to be saying in *Paramount v. Time* was that the board should not have to choose between short-term and long-term gain. But why not? What if a bidder approaches the Target and offers a terrific price? Does the board have to consider it? It has to at least deliberate on it and make some sort of passing determination that pursuing the current course is in the best interest of the shareholders. In fact, on a regular basis boards should consider the company's long-term strategic plan and the potential value to shareholders. If it were to do this, it would be in a better position to respond to the unsolicited offer. Odds are that if the Target is in shaky condition, or its long-term prospects do not look so good, the board will want to consider the offer anyway.

One would think that the analysis should be no different if the Target has decided to merge, whether for cash or whether for stock in a no-change-of-control situation as in *Paramount v. Time*. Something big is going to happen one way or the other, and it cannot be said that the process will distract the board from its path of guiding the future of the Target on its current course.

In that situation, one would think the proper analysis would be that more serious consideration should be given to the new bidder. The board should be required to examine in more detail and more carefully whether the shareholders are better off taking the cash now, as opposed to sticking with the company's strategic plan. As we have seen in our discussion of corporate finance concepts, long-term value equates to current value appropriately discounted for the time value of money (and risk).

There is ample room in each of these exercises for application of the business judgment rule. If the board has considered whether to pursue various alternatives, perhaps the courts should leave the board alone because these judgments are so difficult and complex.

So, to answer the question posed, a board should be advised in the situation where a feeler comes in from a third party that it should at least consider whether a sale of the company would be appropriate at the time. But it need not agonize over it and spend a lot of money on bankers and lawyers unless there is reason to think that a great deal may result.

Provided that a board acts with due care in a disinterested manner in considering any offers that are made, a board can reject them for any legitimate business reason including, for example, inadequacy of the offer in terms of dollar amount; the nature and timing of the offer; the quality of any securities being offered in exchange for the company's stock; the lack of a compelling strategic fit with the proposed Buyer; any questions of illegality in connection with the proposed transaction; any risks of nonconsummation; the impact on constituencies other than shareholders (i.e., creditors, customers, employees, and perhaps the community generally), at least to the extent such impact could affect shareholder value; the basic shareholder interests at stake (long-term investors versus short-term speculators); or a more fundamental determination, taking into account all relevant circumstances, that the time is simply not right to sell the company.

Where a big transaction is inevitable regardless of its form, Targets should very carefully deliberate and perhaps even spend a lot of money on bankers and lawyers.

So if the board decides to take an offer, and assuming that it has been diligent in its prior actions, what lock-ups and similar devices are appropriate? In public company acquisitions, the practice that has evolved and continues to evolve is to allow deal-protection devices that adequately compensate the Buyer for its time and effort if the deal fails and that make it difficult, but not impossible, for another bidder to come in. If at all possible, before signing an acquisition agreement, the Target should try to do a market check by inquiring of the most logical bidders whether there is any interest in acquiring the Target. If there has been no shopping and no market check, the Targets should argue for the weakest versions of the deal-protection devices. As discussed earlier, these devices commonly include fiduciary outs, no-shop agreements, and breakup fees.

A no-shop clause requires the Target not to shop the deal to other bidders pending the anticipated receipt of the Target shareholder approval and closing. But the Target may have an out in the merger agreement that permits it to consider a better offer if one comes along without having been solicited by the company, or a *window-shop*. To compensate the Buyer for the weakened form of deal-protection devices, the no-shop is combined with a breakup fee—that is, if a better offer comes along and the Target agrees to take it, then it has to pay the first Buyer a substantial amount of money for its efforts (often financed by the second Buyer), sometimes only on the closing of the other deal, and sometimes to terminate the first agreement whether the new second deal closes or not. There are multiple varieties of these clauses. A Target should always examine the public SEC filings of the particular bidders to see what deal-protection terms other Targets have negotiated with that bidder in the past.

Another emerging area is how these issues are handled in acquisitions of private companies. In contrast to public-to-public acquisitions, in private company acquisitions, preclusive lock-ups, like locking up the shareholder vote on signing, are still seen as a matter of commercial practice if not legal theory. Those practices are evolving and are under attack. One recent interesting case that bears on that question in private company acquisition practice is *Omnicare v. NCS Healthcare.*

Omnicare v. NCS Healthcare   NCS was a troubled company that entered into a merger agreement with Genesis Health Venture. NCS was a public company but was controlled by two individuals who owned a majority of the stock. After extensive back and forth, NCS and Genesis entered into a merger agreement that did not have a fiduciary out but allowed NCS to talk to a bidder that offered what the NCS board determined to be a superior proposal. The merger agreement required NCS to submit the Genesis merger agreement to its shareholders *come hell or high water*, which is how such restrictive contractual language is commonly referred to. More importantly, the two controlling shareholders of NCS agreed to vote for the merger also *come hell or high water*. Omnicare submitted a superior proposal, the NCS board withdrew its recommendation of the merger, and the advisers withdrew their fairness opinion. Even though NCS could talk to Omnicare, it could not terminate the merger agreement because the agreement did not contain a fiduciary out. Omnicare sued to block the holding of the shareholders meeting, among other things.

The court's majority held that the combination of the inability to terminate either the merger agreement or the voting agreements constituted preclusive and coercive lock-ups, which it decided in effect were per se impermissible. The minority thought that the board and controlling shareholder could totally lock up a deal in these circumstances—the board risked losing everything (particularly here where NCS was a troubled company on the brink of bankruptcy) if it did not accede to the bidder's request for a preclusive lock-up.

One very interesting aspect of this case is how it is to be applied to private transactions. What about a situation exactly like Omnicare, but where immediately after the merger agreement is signed, the majority shareholders execute a written consent in lieu of meeting, thereby making the merger a done deal subject only to other closing conditions like HSR clearance? This technique is generally available in acquisitions of private companies. Is the majority in Omnicare protecting the shareholders' right to vote, or is it saying that in all circumstances the courts will insist on the ability of a higher bidder to upset a deal before the deal has closed (as opposed to the shareholders having voted)? If it is the former, the simultaneous vote will work. If it is the latter, it will not.

There is an unpublished Delaware case that says that stockholder approval must come *after* the board has approved the deal and the merger agreement has been signed. So, one approach is for the agreement to contain a provision that says if the Target's shareholders do not approve the deal within a very short time frame, then the Buyer can terminate the agreement. One could add in the bells and whistles of a breakup fee and the like, but odds are that such an approach is overkill in the typical private company acquisition.

Some Practical Considerations

If the Delaware takeover cases are mind numbing as to their actual rationale and reach, there are nevertheless a number of clear lessons from them as to how Targets and bidders should conduct themselves in an acquisition situation.

Documentation   All of the board's meetings and actions in connection with a proposed merger or buyout should be clearly and carefully documented in minutes that are created contemporaneously with the board's deliberations. It is essential that a record be created that will withstand scrutiny in a litigation context. The Delaware courts come out differently where the board can demonstrate that it acted with due care and deliberation.

Duty of Care   Although it does not happen often, there have been cases where the failure of a board of directors to comply with basic procedures designed to allow the directors to exercise their duty of care has resulted in the Delaware courts not just invalidating a board decision in a merger context, but finding directors to be personally liable to the Target's shareholders for such failure. The argument is sometimes made by Buyers that the definitive merger agreement should contain the strongest lock-ups possible and that the Target should not really care what the lock-up devices are because the court will just invalidate them if they are too harsh. The risk of director liability undercuts that line of reasoning. What if the bidder agrees to indemnify the Target board against that liability?

Van Gorkom is particularly instructive as to the types of procedures that companies should put in place to assure that they comply with their duty of care in a premerger context. Among these procedures should be:

- *Directors should avoid not only haste but also the appearance of haste.* Directors should have a full opportunity to review and discuss all aspects of a proposed transaction. This may well take more than one meeting.
- *Directors should carefully review materials relevant to the decision.* Relevant information should be distributed to the directors as far in advance of the meeting as is practicable under the circumstances.

The board should review all relevant documents, or summaries thereof, before approving them. The board should at least read the key provisions of the key agreements.

■ *The board should seek the advice of competent outside experts.* Such experts would include, for example, outside counsel and investment bankers to provide guidance regarding the board's legal obligations, the fairness of the proposed transaction from a financial point of view, and such other matters as the directors may consider relevant to their analysis or decision. While neither the advice nor a formal opinion of an investment banker is an absolute legal requirement, such advice may assist the board in assessing a proposed transaction from a financial point of view. In fact, it has become quite standard for fairness opinions to be issued in acquisition transactions, at least where the particular board is recommending a deal to the Target's shareholders.

■ *The board should not take information and advice at face value.* Instead, it should actively question, probe, and evaluate the information and advice presented to it and document that it has done so in the board meeting minutes.

In many cases the board of directors will face the prospect of a strategic merger with another industry player rather than a buyout of the company for cash. In those instances, the board's deliberations should include consideration and analysis of the Target's existing strategy and prospects and the proposed strategy of the combined entity, the relative likelihood of achieving the benefits of the proposed merger, and whether the proposed strategy for the combined entity is consistent with the board's view of an appropriate strategic direction.

Duty of Loyalty   The duty of loyalty requires that companies be attuned to the possibility of financial interests or other special motivations of officers and directors that may make it difficult for them to act disinterestedly and independently in a particular situation. An obvious example of such a situation would be if a Target director is also a director, employee, or substantial shareholder of a potential Buyer. A less obvious example would be if a director is a major shareholder of one of the Target's suppliers, whose position may be threatened if a proposed transaction is consummated. The board needs to ferret out these potential conflicts, and should consult with outside counsel to determine whether and to what extent a director should be removed from the decision-making process. At a minimum, decisions relating to proposed transactions must be made by vote of a majority of the disinterested directors.

Obviously, the inherent conflict of interest of management directors in connection with a proposed transaction that may jeopardize their employment must be taken into account. This can be done by assuring that outside, independent directors take an active role in the decision-making process. Under certain circumstances, at some point in a negotiation with a prospective merger partner, counsel may advise that one or more of the management directors step away from the process altogether. But ordinarily, management directors should be able to participate in discussions regarding prospective transactions, as long as the conflicts and potential conflicts are fully disclosed and all actual decisions are made by a disinterested majority of directors.

Director Committees   The preceding considerations—the need for active director involvement in the evaluation process and the need to control conflicts of interest—mean that it is usually advisable for a Target to establish a committee of directors to take the leadership role in premerger or buyout situations. Such a committee ideally would consist of a majority of outside, independent directors and may include the Target chief financial officer and chief executive officer, although the members of management, if directors, should be prepared to step back if a particular proposal raises a conflict of interest issue. The committee should deal directly with the Target investment bankers (if any), outside counsel, and other advisers in connection with its activities, and may provide an active interface with potential acquirers. The ultimate decision to accept or turn down a formal offer to buy or merge with the Target should be made by the full board, after compliance with the procedures previously described.

Cleansing Vote of a Majority of the Minority   Another procedural protective device that boards should consider is to require as a condition to the Target's obligation to close a transaction that a majority of the shares held by disinterested shareholders of the Target vote to approve the transaction. Such a procedure has been endorsed in several contexts by the Delaware courts. Of course, although that vote would be nice to have, what happens if you ask for it and don't get it? As a result, there is often reluctance to use this device.

Sample Memorandum to the Board of Directors   It is customary and appropriate, in the face of a bid for a public company, for the Target's counsel to prepare a written memorandum on the board's duties relating to deal-protection devices and to walk the board through the memorandum at a board meeting. A sample memorandum discussing these duties is contained in the appendix to this chapter.

SECURITIES LAWS AND PUBLIC COMPANY ACQUISITIONS

Disclosure of Merger Negotiations

As noted earlier, the issue of when a public target is under an obligation to disclose merger discussions or an agreement in principle is one of the most difficult judgment calls a Target and its lawyers are required to make. As we have said, there is a great reluctance on the part of both the Target and the Buyer to make disclosure because of the significant impact the disclosure will have on various corporate constituencies and the potential significant impact of a later disclosure that the parties failed to come to a deal.

Because such judgments are so difficult, in the past M&A lawyers relied on certain court decisions that created a bright-line test. The test was that disclosure was not required unless the parties had reached agreement in principle on price and structure. For that reason, in public company deals, letters of intent were not typically used, and instead a term sheet was used that left the purchase price blank. This approach was for the ostensible protective purpose of later demonstrating that there was no agreement on price and structure and therefore there was no need for disclosure.

This approach was turned on its head in the 1988 Supreme Court decision in *Basic, Inc. v. Levinson*. In that case, the parties had been flirting with one another for quite some time. Merger discussions were sometimes on and sometimes off. The issue arose because during one of the times that there were discussions, Basic released public statements that said that there was nothing going on.

The Court was asked to apply the materiality standard of SEC Rule 10b-5, the rule that prohibits the making of misleading statements and omissions in connection with the purchase or sale of a security or in public reports. The district court had ruled that the mere existence of merger discussions was not material. The court of appeals reversed, saying that the affirmative denial that there were merger discussions, because of its specificity, was materially misleading.

The Court at the outset noted the difficulty of the issue:

The application of this materiality standard to preliminary merger discussions is not self-evident. Where the impact of the corporate development on the target's fortune is certain and clear, the TSC Industries materiality definition admits straightforward application. Where, on the other hand, the event is contingent or speculative in nature, it is difficult to ascertain whether the "reasonable investor" would have considered the omitted information significant at the

*time. Merger negotiations, because of the ever-present possibility
that the contemplated transaction will not be effectuated, fall into
the latter category.*

The Court viewed the issue as involving a judgment as to what is
material in the context of merger discussions, not whether there is duty to
disclose:

> *We need not ascertain, however, whether secrecy necessarily maxi-
> mizes shareholder wealth—although we note that the proposition is
> at least disputed as a matter of theory and empirical research—for
> this case does not concern the* timing *of a disclosure; it concerns only
> its accuracy and completeness. We face here the narrow question
> whether information concerning the existence and status of prelim-
> inary merger discussions is significant to the reasonable investor's
> trading decision. Arguments based on the premise that some disclo-
> sure would be "premature" in a sense are more properly considered
> under the rubric of an issuer's duty to disclose. The "secrecy" ratio-
> nale is simply inapposite to the definition of materiality . . .*
>
> *We therefore find no valid justification for artificially excluding
> from the definition of materiality information concerning merger
> discussions, which would otherwise be considered significant
> to the trading decision of a reasonable investor, merely because
> agreement-in-principle as to price and structure has not yet been
> reached by the parties or their representatives.*

The Court abandoned the bright-line test of agreement in principle on
price and structure and adopted a different standard, stating that materiality

> *will depend at any given time upon a balancing of both the indicated
> probability that the event will occur and the anticipated magnitude
> of the event in light of the totality of the company activity.*

The Court summarized its holding as follows:

1. *We specifically adopt, for the § 10(b) and Rule 10b-5 context,
   the standard of materiality set forth in* TSC Industries, Inc. v.
   Northway, Inc.
2. *We reject "agreement-in-principle as to price and structure" as
   the bright-line rule for materiality.*

3. We also reject the proposition that *"information becomes material by virtue of a public statement denying it."*
4. Materiality in the merger context depends on the probability that the transaction will be consummated, and its significance to the issuer of the securities. Materiality depends on the facts and thus is to be determined on a case-by-case basis.

The Court put M&A lawyers on the hot seat without much help. The seat is so hot partly because all of these decisions are judged by 20/20 hindsight.

What has happened as a practical matter as a result of this decision? First, the pressure remains to keep merger discussions private until there is agreement on price and structure. Second, in order to minimize the period of pressure around the disclosure issue, there is enormous pressure of another sort—to get the deal signed up and disclosed in a matter of days or over a weekend. Third, no one should make any denials that are false. The only proper response to questions about merger discussion is "No comment." In theory, that may not be good enough. But it usually suffices as a practical matter.

SEC's Proxy and Tender Offer Rules

Tender Offers and Stock Ownership Reporting The Securities Exchange Act of 1934 and related rules contain provisions regulating the substance of tender offers, as well as disclosures related to a person or group accumulating a significant percentage of a class of securities registered under the Exchange Act. These provisions were added to the Exchange Act by the Williams Act.

Schedules 13D and 13G One of the premises of the Williams Act was that the public is entitled to know if significant positions are being accumulated in a public company's stock and whether the persons acquiring that stock have acquisition intentions.

The SEC's Regulation 13D-G and Schedules 13D and 13G thereunder generally provide that if any person or group acting in concert acquires a 5 percent or greater position in a company with securities registered under Section 12 of the Exchange Act, then such person or group must file a Schedule 13D with the SEC within 10 days, unless they are exempt from filing under Rule 13(d)(6). Schedule 13D requires information about the acquiring person or group, including whether it has any plans to influence the conduct of the Target's business or for the acquisition of the Target.

Tender offers often begin with an accumulation of the Target's securities by purchases in the open market or from large Target shareholders. This is done for several reasons:

- If the Buyer plans to acquire the Target, it is usually cheaper to acquire shares early in order to avoid paying the premium that usually accompanies public company acquisitions.
- It gives the Buyer increased negotiating leverage and may give the Buyer a leg up on other potential bidders.
- The Buyer may make a substantial profit on those shares if another bidder buys the Target for more than the Buyer paid for the shares.

Of course, if no deal happens, the Buyer may get stuck with the stock it bought and have to sell it at a loss. Also, word can leak out of the Buyer's interest, causing a run-up in the Target's stock price and making a subsequent acquisition more expensive.

For the purposes of a Schedule 13D filing, *beneficial ownership* exists when a person possesses or shares, directly or indirectly, alone or with others, the power to vote, sell, or determine the disposition of a security. Additionally, a person shall be deemed to be a beneficial owner of a security if that person has the right to acquire such security within 60 days. This includes the right to acquire beneficial ownership through the exercise of any option, warrant, or right; through the conversion of a security; pursuant to the power to revoke a trust, discretionary account, or similar arrangement; or pursuant to the automatic termination of a trust, discretionary account, or similar arrangement. The SEC interprets beneficial ownership broadly. For one thing, members of a group that act together are deemed to beneficially own each other's securities. If the aggregated ownership exceeds 5 percent, then the group must file a Schedule 13D.

The Schedule 13D requires the following disclosures:

- The title of the class of equity securities
- The identity of the beneficial owner and its officers, directors, and controlling persons
- The source and amount of funds for a planned acquisition
- The beneficial owner's acquisition or other intentions with respect to the Target
- The beneficial owner's ownership of the Target's shares (including a description of recent purchase transactions)
- Any contracts or understandings the beneficial owner has relating to the Target's securities

The Schedule 13D must be signed by the reporting person or an authorized representative. The beneficial owner must "promptly" report any material change in the reported information (e.g., any acquisition or disposition of more than one percent of the Target's shares).

A person or group of persons who are the beneficial owners of more than five percent in a company with securities registered under the Exchange Act at the end of a calendar year and not required to filed a Schedule 13D must file a Schedule 13G. This may occur when the acquisition was exempted from Section 13(d) of the Exchange Act pursuant to Section 13(d)(6). Additionally, certain institutional and passive investors may file a Schedule 13G in lieu of a Schedule 13D. Institutional investors that acquire securities in the ordinary course of business without the purpose or effect of changing or influencing the control of the issuer may use the Schedule 13G. Passive investors that beneficially own less than 20 percent of a covered class of securities and are not seeking to influence control of an issuer may also file a Schedule 13G instead of a Schedule 13D. The information contained in a Schedule 13G is often less extensive than the information in a Schedule 13D, and in certain situations, many of the required disclosures are not applicable. Typically, if persons are eligible to file a Schedule 13G, they prefer to do so over filing a Schedule 13D.

Once the beneficial owner beneficially owns more than 10 percent of any publicly traded class of the Target's equity securities, it becomes an insider and will have to file an additional report with the SEC under Section 16(a) of the Exchange Act, and thereafter will have to report trades in the Target's shares within two business days of executing them. Insider status also subjects the beneficial owner to the extremely treacherous *short-swing* profits provisions of Section 16(b) of the Exchange Act. This rule requires an insider to turn over to the Target any profits made from purchases and sales, or sales and purchases, of the Target's securities within any period of six months. The provision applies to executive officers and directors of the Target in addition to 10 percent owners. Mistakes in the Section 16 area can be catastrophic.

In making initial purchases of outstanding Target shares, the Buyer must take care that its purchases are not deemed to be a tender offer subject to the Exchange Act rules or a takeover bid as defined in state takeover statutes. There are no precise rules on what constitutes a tender offer, but there are certain indicia of a tender offer, depending on the Buyer's behavior. *Wellman v. Dickinson* set forth an eight-factor test for whether a tender offer has been made. These factors are: active and widespread solicitation of shareholders; solicitation made for a substantial percentage of the issuer's stock; the offer to purchase is made at a premium over market price; non-negotiable offer terms; contingency of the offer on the acquisition of a fixed percentage of shares; time constraints on potential sellers; pressure to sell one's stock; and publicity of the offer.

Substantive Tender Offer Rules Sections 14(d) and 14(e) of the Exchange Act cover the timing and procedures of regulated tender offers. A disclosure document must be filed with the SEC at the same time that the tender offer commences. In the case of an exchange offer, the Buyer must have already filed a registration statement with the SEC.

The tender offer must remain open for at least 20 business days, and during that time the shareholders of the Target who tendered their shares may revoke their decision. Buyers cannot purchase shares outside of the tender offer while it is ongoing, and must treat all tendering shareholders alike. If the Buyer is seeking less than all of the Target's shares, and if more than the amount being sought by the Buyer is tendered during the offer, the Buyer must buy the shares on a pro rata basis. If the Buyer significantly changes the terms of the tender offer, it must extend the tender offer period.

The Exchange Act rules impose disclosure requirements on the Buyer in addition to the foregoing substantive requirements, including the obligation to disclose information about its management and any prior dealing with the Target, financial information under certain circumstances where it is relevant, and its intentions with regard to the business of the Target. The Buyer must also disclose any material inside information that it has obtained relating to the Target.

The SEC has an additional rule, Rule 13-e3, that applies to transactions between a company and an affiliate that result in the elimination of a public trading market for the company's shares. This rule requires more extensive disclosures relating to the deal and the parties.

Regulation M-A

Traditional SEC rules created traps for those who *wanted* to discuss a proposed deal and furnish more information to the public. These actions were considered to implicate the SEC prohibition on gun jumping, or offering securities before a registration statement was filed. Similarly, under the tender offer rules, there were strict prohibitions on the timing of the filing of the tender offer statement. The tension here was whether statements by a bidder unintentionally created a commencement for purposes of the tender offer rules.

Rules 425 and 165 The SEC adopted Rules 425 and 165 to clarify and liberalize these practices. Buyers can now make communications about the proposed deal after the initial public announcement of the deal and before the requisite SEC filing is made as long as they file a copy of the communication with the SEC under Rule 425 on the date the communication is first used. A public announcement is defined by Rule 165(f)(3) as any oral or written communication by a participant that is reasonably designed to inform or has the effect of informing the public or security holders in general about the business combination transaction. A business combination may include a merger, consolidation, joint venture, lease, sale, dividend exchange, mortgage, pledge, transfer, or other disposition.

Rule 165 also applies after the filing of the registration statement in a business combination transaction. Rule 165(a) provides that any written communications in connection with a business combination transaction made between the filing of a registration statement and its effective date need not satisfy the prospectus requirements of the Securities Act so long as they are filed with the SEC according to Rule 425.

Written communications required to be filed with the SEC include the initial public announcement publicizing the transaction and virtually every other subsequent communication. It is current practice to err on the side of filing under the rule.

Proxy Rules Rule 14a-12 was revised in 1999 to permit both written and oral communications relating to a proposed acquisition transaction before the filing of a proxy statement, as long as all written communications are filed with the SEC on the date of first use. However, oral communications do not need to be filed with the SEC. This rule change is designed to allow better communication between management and shareholders about important corporate events.

At one point, confidential treatment was available for all merger proxy materials filed with the SEC. In a business combination transaction, if public disclosure is limited to the basic disclosures permitted by Rule 135, confidential treatment is still available for merger proxy materials.

Tender Offer Rules In order to put cash and stock tender offers on a more level playing field, Regulation M-A permits both issuer and third-party exchange offers to commence as early as the filing of a registration statement. Rule 14e-8 of the Exchange Act prohibits Buyers from announcing an offer without the intent or means to complete the offer within a reasonable time.

Rule 162 permits offerors to solicit tenders of securities in an exchange offer after filing but before a registration statement is effective as long as the other requirements of the rule are met. However, no securities may be purchased until the tender offer has expired and the registration statement has been declared effective.

Miscellaneous

Stock Exchange Requirements In addition to SEC rules and regulations, companies that list on a stock exchange are subject to the rules of those organizations. Historically, SEC rules regarding public companies related solely to complete disclosure about corporate events and to certain trading practices by market participants. The approach changed somewhat with the passage of the Sarbanes-Oxley Act, which we will discuss momentarily.

The principal source of regulation of the substantive conduct of public companies, other than the state corporation statutes and related case law, has been the stock exchanges, which impose corporate governance requirements for a company to be initially listed and to stay listed. When a company lists on Nasdaq or another stock exchange, it is required to sign a listing agreement that imposes a number of substantive requirements, either directly or by reference to the governance rules of the exchange.

After the Enron and other corporate scandals, Congress concluded that the regulatory scheme of the state corporate statutes, the SEC, and the self-regulatory organizations (SROs), like Nasdaq and the other exchanges, was too lax. It enacted the Sarbanes-Oxley Act in response to these scandals in 2002. Many commentators believe Congress went drastically overboard and did not appreciate the huge cost and management distraction caused by the new rules.

Sarbanes-Oxley (SOX) imposed a number of substantive requirements on public companies. The most intrusive were requirements for the composition of audit committees and stringent expanded requirements for internal controls to make sure that the books and records of the company reflect all transactions. CEOs and CFOs were personally required to certify that the company's financial statements and other SEC disclosures are complete and correct—even though many CEOs have little or no accounting background. Interestingly, the SEC did not directly require that companies comply with the plethora of other substantive requirements mandated by SOX. The mechanism was that the SEC required the stock exchanges to impose these substantive requirements.

The historical SRO rules and the newer SOX-mandated rules have little to do with mergers and acquisitions practice, although there are a few important requirements. Principal among them is the requirement that acquisitions by a Buyer involving significant issuances of Buyer stock over a specified threshold be approved by the Buyer's shareholders even if not required by the state corporations statute.

State Anti-Takeover Laws The most common state anti-takeover statutes were adopted in three historical waves and are often referred to as first-, second-, and third-generation statutes. First-generation or *disclosure* statutes regulated tender offers per se before the U.S. Supreme Court, in *Edgar v. MITE Corp.*, invalidated virtually all disclosure statutes on the basis of Williams Act preemption and Commerce Clause violations. However, a number of states have not repealed their disclosure statutes entirely.

Second-generation or *control share* statutes were adopted largely in response to *MITE* and were generally validated by the Supreme Court in 1987 in *CTS Corp. v. Dynamics Corp. of America.* The control share statutes were drafted to deal with hostile offers by regulating voting rights and other traditional areas of corporate governance.

Third-generation or *business combination* statutes were adopted largely after *CTS* and generally prevent a raider who accumulates a substantial stock position from effecting a merger without first obtaining approval of the Target's board. Business combination statutes are considered the most effective of the three common forms of anti-takeover legislation.

In addition to or included within certain of these widely adopted anti-takeover statutes, many states have adopted special-purpose statutes controlling shareholder rights, such as *cash-out* or *fair-price* laws to protect against coercive two-tier offers or *disgorgement* statutes to protect against other forms of short-term profit-taking. Many more states have directly regulated the powers of management to discourage takeovers by limiting directors' abilities to cooperate with an acquirer through anti-greenmail statutes (greenmail is buying out a threatening raider for a premium); taking advantage of compensation restriction laws; continuing labor contract provisions; or increasing director discretion to resist acquisitions by authorizing staggered boards, enabling *poison pills,* and relaxing directors' duties in the face of a takeover bid.

A large number of states, including Delaware, have enacted business combination statutes. Unsurprisingly, Delaware's post-*CTS* business combination statute has become the de facto standard. Delaware's statute has had special significance because half of the corporations listed on the New York Stock Exchange are incorporated in Delaware; other states look to Delaware in developing and interpreting their corporate law; and the Delaware business combination statute has survived several court challenges.

The professed goal of the Delaware statute, which is discussed in detail in the next section, is "to strike a balance between the benefits of an unfettered market for corporate shares and the well documented and judicially recognized need to limit abusive takeover tactics." It has been noted that the Delaware legislature actively chose to limit the ability of Buyers to succeed with bids considered to be inherently coercive, such as front-end-loaded, two-tiered tender offers.

Miscellaneous Statutes

Cash-Out Statutes Yet another approach to state regulation of takeovers, the cash-out requirement, has been adopted by several states. Generally, a cash-out provision requires the *raider,* rather than the corporation, to purchase dissenting shareholders' shares at a fair price.

Fair-Price Statutes A number of states have adopted fair-price statutes. These statutes generally preclude a raider who crosses a specified ownership threshold from engaging in a merger or other business combination with the Target company unless a statutory fair-price test is met or the raider obtains board approval and a supermajority vote of the shareholders. The primary effect of fair-price statutes is to protect shareholders from two-tier bids.

Disgorgement Statutes A few states have also adopted disgorgement provisions. These provisions require certain controlling shareholders to return to the Target corporation profits earned on certain dispositions of the Target's stock. The purpose of such statutes is to protect corporations from the threat of greenmail and discourage speculators from putting companies in play in order to collect speculative profits.

Internal Affairs Statutes Many states have enacted anti-takeover legislation aimed at discouraging director collusion with raiders and/or increasing director discretion in defending against raiders. Under the internal affairs doctrine, a Target company's state of incorporation has the primary authority to regulate that company's corporate governance and fiduciary standards. The state's rules will affect the Target's defensive position and flexibility in numerous ways. The state may permit a staggered board, enable poison pills, prohibit greenmail, regulate director and/or employee compensation (subject to preemption concerns), require the continuation of labor contracts, or allow the board to consider a variety of constituencies in responding to a takeover bid.

Staggered Boards Virtually all states permit the adoption of staggered boards, which lengthens the time period required for a raider to replace the existing directors upon obtaining control. Some states, however, require a minimum number of directors in order to permit staggering.

Poison Pill Enablement A number of states have enacted poison pill enablement statutes. Generally, the pill-authorization statutes have taken the form of amendments to existing provisions that permit a corporation to issue rights or options with respect to its shares (whether or not in connection with the issuance and sale of any of its securities) on terms and conditions determined by the board, thereby making an acquisition prohibitively expensive for a Buyer. Under these statutes, the terms and conditions may include restrictions that preclude or limit the exercise, transfer, or receipt of such rights or options by the holder of a specified number or percentage of outstanding common shares (i.e., a potential Buyer) or other securities of the corporation, or any transferee of such person, or that invalidate or void rights or options held by any such person or transferee.

Anti-Greenmail Several states have enacted anti-greenmail statutes, which provide that a corporation cannot pay a premium over market value for the shares of a shareholder who has acquired a certain percentage (3 to 10 percent) of the corporation's shares and who has held those shares for less than a certain number of years (two or three).

Director/Employee Compensation Several states have enacted some form of compensation restrictions. A couple of the statutes are intended to prevent boards from voting golden parachutes for themselves. In the event of a corporate takeover, a golden parachute is a large termination payment that will shield executives from the takeover's effects.

Directors' Duties Finally, a number of states have enacted statutes expanding the factors that directors may properly consider in the performance of their fiduciary duties during a takeover attempt. With the takeover explosion in the 1980s, some participants and observers were concerned that boards of directors were pressured in takeover situations to place undue emphasis on the immediate maximization of shareholder value (i.e., usually through the sale of the Target). Inadequate attention, it was argued, was given to the Target's long-term stock value and to its other relevant constituencies, including employees, customers, and local communities. Virtually all of these states now expressly allow for consideration of, among other things, employees, customers, suppliers, creditors, the economy of the state, and community effects, rather than solely shareholder value.

ANTI-TAKEOVER DEVICES

It has become customary for a private company to adopt selected anti-takeover measures when it goes public. At one point, there was some resistance on the part of the initial public offering (IPO) customers—the institutional buyers that purchase the large part of IPOs—but certain normal anti-takeover devices have become accepted practice. It is simple to put these devices in place at the time of an IPO, but for most of the devices, it is extremely difficult to adopt them after the company is public and subject to the difficulties of rounding up sufficient votes among the company's institutional shareholders to approve the anti-takeover devices.

Those factors are not present in the post-IPO adoption of a poison pill, on the other hand, because poison pills, or shareholder rights plans, can be adopted by the board of directors without shareholder approval. Thus, it is relatively uncommon for companies going public to adopt poison pills at the time of the IPO. If a threat emerges after the company goes public, the board can adopt a poison pill then. Many IPO companies reexamine the advisability of having a poison pill after a significant drop in the company's stock price makes them more attractive to corporate raiders.

Staggered Boards and Other Structural Changes

Poison pills are discussed in the next section. In this section, we briefly outline the other common defensive measures and their rationales. Note that the adoption of any anti-takeover provisions in the face of a hostile takeover will face enhanced scrutiny by a Delaware court, as was seen in *Unocal*.

The panoply of anti-takeover measures includes:

- Staggered board of directors
- *Blank check* preferred stock
- Charter provision allowing the board to consider broad interests in evaluating a takeover proposal
- Charter or bylaw provision requiring advance notice of shareholder nominations for directors
- Charter provision that prohibits written consent of shareholders
- Supermajority shareholder voting requirements for charter and bylaw amendments and for removal of directors without cause
- Fair-price provision requiring merger consideration to be the highest price paid by the Buyer within a specified period
- Adoption of Delaware anti-takeover statutory provisions

Classified or Staggered Board   In a staggered board, the directors are generally divided into three classes, with each class serving a three-year term and with one class being elected at each annual meeting. In the first election after a staggered board is approved by shareholders, one class is elected for one year, another for two years, and the third for three years. In addition, the bylaws of a public company provide that directors may be removed only for cause and only by the holders of a supermajority of the outstanding stock. The operative effect of these provisions is to make it more difficult to change the composition of the board via a proxy contest by a raider. Given the staggered terms, it will take two years to effect a change of control of the board.

Authorization of Blank-Check Preferred Stock   The authorization of blank-check preferred stock enables the board of directors to issue, in its sole discretion, preferred stock in one or more series of preferred stock and to determine the rights and preferences of such preferred stock at the time of issuance. No shareholder action is required for the board of directors to issue the blank-check preferred stock. The operative effect of this provision is to allow the board, when faced with a threat, to issue preferred stock with deterrent provisions to a friendly third-party investor.

Factors to Consider in Determining the Best Interests of the Corporation   The charter can have provisions that deal with the authority of the board, when evaluating any tender or exchange offer or business combination, to consider any factors it determines to be relevant. The effect of this provision is to take away the handcuffs placed on the board by *Revlon* and similar provisions that frown on any actions that do not "maximize shareholder value."

These provisions typically allow the board to consider the interests of the shareholders; the proposed consideration as it relates to the current market price of the company's capital stock; the market price of the company's capital stock over a period of years; the estimated price that might be achieved in a negotiated sale of the company; the premiums over market price for securities of other companies in similar transactions; other factors bearing on securities prices and the company's future prospects; and the social, legal, and economic effects of the proposed transaction upon employees, suppliers, customers, creditors, the communities in which the company conducts its business, and the economy of the state, region, and nation.

Advance Notice of Board Nominations   Because some raiders engage in proxy fights to convince a Target's shareholders to elect the raider's proposed directors instead of the Target's current directors, a requirement is sometimes added to the company's bylaws that proposed shareholder nominations for directors be announced to the company no later than a certain date prior to the meeting at which directors are to be elected. This requirement will eliminate the surprise element of proxy contests.

Prohibition on Written Consent of Shareholders   This charter provision provides that shareholders may not take any action by written consent. Thus, all matters requiring shareholder action must be taken at a meeting of the shareholders. This also has the effect of delaying the ability of a raider that has acquired a significant voting block to act quickly via the written consent route. Although this provision is standard for public companies, since the only thing it accomplishes is delay, it is not a particularly effective anti-takeover measure.

Supermajority and Fair-Price Provisions   Supermajority voting requirements generally provide that if the Target's board does not approve the proposed merger with the raider, a higher percentage of shareholder approval than is required by law will be required for the merger, unless the price paid for all shares of the Target's stock is a specified amount or at least equal to the highest price paid by the raider for any of the shares it has acquired before or pursuant to the tender offer.

Fair-price provisions are less useful and less prevalent as a takeover defense than was the case in the past. This is due to the advent of poison pill plans (which accomplish essentially the same result and can be adopted unilaterally by the Target's board) and to the recent enactment in several states of statutory fair-price provisions. Delaware's anti-takeover statute does not contain such a provision.

Delaware's Business Combination Statute   Section 203 of the General Corporation Law of the State of Delaware regulates certain business transactions involving corporations organized under the laws of Delaware and their shareholders. The purpose of Section 203 is to regulate hostile takeovers of Delaware corporations. Section 203 restricts for a three-year period certain transactions involving raiders who acquire between 15 and 85 percent of the Target's stock. Absent the consent of the Target, raiders are prohibited from engaging in "business combinations" with the Target, including mergers and consolidations, dispositions of 10 percent or more of the assets, or otherwise engaging in a "self-interested transaction" with the Target.

Section 203 applies to all Delaware corporations that have a class of voting stock listed on a national exchange, authorized for quotation on certain interdealer quotation systems, or held of record by more than 2,000 shareholders.

Business combinations include certain mergers and consolidations, dispositions of assets, issuances of stock, and other transactions with the interested shareholder or a party controlled by it, except for those transactions that result in a person becoming an interested shareholder and simultaneously acquiring at least 85 percent ownership of the Target. An interested shareholder may assert control of the Target by continuing the Target's ordinary business, so long as any transactions with the interested shareholder or a party controlled by it, or which result in a financial benefit to the interested shareholder (except proportionately as a shareholder of the corporation), are with the consent of two-thirds of the disinterested shareholders. Furthermore, prohibited transactions do not include proxy contests or the election of directors.

An *interested shareholder* is generally defined to include any person who acquires 15 percent or more of the Target's outstanding voting stock, and any affiliate and associate of such person.

There are several major exceptions to Section 203's application:

- *Eighty-five percent ownership.* Section 203 will not apply to a person who owns at least 85 percent of the corporation's outstanding voting stock (excluding stock owned by officers and directors of the corporation and certain employee stock plans) upon consummation of the transaction, including a hostile tender offer, in which such person becomes an interested shareholder.
- *Pre-acquisition board approval.* Section 203 does not apply if, prior to the time at which a person becomes an interested shareholder, the board of directors approves either the business combination or the transaction that results in the person becoming an interested shareholder. Section 203 is silent on the extent to which approval of a business combination or transaction will be inferred from a board's acts. However, references elsewhere in Delaware General Corporation Law would suggest such approval requires an affirmative and formal action of the board. Directors should note the possibility that a transaction that results in an interested shareholder becoming such may be broadly interpreted to include issuances of shares, warrants, and convertible securities, and certain contingent agreements.
- *Post-acquisition approval.* After the acquisition that resulted in a person becoming an interested shareholder, a subsequent business combination may only proceed with the approval of the board of directors and the affirmative vote of 66.2 percent of the Target's outstanding voting stock, excluding stock owned by the interested shareholder.
- *Additional exceptions.* Section 203 applies if the Target has a class of stock listed on a national securities exchange or held of record by more than 2,000 shareholders. If the Target fails to meet these criteria due to action taken by the interested shareholder, Section 203 will still apply. Additionally, an exception will apply to allow an interested shareholder to propose and complete what is defined as a "competing proposal" to certain existing business combinations supported by the Target's board of directors. Furthermore, Section 203 will not restrict a business combination with an interested shareholder who became an interested shareholder at the time when the Target was not subject to Section 203, unless the Target's certificate of incorporation contains a provision electing to be governed by Section 203.
- *Provisions.* A Delaware corporation may elect not to be governed by Section 203 by so providing in its original certificate of incorporation. Any election to opt out after this initial opportunity has passed is subject to certain limitations. Such post-organizational election requires a

charter or bylaw amendment approved by at least a majority vote of the corporation's shareholders. In addition, the election would not be effective until 12 months after the amendment and would not apply to a business combination with any person who became an interested shareholder prior to the adoption of the amendment, except in the case of a corporation that has never had a class of voting stock that falls in the categories previously described.

Despite a prior decision to opt out of Section 203, a corporation may elect, by amending its certificate of incorporation, to be governed by Section 203. However, such an amendment would not apply to restrict a business combination between a Target and any interested shareholder that became such prior to the effective date of the amendment containing the election to opt in.

Poison Pills

How Do Poison Pills Work? Poison pills, or shareholder rights plans, were enormously innovative when they were first adopted in the early takeover wars, and in 1985 the Delaware Supreme Court found them to be valid. Essentially, the purpose of a poison pill is to put a decisive defensive measure into the hands of the board of directors of the Target.

In the heyday of the hostile takeover, raiders had a panoply of weapons that were thought to be abusive in their ability to coerce shareholders to accede to a takeover attempt. Foremost among these was the front-end-loaded, two-tier tender offer. That technique involved a raider starting a tender offer for a majority of the Target's shares for a specified above-market price. At the same time that the tender offer was announced, the raider also announced that after it obtained majority control and was able to force a squeeze-out merger, it would offer consideration, usually noncash consideration, considerably lower than the initial cash tender. That put shareholders between a rock and a hard place: If a shareholder did not accept the offer, it risked having all of its shares purchased at the lower price in the back-end merger. Boards were largely defenseless because the tender offer was directed to the Target's shareholders, not to the board.

The poison pill was devised to give back to the board its power to decide on, or at least have an effective role in, situations where takeover attempts take place, particularly those employing abusive tactics.

Poison pills are essentially a dividend of rights declared by the board of directors, giving a company's shareholders (*excluding* the raider) the right to acquire additional securities of the company (or of the successful raider) at a discount from the market price. The rights are triggered when a raider acquires a specified percentage of the company's stock without board approval. The board of directors retains the power to redeem the rights for a defined period of time after the rights are triggered (or the "pill explodes"). This gives the board the ability to be actively involved in the takeover process by either negotiating with the raider for a better price or giving it the time to seek a better offer and then redeem the rights.

Poison pills are not considered to be anti-takeover devices in the purest sense. Market realities put such enormous pressure on boards to sell the company in the face of a takeover threat that the poison pill is thought to be a device merely to postpone the takeover process and give the board some breathing room.

Poison Pill Sequence The typical sequence of events in adopting a poison pill is as follows:

1. The company's board declares a dividend of rights ("Rights") to purchase stock (common stock or preferred stock) of the company. As with a dividend of common stock, the Rights can be issued without shareholder approval if there is sufficient authorized but unissued common stock or blank check preferred stock. The Rights are initially traded with the company's common stock (i.e., the Rights are automatically transferred with the stock in trades and other sales) and have little or no value. They become exercisable upon the occurrence of certain triggering events, as described next.

2. The Rights are redeemable at a nominal price by the board until 10 days after a "triggering event" occurs (e.g., the raider acquires 20 percent of the company's stock or announces or commences a tender offer). The potential lapse of the redemption feature encourages the raider to negotiate with the board. By time-limiting the discretion of the Target's board, the 10-day fixed redemption period discourages the raider from engaging in the triggering event, on the theory that the raider knows it will not be able to enter into extended negotiations with the board to try to convince it to redeem the Rights. Many plans provide for a longer redemption period or for none at all in order to give the Target board more or less flexibility in its deliberations.

3. The Rights detach from the common stock, trade separately, and become exercisable (other than by the raider), but their initial exercise price (typically 200 to 300 percent of the market price at the time the board of directors adopts the plan) discourages their exercise until the raider actually gains control of the Target by merger or otherwise.

4. The raider "swallows" the pill by actually taking over control of the Target. This releases the "poison": If the Raider acquires control of

the Target or if the Target is the legal survivor in a back-end merger with a subsidiary of the raider, then the Rights convert into the right to buy the Target's stock at a certain percentage (typically 50 percent) of the market price at the time of the takeover ("flip-in plans"); if the Target disappears in the merger, then the Rights convert into the right to buy the raider's stock at a certain percentage (typically 50 percent) of the current market price ("flip-over plans"). There are many variations of these plans.

Legal Aspects of Poison Pill Plans It is now widely accepted that the board of directors of a company may act to protect the company's shareholders by discouraging coercive, two-tiered bids and encouraging potential raiders to negotiate the terms of a takeover.

The time at which a poison pill plan is adopted may affect the ability of the plan to withstand a legal challenge. It has been argued that it is better for the board to adopt a poison pill plan before a Target faces a takeover threat in order to avoid a challenge that the plan was implemented to entrench the Target's management and therefore violates the fiduciary duty of the Target's board to the Target's shareholders.

However, recent Delaware cases suggest that a plan may be adopted in the face of a takeover threat without being challenged successfully in court if it is determined that the plan is in the best interests of the Target's shareholders and is not primarily designed to entrench management. Delaware courts apply the *Unocal* two-prong standard when a poison pill plan is at issue: The board must have reasonably believed that a danger to the corporation existed and the board's response to the perceived threat must have been reasonable. If these elements are met, then the business judgment rule will apply. This determination is made by a court with a certain amount of hindsight, and the plan is not certain to withstand challenge under the enhanced standard of judicial scrutiny.

The Target's board of directors will also face substantial pressure in deciding whether to redeem the Rights in the face of a takeover attempt. A board of directors must properly determine that a particular offer is inadequate or coercive.

Delaware courts have also considered the validity of poison pills in two non-takeover situations (i.e., where there has been no offer to purchase a company): asset protection and corporate culture protection. In *Versata Enterprises Inc. v. Selectica, Inc.*, the Delaware Supreme Court ruled that a low-threshold poison pill can be used to protect corporate assets. The Court, using the *Unocal* standard, found that Selectica's decision to amend its poison pill trigger from 15 percent to 4.99 percent in an attempt to protect its net operating loss (NOL) carryforwards, when a competitor had recently purchased more than 5 percent of Selectica's shares, was reasonable.

In *eBay Domestic Holdings, Inc. v. Newmark*, the Delaware Court of Chancery found that the use of the poison pill in closely held corporations to protect the corporate culture was not valid. eBay acquired a 28.4 percent ownership interest in Craigslist, becoming one of three shareholders in the company. eBay then launched a competitor site to Craigslist, and the other two Craigslist owners implemented a shareholder rights plan that prevented eBay from purchasing additional Craigslist shares and limited eBay's ability to sell shares to third parties. eBay challenged these defensive measures, and the Court ultimately found that the adoption of the shareholder rights plan was not a reasonable defense to a perceived threat to Craigslist's corporate culture.

Advantages of Poison Pill Plans   A poison pill plan serves a number of purposes, as follows:

- It signals the Target board's determination to resist inadequate or potentially abusive stock accumulations and takeover attempts.
- It discourages partial tender offers without discouraging fair offers for all of the Target's common stock or for the Rights as well as the common stock.
- It creates uncertainties about the ultimate cost of the Target to the raider.
- Because poison pill plans are often challenged in court, they give the Target's board time to solicit better bids or to adopt other strategies.
- Because the exercise price of Rights is so far out-of-the-money prior to a triggering event, Rights have no balance sheet, income statement, or cash flow effects prior to exercisability or redemption.

Disadvantages of Poison Pill Plans   There are, however, a number of negative aspects of poison pill plans, as follows:

- They do not deter (and may even encourage) proxy contests. If a raider simply wants to control a Target or change its management, as opposed to selling substantial assets or extracting greenmail, a proxy contest may be an attractive alternative. Accordingly, staggered boards have become a common anti-takeover device to counter this threat.
- Adoption of a plan may inflame a company's shareholders, who might prefer the board to entertain takeover bids. Shareholder proposals to

rescind or redeem Rights or to submit poison pill plans to shareholder approval are frequently included in proxy statements. The best time for already-public companies to adopt a plan is after shareholder proposals can no longer be submitted for a particular year.

- The law governing poison pill plans is currently undergoing another phase of rapid development. As a result, a plan adopted now may require amendment or repeal in the near future.

- Depending on the terms of the plan, the financial flexibility of the board of directors and the possibility of negotiating a friendly white-knight transaction may be severely inhibited should the Rights ever become nonredeemable.

APPENDIX

The following appendix is located on the website that accompanies this book. For information on the website see the "About the Website" section at the back of this book.

Appendix 6A, Sample Memorandum to Board of Directors on Fiduciary Duties in Connection with an Acquisition

Leveraged Buyouts (Structural and Tax Issues) and Acquisitions of a Troubled Business (Creditors' Rights and Bankruptcy)

LEVERAGED BUYOUTS: STRUCTURAL AND TAX ISSUES

Introduction

What is a leveraged buyout (LBO)? The term usually is used to describe a transaction where equity investors form a shell company, often including management of the company to be acquired, which acquires an operating business or division using significant debt financing to fund the purchase price. Since the shell company has little borrowing capacity, the borrowing is based in large part on the value of the assets and expected future cash flows of the business to be acquired. The organizer of the LBO is typically an LBO fund. Where there is significant management participation, the transaction is called a management buyout (MBO).

Leveraged buyout funds historically have generated extremely high returns for their investors. If that is the case, then why don't the management and selected shareholders of the Target do the same thing without the LBO fund? The answer is they do—via a leveraged recapitalization. A *leveraged recapitalization* or *leveraged recap* is a transaction where an operating company levers up and borrows a significant amount of money, using the proceeds to pay a special dividend to its shareholders or buy back some of its shares.

Leveraged buyouts are highly complicated transactions, not because there are unusual elements not seen in other transactions but rather, because the transaction is composed of multiple familiar steps, each of which has to be meshed with the others in real time. LBOs are essentially just a combination of mergers and acquisitions practice; debt financing and the relationship between different debt tiers; and the finance and equity elements of starting a new business. There are a few unique issues, however, which we cover here in more depth.

Leveraged buyouts can be used to acquire public companies or private companies. Acquisition of a public company is much more complicated, for two basic reasons: The sale is regulated by the Securities and Exchange Commission (SEC) and public transactions attract more scrutiny of the Target's board of directors regarding fulfillment of its fiduciary duties to the Target's stockholders. The board has the same duties in public and private transactions, but, as discussed in Chapter 6, public acquisitions are more visible and there are many more shareholders who are scrutinizing the performance of the Target board in getting maximum value for the shareholders (and who are willing to sue). Public transactions also attract rival bidders that must find a way to upset the original deal. In private companies, frequently the board members are the representatives of the major shareholders, so there is no real practical dichotomy between the board and the shareholders. Even in our society, you can't sue yourself. Director duties in the acquisition context are discussed in detail in Chapter 6.

Only companies with significant free cash flow, ideally highly predictable cash flows, are LBO candidates. The economics of an LBO are that the free cash flow above interest payments of the new or reorganized company is used to pay down the principal on the debt. Even where the business does not grow, the equity sponsors and management can still make money as the debt is paid down and the equity value approaches the original *enterprise value*. Essentially, the Buyer is using the business's own cash flow to pay for the business on a deferred basis. Sometimes the debt is paid down after the acquisition from the proceeds of sales of unwanted assets of the acquired business in order to make the numbers work.

From the global/economic/policy perspective, why do these deals make any sense? There can be no operating synergy since the acquirer is a shell, and management frequently is not replaced.

One explanation relates to the tax efficiencies that result from the use of leverage: the interest payments are deductible. Also, because management usually significantly increases its equity stake, management may be more motivated to devote more time and energy to the business. Further, management has a new set of bosses, who are highly intolerant of mediocre performance. If a public company is acquired and thereby becomes a private company, management is free to devote itself to growth in real value versus the short-term returns rewarded by the public markets. Another reason is that the new leveraged finance structure is more appropriate for the type of business (cash-flow oriented) that is being acquired.

LBO Structures and Their Tax Consequences

In an LBO, the equity sponsor (and management) want to end up with ownership of all or substantially all of the equity securities of the Target. The Target is being bought partly with the new money supplied by the equity sponsor and partly by using the value of the Target's assets and expected future cash flows to borrow funds that will be used to buy out the existing equity owners. The basic structuring challenge in an LBO is to solve the following conundrum: the Buyer needs to borrow based on the Target's assets to generate the cash to buy the business, but the Buyer cannot borrow against the Target's assets until it owns the Target. How do you get the money out of the Target to use the Target's own value to buy it?

There are only so many ways to structure an acquisition. So, in an LBO, the structures are pretty much the same as we have already discussed. There are, however, significant tax, finance, and accounting differences that become applicable because of the use of a large amount of debt. As discussed in Chapter 4, different structures with the same economics can have significantly different tax results. So, with the assistance of a tax lawyer, all possible transactions must be examined to determine the optimal tax result. The structure yielding the optimal tax result may not be the structure that yields the optimal nontax result. The right balance has to be struck.

Because an LBO buyer uses (or is itself) a newly formed shell corporation to effect the acquisition, in the following discussion we will refer to the shell as "Newco."

The most common LBO structures are:

- Newco merges directly into the Target, and Newco borrows money.
- Newco's newly formed shell subsidiary (Newco Sub) merges into the Target, and Newco borrows money.
- Newco's newly formed shell subsidiary (Newco Sub) merges into the Target, and Newco and Newco Sub borrow money.
- Newco purchases part of the Target's stock, and the Target redeems the rest using existing cash and/or borrowed funds.

We have seen each of these structures before in Chapter 3. All that is different is adding in the borrowing of funds. Exhibits 7.1 through 7.4 are the same as those exhibits in Chapter 3 with the addition of leverage.

The tax consequences of these types of transactions tend to follow the economics. Where Newco disappears, it is largely ignored.

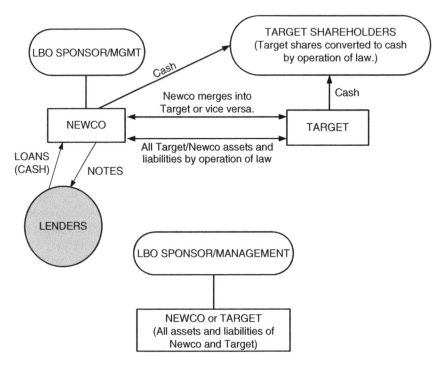

EXHIBIT 7.1   LBO Direct Merger for Cash

In economic terms, the *direct merger* (Exhibit 7.1) can be considered to be a borrowing by the Target because Newco is ignored. The Target, in order to cash out the Target shareholders, redeems its outstanding stock. If there is not a complete termination of interest of the Target's shareholders ownership position, dividend treatment is possible. If the Target's cash is used to effect the buyout, as well as borrowings by the Target, the economics resemble a part purchase by Newco and a part redemption by the Target. The tax analysis required to determine which is the optimal treatment is complex and involves, for example, whether the Target has earnings and profits and whether the Target's shareholders are corporations entitled to receive the intercorporate dividend deduction.

In economic terms, the *subsidiary merger* (Exhibit 7.2) where Newco is the borrower can be looked at differently because there are two corporations in the picture. Because Newco survives as an entity, the substance resembles a purchase by Newco of all of the Target's shares from the shareholder. If, however, some of the Target's shareholders retain a portion of their

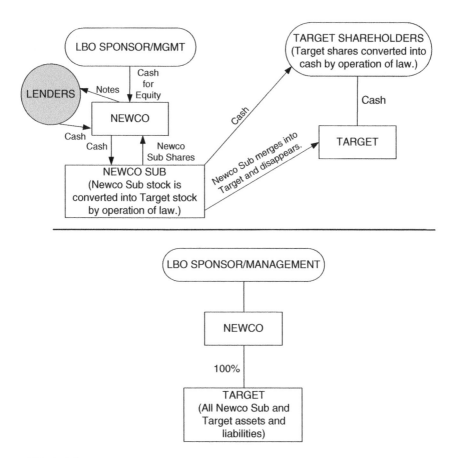

EXHIBIT 7.2   LBO Reverse Triangular Merger for Cash (Debt at Newco Level)

equity interest in the business, the transaction can be looked at as a contribution of those shareholders' shares to the equity of Newco in an IRC Section 351 formation transaction for cash and Newco shares. Also, it could be looked at as a sale of those shareholders' shares to Newco and the purchase of new Newco shares with a portion of the after-tax proceeds of sale.

One problem with this structure, as discussed in Chapter 3, is that Newco is the borrower and it has no real assets except its stock in the Target. Newco winds up as a holding company. As we said, lenders like to lend to the entity with the assets, and here the assets are in the Target, which is not the borrower.

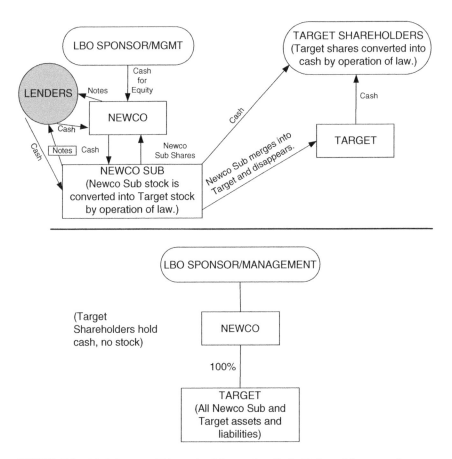

EXHIBIT 7.3   LBO Reverse Triangular Merger for Cash (Debt at Newco and Newco Sub Levels)

In economic terms, the subsidiary merger where Newco and Newco Sub are both borrowers (Exhibit 7.3) can be looked at partly like a combination of the first two transactions—part redemption and part stock purchase.

In economic terms, the *part purchase/part redemption* transaction (Exhibit 7.4) also is much like the preceding example.

In all of these cases, if management of the Target is to continue with an equity position in the business after the transaction, it is in management's best interest to obtain IRC Section 351 treatment by the rollover of all or a portion of management's Target stock into Newco stock—in other words, management uses its Target stock to pay for its Newco stock. The rollover

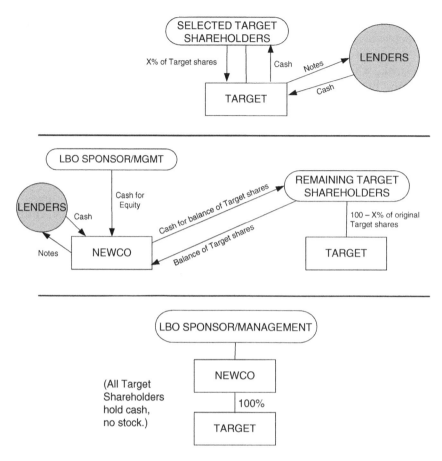

EXHIBIT 7.4 LBO Direct Redemption Plus Sale

has to be part of the Section 351 plan, and there should be some time gap between the contribution to Newco by management of its Target stock and the acquisition transaction. This topic is discussed in Chapter 4.

ACQUISITION OF A TROUBLED BUSINESS GENERALLY

Acquisitions of troubled businesses present unique problems. Nevertheless, troubled businesses present a tempting target for Buyers convinced that they can do better with new management or a better business model. The added possibility of cherry-picking assets, and even leaving some of the liabilities of the old business behind to give it a fresh start, can make the Target's business attractive in spite of a troubled past.

As we have seen, the simplest method to acquire a business is to buy the stock, whether by direct stock purchase or by merger. If that is done, then the Buyer gets all of the assets of the Target but also inherits all of the Target's liabilities. Also, a stock purchase may not be feasible because presumably the Buyer is not willing to pay very much for a troubled business and the shareholders of the Target may not want to bother to sell their stock for a distressed price. If the Buyer acquires control of the business through a purchase of new equity at a very low price, shareholders might challenge that transaction as a breach of the Target board's duty. If the Buyer buys a majority position from existing shareholders followed by a squeeze-out merger, the squeeze-out merger might be challenged on the entire fairness standard.

An asset deal possibly leaves behind all or selected liabilities, but because of state fraudulent transfer laws and the bankruptcy law equivalent, doing an acquisition where creditors don't get paid in full can be a risky proposition. In theory, the assets of the business could legally be sold for their fair market value, but the determination of what is really fair market value is in the eye of the beholder. It will be hard to convince the creditors of the Target who are losing all or part of their money that the transaction is really for fair market value. Creditors who have been shortchanged can put the Target into bankruptcy after the sale, and there is the possibility that the bankruptcy court would invalidate the sale as a fraudulent transfer. Short-changed creditors may also be critical suppliers to the Target and may insist on getting paid before they will continue to do business with Target.

Another issue in an asset purchase is recourse to the seller if it turns out that there were misrepresentations made to the Buyer. As discussed, that recourse is only as good as the existence and solvency of the seller, and in a distressed situation there are multiple creditors looking at the same assets as the source of recovery on their claims. One technique that may serve to insulate the Buyer is to pay all or part of the purchase price by a note. The documents would provide that subsequent claims by the Buyer would allow it to reduce its payments on the note by a right of offset. With certain caveats, these offset rights are generally respected in bankruptcy.

In a distressed business, the assets are likely to be subject to one or multiple liens, and in order to get clear title to such assets, those liens must be discharged, but the secured creditors holding the liens may insist on getting paid in full or close to it in order to agree to voluntarily release their liens. That then brings us back to the fundamental problem that the business may not be worth buying if liabilities have to be assumed or paid off. Compromises can be sought with the creditors before or after an acquisition, but there can be no assurance of success.

All of the other elements of buying a business are present in this situation. Consider the following:

- Can key employees be retained, and on what terms?
- Are there arrearages in debts to employees, landlords, equipment lessors, and mortgagors that must be satisfied? Do the leases have defaults that cannot be cured even if the Buyer were willing to do so?
- Will vendors continue to do business after the acquisition?

So what are some of the unconventional techniques that are used in this situation? One possibility is for the Target to make an assignment for the benefit of creditors. This is a state law process that is similar to a bankruptcy filing, which is a federal law proceeding. The Target, with the approval of its board, assigns all of its assets to an assignee who acts as a fiduciary to the Target's creditors. The process allows an orderly liquidation of assets, including a possible sale of assets to the Buyer, but the process may be interrupted by creditors who file an involuntary bankruptcy petition.

Another possibility is for the secured creditors of the Target to foreclose and sell the Target's assets to the Buyer in a foreclosure sale. An aggressive move would be for the secured lender to sell the assets to the Buyer in a private sale for the debt owed to the secured creditor. The theoretical result of this course of action is that the Buyer acquires all of the assets of the business (assuming all are subject to a security interest held by the foreclosing lender) and avoids all liabilities other than the secured obligations. This is possible but risky since the actions of the secured creditor must be commercially reasonable and undertaken with the intent to maximize value of the assets being sold. If other creditors get shortchanged, this sleight of hand tends to provoke litigation or an involuntary bankruptcy filing. It is particularly infuriating to creditors if the management or shareholders of the insolvent business emerge with ownership in the new entity in a transaction where junior secured or unsecured creditors receive little or no recovery. Another possibility is for the secured creditor to conduct a public auction with proper notice to all potential buyers. That is less risky but, as in bankruptcy, the Buyer may be the one who walks away with nothing once competitive bidders can enter the picture.

The last possibility is for the Target to file for voluntary bankruptcy. That topic is the subject of the section following the next one.

FRAUDULENT TRANSFERS

Whether forming a new entity, obtaining debt financing, or structuring or implementing a merger, stock purchase (or repurchase), or asset sale, care must be taken to minimize the risk of fraudulent transfer liability. Failure to do so may cause a transaction—referred to as a *transfer* in fraudulent transfer law—to be *avoided,* or unwound, sometimes years after the fact. Avoidance of a fraudulent transfer may also expose both the immediate transferee and any subsequent holders of the property to a *recovery* action, brought either by a creditor under applicable state law or by a debtor or trustee in bankruptcy. Such an action allows a plaintiff to recover—either for its own benefit (if an individual creditor) or for the benefit of all creditors of the transferor who once held the property (if in bankruptcy)—the full value of the transferred property. This is so even if the defendant no longer holds the transferred property or its proceeds.

So what is a fraudulent transfer, and why does the law provide such draconian measures of relief? To begin to understand the issues involved, it helps to consider some of the bedrock principles of corporate law. Creditors have bargained for repayment of their debt, generally with interest over time and, in the pure case, with no opportunity to capture any upside if the debtor realizes unexpectedly high profits. The creditor makes its decision to lend based not only on the debtor's promise to repay the loan but also on an informed evaluation of the debtor's ability to honor its promise. That evaluation, in turn, is based in large part on a consideration of the debtor's assets, liabilities, and business prospects at the time the loan is made.

Fast-forward now, from the date the loan was made to the date repayment is due. The debtor now informs the creditor that payment must be delayed, or that payment will not be made at all. The debtor's business plan did not work out, and its business is failing or perhaps already in liquidation. The creditor's first inkling that the promised payment will not be forthcoming is a bankruptcy court notice or the filing of a "suggestion of bankruptcy" in a pending civil action. Adding insult to injury, the creditor learns that significant assets of the debtor—on which the creditor relied in extending credit in the first place—are no longer on the balance sheet, having been transferred to a third party (or, even worse, to an insider of the debtor)— for little or no consideration. The creditor's likely reaction to this news is readily predictable.

Fraudulent transfer law is designed to maintain the expected order of things. Holders of equity, not debt, should bear the effects of corporate failure, just as they reap the upside if the business prospers. Thus, creditors have a higher payment priority than shareholders. In particular, fraudulent transfer law intervenes when the assets upon which a creditor relied in agreeing to provide debt financing—whether in the form of trade debt or secured loans—are depleted without a corresponding increase in the debtor's equity cushion. Creditors accept ordinary business risk, but they do not bargain for the risk of transfers that lack a rational business purpose from the standpoint of a reasonable debtor-transferor.

Fraudulent transfers take two forms. The easiest to conceptualize, if not always to prove, is the transfer made with actual intent on the part of the debtor-transferor to hinder, delay, or defraud a creditor or group of creditors. This sort of transfer may verge on fraud in the traditional sense of the term, where a debtor secretly moves an asset, or transfers title to an asset, with the understanding that the debtor can retain the use of the asset or reclaim it later, after the creditor has been effectively short-changed. Since it is the rare debtor that will admit to having transferred a valuable asset with such a purpose in view, proof of an actual fraudulent transfer will typically entail a search for one or more badges of fraud, including:

- A transfer that occurred after the debtor was sued or threatened with suit, or shortly before or after a substantial debt was incurred;
- A purported transfer of substantially all of the debtor's property;
- Insolvency or other unmanageable indebtedness;
- An insider relationship between the debtor and the transferee; and
- After the transfer, retention by the debtor of the property involved in the putative transfer.

Conceptually, the second type of fraudulent transfer can be far more complex. This is the *constructively* fraudulent transfer, in which the debtor transfers property for less than "reasonably equivalent value" (articulated by some state statutes as "fair consideration") where the debtor-transferor:

- Was insolvent at the time of the transfer;
- Was rendered insolvent as the result of the transfer;
- Was engaged or about to engage in a transaction for which its remaining capital was unreasonably small; or
- Intended to incur or believed that it would incur debts that would be beyond its ability to pay as those debts matured.

This type of transfer focuses not on the transferor's intent, but on the twin questions of asset valuation and insolvency. In short, the issue is whether the transfer improperly shifted unbargained-for risk to a corporation's creditors by altering the corporate structure on which they relied in extending credit.

Principal sources of fraudulent transfer law in the United States include Sections 544 and 548 of the Bankruptcy Code (11 U.S.C. §§ 544, 548) and state statutes predicated on uniform laws such as the Uniform Fraudulent Conveyance Act (UFCA) or its younger sibling, the Uniform Fraudulent Transfer Act (UFTA). All 50 states have enacted some form of fraudulent transfer law.

There are fine points of distinction between federal bankruptcy law and state statutes in this area, but as a general matter, both federal and state statutes allow creditors or estate fiduciaries in a bankruptcy case (either a trustee appointed by the U.S. Department of Justice or a debtor-in-possession) to file a complaint to avoid actual and constructively fraudulent transfers occurring within a window of time prior to the commencement of a civil action or a bankruptcy case, as applicable, and recover the value of the transferred property for the benefit of the creditor-plaintiff or the bankruptcy estate, as the case may be. The defendant in the action typically is not the transferor who parted with the property, but the transferee who received it.

The window of time within which such transfers remain vulnerable to avoidance varies by statute. Under the UFTA, the reach-back period for avoidance actions is four years from the date of the transfer. By contrast, under the UFCA the reach-back period varies depending on the nature of the transfer to be avoided; for example, if the challenged transfer was a contract under seal, applicable state law may allow the transfer to be avoided 20 years after the date of the contract. Federal bankruptcy law effectively piggybacks on state statutes. Under Section 544 of the Bankruptcy Code, an estate representative (a trustee or debtor-in-possession) may take advantage of the reach-back period under the applicable state statute. At the same time, the estate representative may use Section 548 of the Bankruptcy Code to bring a fraudulent transfer within a two-year reach-back period even when the requirements for a state law cause of action cannot be satisfied.

Changes in federal bankruptcy law expanded the reach-back period under fraudulent transfer law and added new provisions that allow the estate representative to avoid any transfer to or for the benefit of an insider under an employment contract or self-settled trust if the transfer was made or incurred within two years before a bankruptcy filing in the case of an employment contract, or within 10 years prior to a bankruptcy filing in the case of a self-settled trust. A transfer made pursuant to an employment contract may be avoided where the debtor-transferor made the transfer with actual intent to hinder, delay, or defraud creditors, or where reasonably equivalent value was not given. The 10-year reach-back applies to transfers to a self-settled trust only where the transferor acted with actual intent to hinder, delay, or defraud creditors.

Fraudulent transfer law casts a wide net. Not surprisingly, given the policy underpinnings of the law, transfers that effect structural changes in an organization may be particularly susceptible to challenge as constructively fraudulent. For example, the LBO has come to be viewed by many as a virtual archetype of constructively fraudulent transfer since the modern Bankruptcy Code was enacted more than 30 years ago. This need not be so, since the mere fact of an LBO does not establish the insolvency prong of the cause of action, but old equity that has been cashed out in an LBO provides a tempting target for a bankruptcy trustee seeking to enhance the value of an estate for the benefit of creditors. When a company is sold, whether to management or an unrelated third party, and the target company's assets are used by the Buyer to secure the seller's right to payment of the purchase price, the value of the Target is immediately reduced, and the lost value transferred to the selling shareholders. There is no sure way to eliminate fraudulent transfer risk in this scenario unless the Target is unquestionably solvent, both before and after the LBO; has sufficient working capital at and after the closing; and no one has acted with actual intent to hinder, delay, or defraud any known creditor.

In addition to the LBO, other fertile grounds for fraudulent transfer risk include:

- *Dividend payments.* When a corporation is insolvent, the discretionary payment of cash or other valuable consideration to shareholders may be avoided as constructively fraudulent as to creditors. Dividend payments are also subject to challenge under state corporation statutes that impose a solvency test on the corporation's ability to pay dividends. Notably, the corporation's directors may be held personally liable for authorizing the payment of dividends when the corporation is insolvent or where such payment will render the corporation insolvent. Moreover, Delaware courts have led the way in imposing on corporate directors a derivative duty to the corporation's creditors when the corporation is insolvent or has entered the zone of insolvency.
- *Stock repurchases.* Like dividends, stock repurchase transactions transfer cash or other valuable consideration to shareholders, here in exchange for the corporation's own stock. With the possible exception of the transfer of a control premium, however, courts have held that a corporation's stock has no value to the corporation, leaving the repurchase transaction vulnerable to a fraudulent transfer challenge.
- *Friendly foreclosure sales.* Corporate insiders may structure an indirect fraudulent transfer by setting up a shell company, borrowing funds from the company's bank to purchase the older company's assets, and inviting the bank to conduct a *friendly foreclosure.* After the bank forecloses on the assets, it flips the assets to the insider-controlled shell company in a collusive auction. The effect of the transaction is to transfer value from the corporation and its creditors to the insiders and the bank.
- *Noncash benefits to selling shareholders.* When a closely held business is sold, it is not uncommon to find that the shareholder has taken out loans from the Target, evidenced (hopefully) by one or more promissory notes.

Unless the borrower-shareholder intends to remain involved in the business after the closing, it is likely that the shareholder will seek loan forgiveness as part of the sale transaction. In this situation, it is generally preferable to structure the transaction as an adjustment to the purchase price, allowing the Buyer to take an assignment of the borrower's loan obligations, rather than simply wiping out the debt. If the Buyer is adequately capitalized, substituting one obligor for another does not deplete the value of the operating company and therefore reduces the threat of a fraudulent transfer challenge. This alternative is not without risk, either, however, since an operating company guarantee will likely be required to provide collateral for the increased price.

- *Transactions involving loans to an affiliated group of companies.* When a group of affiliates enter into a transaction with a lender, almost inescapably fraudulent transfer risk will arise. Commonly, some members of the affiliated group receive the benefits of the loan while other members of the group incur liability on the debt. A wise lender will ensure that the proposed business plan makes economic sense for every member of the group before making the loan.

- *Guarantees (secured and unsecured).* A related point: where the person or entity whose performance is guaranteed is a wholly owned subsidiary of the guarantor, there will be no issue—any resulting appreciation in the value of the entity whose performance is guaranteed likely indirectly benefits the guarantor holding its stock or member interests. Similarly, there is little fraudulent transfer risk if the guarantor is not the sole owner but receives some other indirect benefit from extending the guarantee. In a holding company context, for example, the opportunity to acquire otherwise unavailable business opportunities may provide an indirect benefit sufficient to take the transaction outside the purview of the fraudulent transfer statutes. However, an *upstream* or *cross-stream* guarantee may not provide reasonably equivalent value to the guarantor.

A decision by the Fourth Circuit Court of Appeals illustrates many of the points discussed here. The case resolved numerous disputes involving the Gleneagles Investment Company. The president of the Raymond Group of companies effected a purchase of the shares of a group of coal mining companies, forming a shell holding company as the vehicle for the acquisition. The shell obtained a loan commitment from a lending group to finance the purchase of the Raymond Group shareholders' interests. Some of the Raymond Group companies served as borrowers and others provided secured guarantees to the lenders. A disgruntled creditor brought an action against everyone involved in the transaction and succeeded in having the guarantees set aside as fraudulent conveyances, whereupon the selling shareholders capitulated and entered into a settlement agreement with the plaintiff-creditor.

When a fraudulent transfer complaint is filed, there are few defenses that can be raised. The issue will focus on the plaintiff's case; the plaintiff will prevail who can introduce persuasive evidence of sufficient badges of fraud to prove that the transferor acted with actual intent to hinder, delay, or defraud creditors. Similarly, the plaintiff will prevail who can introduce persuasive evidence of the insolvency of the transferor and lack of reasonably equivalent value received. The only defense, *per se*, is showing that the defendant took for value and without knowledge of the voidability of the transfer. By definition, of course, a defendant-transferee who received a constructively fraudulent transfer did not give sufficient value to constitute a complete defense, even where the transferee's motives were pure.

Predictably, arguments regarding both insolvency and reasonably equivalent value (or lack thereof) do not remotely suggest an exact science. With respect to insolvency, the debate may focus—depending on the particular statute under which the action is brought—on balance sheet insolvency (whether the transferor's liabilities exceeded its assets at the time the transfer was made, excluding the transferred asset in question); equitable insolvency (whether the transferor was able to pay its debts as they came due); or the unreasonably small capital test (focusing on the transferor's financial requirements at the time of the transfer, its business plans for the future, and its expectations as to the future debts it might incur). Typically, both sides will offer expert testimony and dueling expert reports will be exchanged. The plaintiff may persuade the court that balance sheet values should be restated years after the fact, with asset values written down and liabilities steeply increased.

With respect to the issue of whether "reasonably equivalent value" was given, similar debates will ensue. The issue of valuation is always a thorny one where there is no market test to serve as a benchmark. The issue is difficult even where cash was exchanged for an asset, but the difficulty will increase substantially when a plaintiff is seeking to unwind a complex commercial transaction, possibly involving multiple actors.

In summary, having reviewed the potential risks and the uncertain standards applied by the courts, what can a party do to insulate itself from fraudulent transfer risk? While there are no easy answers, the following suggestions may be helpful:

- Whenever possible, plan ahead. If contracts and agreements are put in place when a client is solvent, a later determination of the client's financial condition may not expose the transaction to attack.

- Whether forming a holding company or restructuring an existing business, be sure that the new or restructured entity is adequately capitalized and has sufficient liquidity. Review the company's business plan and ensure that, at all times, the new or reorganized company is likely to have sufficient assets, including working capital, to execute the plan. If possible, arrange to have a solvent entity guarantee existing debt obligations.
- Pay special attention to transactions like LBOs that are likely to attract the attention of a disgruntled creditor. Try to anticipate, as far as possible, whether an existing trade or judgment creditor could assert a reliance interest based on the old capital structure.
- Watch out for the actual fraudulent transfer, particularly when dealing with close corporations and other situations that involve insiders.
- When executing a transaction that requires a number of steps, analyze each step and be sure that you can articulate a reasonable business purpose for that step. Then collapse the transactions and determine whether you can identify particular creditors, or groups of creditors, who may be able to argue that they relied on the existing capital structure before the transaction occurred. These creditors (or their successor-in-interest, the bankruptcy trustee) may be able to avoid, or unwind, any piece of the transaction or the entire series of transactions as a fraud on creditors.
- In assessing a proposed transaction, whether it be an LBO, asset purchase, or stock dividend, remember that if the deal looks too good to be true, it may be a fraudulent transfer in disguise.

ACQUISITIONS OUT OF BANKRUPTCY

Overview

Acquisitions of troubled businesses are a special case. The first question one might ask is, why should a Buyer acquire a Target that is a troubled business in the first place? The answer is that some assets are best redeployed to other (or higher and better) uses; society benefits from the efforts of an entrepreneur who can unlock the hidden value of assets being underutilized. Valuable assets being used in the wrong way present a tremendous opportunity for the savvy businessperson. Some of these assets are often intertwined in a business with too many liabilities; if the Buyer does not want to assume, directly or indirectly, all of the liabilities of the business to obtain the asset, one alternative is a sale in bankruptcy.

As we have seen in the discussion of fraudulent transfer laws, liabilities cannot effectively, or certainly easily, be avoided by structural sleights of hand. So, where liabilities have to be reduced for an acquisition to make sense, there are two basic alternatives: putting the company into bankruptcy and having liabilities discharged through the bankruptcy process, or attempting to make arrangements with creditors outside of bankruptcy. The advantage of the former is that the bankruptcy mechanism can often be used to jawbone reluctant creditors; the disadvantage is that the process is costly and may be lengthy, and once you start you cannot get out—effectively, you lose control of the process and other bidders can steal the deal. In a private arrangement, the costs and lack of control of a bankruptcy are avoided, but such deals are difficult to do because of the voluntary aspect. A blend of the two techniques is the so-called bankruptcy, negotiated sale where a deal is worked out in advance with the principal creditors and then the bankruptcy process is used to bring the minority along.

Purchasing of Assets out of Bankruptcy

The Bankruptcy Code contains several provisions that relate to the purchase and sale of assets in a bankruptcy case:

- The debtor may sell its assets in the ordinary course of its business without notice or a hearing pursuant to Section 363(c)(1).
- The debtor may sell its assets outside of the ordinary course of its business after notice and a hearing under Section 363(b)(1).
- The debtor may sell some or all of its assets pursuant to the terms of a confirmed plan of reorganization under Sections 1123(a)(5) and 1123(b)(4).

Sales in the Ordinary Course of Business Although the Bankruptcy Code does not define the term *ordinary course of business,* most courts addressing the issue of whether a transaction falls within the ordinary course of business now apply a test that calls for the consideration of the *vertical dimension* and/or the *horizontal dimension* of the transaction. The vertical dimension or *creditors' expectation test* examines the debtor's proposed transaction from a hypothetical creditor's point of view and inquires whether the transaction is similar to the types of transactions that the debtor undertook pre-filing so that the proposed transaction does not upset creditors' reasonable expectations. The horizontal dimension or *industrywide test* examines the debtor's proposed transaction from the perspective of the debtor's industry as a whole and asks whether the post-filing transaction is of a type that other similar businesses would engage in, in the ordinary course of business.

Given that the Bankruptcy Code (in Section 549(a)) provides for the avoidance of transfers that occur after the commencement of the case that are not authorized by any provision of the Bankruptcy Code or by the court, most commentators advise erring on the side of caution by seeking court approval any time a transaction is anything other than a clear continuation of the debtor's regular business operations.

Sales Outside of the Ordinary Course of Business The transactions we are concerned with here for the most part will involve a sale "other than in the ordinary course of business," and will require notice and a hearing. *Notice and a hearing* is spelled out as "such notice and such opportunity for a hearing, as is appropriate in the particular circumstances."

The Federal Rules of Bankruptcy Procedure governing a sale of property outside of the ordinary course of business call for a 21-day notice to all creditors and other parties in interest, including trustees and creditors' or equity committees, "unless the court for cause shown shortens the time." Notice is to be sent by mail, unless the court directs otherwise, and includes the time and place of the public sale, the terms and conditions of any private sale, the time fixed for filing objections, and a general description of the property being sold.

Bankruptcy courts have authority to regulate the time and manner of notice to creditors and parties in interest. In addition, the Bankruptcy Code allows the court to grant the relief requested without a hearing if notice is properly given and no request for a hearing is timely made. Furthermore, a court can grant the requested relief without a hearing if notice is properly given, even if a request for a hearing is timely made, where the court finds that insufficient time exists in which to hold such a hearing. Perishable goods are often sold this way without a hearing.

In order for the bankruptcy court to determine whether a sale outside of the ordinary course of business should be approved, the debtor must present to the court some articulated business justification for the proposed sale. As proponent, the debtor typically bears the burden of proof at a hearing on the approval of a proposed asset sale. If the debtor is selling substantially all of its assets, the moving party must satisfy the four elements of the *sound business purpose* test:

1. A sound business purpose or emergency justifies the sale.
2. The sale has been proposed in good faith.
3. Adequate and reasonable notice has been provided to interested parties.
4. The price is fair and reasonable.

As noted, a bankruptcy sale occurring outside the ordinary course may be by private sale or by public auction. As a practical matter, most of the out-of-the-ordinary-course sales conducted during a Chapter 11 proceeding will be a negotiated private sale to a specified purchaser and will be subject to higher and better offers. Public auctions are sometimes favored by courts due to the fact that the purchase price usually more closely reflects the true market value of the assets being sold, and the procedure may involve one "last and final" sealed bid from each party or an open auction. Generally speaking, a public sale will be sufficient to establish that a purchaser has paid adequate value for the assets being transferred.

Although there is no provision in the Bankruptcy Code or Bankruptcy Rules requiring that a notice of private sale solicit higher counteroffers, the debtor has a fiduciary obligation to "maximize the value of the estate and protect the interest of the creditors." As a result, trustees and debtors typically solicit such counteroffers.

Once a fair price is established, the primary reason for a sale in bankruptcy is that the Bankruptcy Code authorizes a trustee or a debtor-in-possession to sell property of the bankruptcy estate *free and clear* of any third-party interest or claim on such property. The provisions of Section 363(f) govern, and are written in the alternative, so that there are actually five different specified methods by which a sale may go forward free and clear of a third-party's interest. If any one of the five conditions set forth here is met, the debtor has the authority to conduct a sale free and clear of any interest in such property:

1. If applicable nonbankruptcy law permits the sale of such property free and clear of interests.
2. If such entity that holds an interest in the property consents to the sale free and clear of any liens. The most common basis for a sale under Section 363(f) is the consent of the parties in interest. Consent under this Section may be expressed or implied, and several courts have held that the failure to object to a proposed sale after receiving proper notice constitutes consent and acceptance by a secured creditor (vigilance by the interest holder is required). As a practical matter, a lien holder will usually consent to a sale going forward if the creditor's lien attaches to the proceeds of the sale. In addition, a lien holder may consent even though its claim will not be paid in full from such proceeds if it is satisfied that the proposed sale is for the highest price available. In such a case, the lien holder is spared the delay and costs associated with obtaining relief from the automatic stay and instituting a foreclosure sale.
3. If the interest is a lien and the price at which such property is to be sold is greater than the aggregate value of all liens on such property. Several courts have interpreted this section as meaning that the sale price must exceed the aggregate face value of all liens on the property, whereas

MERGERS AND ACQUISITIONS

other courts have held that value means actual value as determined by the bankruptcy court.

4. If such interest is the subject of a bona fide dispute as to whether the creditor actually holds an interest in the property subject to sale.
5. If the party holding the interest could be compelled, in a legal or equitable proceeding, to accept money in satisfaction of such interest. Courts are divided on the issue of whether this condition requires the full satisfaction of a lien holder's debt. Several courts interpreting this section have held that the requirements are satisfied in situations where the debtor can demonstrate that the creditor is receiving what it could be compelled to accept under the relevant terms of the Bankruptcy Code (i.e., a *cramdown*).

When a debtor decides to sell an asset, its main responsibility, and the primary concern of the bankruptcy court, is the maximization of the value of the asset sold. In proposing a sale, the debtor has an affirmative obligation to present evidence that the proposed purchase price is adequate and that the sale is being proposed in *good faith*. A good-faith showing is a prerequisite to affording a sale the protections of the Bankruptcy Code (Section 363(m)), which will moot any appeal of an order approving a sale absent the issuance of a stay.

Within these parameters, the business judgment rule affords a debtor a fair amount of discretion in formulating the terms of a proposed sale transaction. Because oftentimes the initial offer is used as a stalking horse offer, subject to counteroffer from any other interested party, the negotiation process involves walking a fine line between the debtor fulfilling its fiduciary obligation to maximize the amount received for the estate's assets, versus satisfying the potential purchaser's desire for some degree of bid protection. In this regard, the initial bidder typically seeks to preclude competitors from piggybacking on its due diligence by inserting into its offer any number of bid-protection devices, including the establishment of minimum overbid requirements, the requirement that any counteroffer mirror the nonprice terms of the initial proposed deal, a minimum deposit requirement, a breakup fee, and window-shop provisions.

Bid-Protection Devices Making a higher bid for assets being sold in a bankruptcy context will subject a potential acquirer to overbid procedures, which are being commonly used by buyers as a protection mechanism. Overbid procedures provide certain protections to an initial bidder against subsequent bidders who may rely on the initial bidder's due diligence and offer only a slightly higher bid.

The rules regarding overbidding are typically established in advance of the sale and are usually set forth in the sale motion. Such sale motions typically set forth minimum amounts that overbidders must offer over and above the initially proposed purchase price, commonly referred to as the *upset price*. Examples of overbid procedures used to protect initial bidders include:

- Requirement of a minimum cash deposit (generally a fixed percentage of the proposed purchase price);
- Provision that the overbidder must accept the same terms as provided in the proposed asset purchase agreement;
- Specification of the increments in which any subsequent bids over and above any initial overbid must be stated; and
- Requirement that additional bidders demonstrate financial ability to consummate the transaction.

Breakup Fee Provisions   Breakup fees, topping fees, stalking fees, or bust-up fees are all designed to provide the initial bidder with some assurance that it will be compensated if the sale transaction is not consummated through no fault of its own. The purpose of a breakup fee is to encourage potential purchasers to spend the time and money to conduct the due diligence to make an initial offer. In a corporate context, courts have repeatedly upheld the granting of breakup fees and expense reimbursement as within the business judgment and discretion of the company's board of directors. In bankruptcy, numerous courts have approved the use of breakup fee arrangements in the Section 363 sale context. In determining whether a breakup fee is appropriate, the bankruptcy courts will consider whether the relationship of the parties who negotiated the breakup fee is marked with self-dealing or manipulation; whether the fee hampers, rather than encourages, bidding; and whether the amount of the fee is reasonable in relation to the proposed purchase price. Today, virtually all courts will authorize the payment of reasonable breakup fees and expenses under the proper conditions.

Appeals, Stays Pending Appeal, and Mootness   Appeals of orders approving sales pursuant to Section 363 are governed by provisions in Section 363(m). That section provides that if an order approving a sale of an asset is reversed on appeal or modified, the good-faith purchaser of an asset is protected, so long as the consummation of the sale was not stayed pending appeal. Most courts hold that an appeal of an order authorizing a sale is moot unless the appellant obtains a stay pending appeal. The mootness rule promotes finality with respect to sales conducted in the bankruptcy court.

The elements for obtaining a stay are whether the movant has made a showing of likelihood of success on the merits; whether the movant has made a showing of irreparable injury if the stay is not granted; whether the granting of the stay would substantially harm the other parties; and whether the granting of the stay would serve the public interest. If a stay is not obtained, the consummated sale of the assets will not be set aside, absent a showing of lack of good faith. Since neither the Bankruptcy Code nor the legislative history defines good faith, the courts have generally adopted the traditional equitable definition of the term and determined that good faith under Section 363(m) refers to one who purchases "in good faith" and "for value."

If the bankruptcy court order approving the sale is not stayed, the sale can generally be consummated even though an appeal is pending. Upon consummation of the sale, most appeals would thereafter be subject to dismissal on the grounds of mootness. Potential purchasers should be careful not to inadvertently waive the protections afforded in Section 363(m) by agreeing to condition a sale upon a "final, non-appealable order."

Bidder Collusion Lack of good faith generally relates to misconduct during the sale process. Such misconduct typically involves fraud or collusion between the purchaser and other bidders or the debtor. In this regard, the Bankruptcy Code specifically provides a trustee with the power to avoid a sale or seek damages if the sale was tainted by collusive bidding. In addition, the court also has the authority to grant punitive damages in the event the sale is determined to be collusive. In this regard, collusive bidders should also be concerned with the U.S. Criminal Code (18 U.S.C. § 151, et. seq), which provides for fines or imprisonment of up to five years or both for anyone who, among other things, knowingly and fraudulently gives, offers, receives, or attempts to obtain any money or property, remuneration, compensation, reward, advantage, or promise thereof for acting or forbearing to act in any bankruptcy case.

Successor Liability Issues Certainly one of the primary benefits of purchasing assets out of a bankruptcy estate is the possibility of purchasing those assets free and clear of the claims that could have been asserted against the debtor before the bankruptcy petition was filed. As previously examined, as a general rule, a properly noticed, arm's-length sale pursuant to Section 363 typically insulates the purchaser of assets from liabilities that could have been brought during the bankruptcy case. However, some uncertainty exists between the courts as to a purchaser's potential liability for claims that are not asserted until after the bankruptcy proceedings have been concluded.

With respect to the postbankruptcy claims, many courts addressing this issue have determined that the bankruptcy court does not have jurisdiction to preclude successor liability claims. In holding that bankruptcy courts do not have jurisdiction to bar successor liability suits relating to claims that are unknown at the time of the sale or reorganization, courts have reasoned that allowing the bankruptcy court blanket power to enjoin all future lawsuits would allow the parties to bankruptcy sales to extinguish the rights of third parties without notice to them or any consideration of their interests. Increasingly, however, bankruptcy courts have permitted a range of claims and interests to be stripped off in Section 363 sales where the party seeking to assert the claim or interest is viewed as having slept on its rights by failing to object to the sale.

Liability under State Law If a bankruptcy court does not have jurisdiction to preclude a successor liability suit, the purchaser will be subject to the substantive state law rule of the forum. Although the general rule continues to be that when one corporation transfers its assets to another corporation, the transferee corporation is not responsible for the liabilities of the transferring corporation, several theories exist that are exceptions to this general rule: where there is an agreement to assume such debts or liabilities; where the circumstances surrounding the transaction warrant a finding that there was a *de facto* consolidation or merger of the corporation; where the transaction was fraudulent in fact; or where the purchasing corporation was a mere continuation of the selling company. If the transfer is found to fall within one of these exceptions, the purchasing corporation may thereby be deemed to have assumed all of the selling corporation's debts and liabilities, whether liquidated or unliquidated.

In addition to the four traditional exceptions to the general successor liability rule, potential purchasers should be made aware that additional exceptions commonly arise in the areas of environmental liability, products liability, Equal Employment Opportunity Commission (EEOC), pension, and other employee-related claims. This topic is discussed in more length in Chapter 3.

Asset Transfers Pursuant to a Plan of Reorganization Though used far less often these days than Section 363 sales, the last method by which a debtor may effectuate a sale of some or all of its assets is through the use of a plan of reorganization. The debtor and/or a potential purchaser of assets from a bankruptcy estate must decide if it is strategically preferable to effectuate the transfer of assets utilizing a plan of reorganization, rather than a Section

363 sale motion, even though the plan process is typically more expensive and time consuming. If permitted to do so, it may be in the best interests of a potential purchaser to propose its own plan of reorganization providing for the transfer of assets.

The major difference between a sale of assets by a Section 363 sale motion and a transfer of assets under a plan of reorganization, and perhaps the greatest benefit, is that the plan of reorganization addresses and resolves all of the claims against the debtor corporation. In addition, the Bankruptcy Code specifically authorizes sale under a plan of reorganization, notwithstanding certain restrictions or prohibitions on transfers imposed by applicable nonbankruptcy law. The statutory framework that provides for the transfer of assets through a plan of reorganization is found in Bankruptcy Code Section 1123, which provides that a plan may sell an asset and distribute the proceeds notwithstanding a prohibition or restriction imposed under applicable nonbankruptcy law.

Another advantage of a plan of reorganization over a Section 363 motion is that pursuant to Section 1145 of the Bankruptcy Code, the registration requirements of Section 5 of the Securities Act of 1933, and of any state or local laws, generally do not apply to the offer or sale of securities pursuant to a plan of reorganization.

Finally, since a sale of assets will generally give rise to potentially significant tax consequences, a potential purchaser should carefully examine the tax consequences of a plan of reorganization, versus a Section 363 sale. In particular, the transfer tax provision of the Bankruptcy Code, Section 1146, may be interpreted less favorably in a Section 363 context, as opposed to a sale under a plan. Since the sale of assets utilizing a plan of reorganization can be structured as either an asset or equity transfer, a debtor and/or potential purchaser should always consider the impact upon the debtor's tax attributes that a confirmed plan may have.

Standing of Potential Buyer   One issue that may arise where a transfer of assets is proposed under a plan of reorganization is whether the potential purchaser may be the proponent of the plan. Section 1121 of the Bankruptcy Code provides that any party-in-interest may file a plan after the expiration of the exclusivity period. Some courts have determined that a potential bidder is not a party-in-interest and, therefore, lacks standing to propose a plan of reorganization. In order to avoid this issue, it may be advisable for a potential purchaser to purchase a claim in the bankruptcy case in order to obtain standing to propose a plan or to challenge a Section 363 sale to another bidder.

Confirmation Issues Where a plan of reorganization provides for the sale of encumbered property either free and clear of, or subject to, an interest in the property, the plan, unlike a motion, must address the rights of the holder of such interest. If the holder of the interest does not consent to the plan, the plan component must attempt to seek plan confirmation under the Bankruptcy Code's *cramdown* provisions. In Section 1129(b), the Bankruptcy Code provides that property may be sold over the objection of a secured (or unsecured) creditor, provided that certain elements of confirmation are met. A potential purchaser should be careful to analyze each of these elements very carefully to determine the likelihood of success at the confirmation hearing.

CHAPTER 8

International M&A

CROSS-BORDER ACQUISITIONS

Acquisitions can have international implications, which in some cases are not obvious. A merger of two domestic corporations can have foreign implications if either company has substantial operations or has shareholders in foreign countries. The more obvious situation is where the parties are located in different countries.

A transaction having foreign implications does not mean that the lawyers involved need to have knowledge of international law. What we are really talking about here is the cross-border acquisition where the substantive laws of a country outside of the United States apply to the transaction. If a foreign client is acquiring a U.S. company, the transaction is handled by the U.S. lawyers much like any other acquisition, subject to certain U.S. federal requirements and cultural matters that come into play, as discussed later in this chapter. If a U.S. client is acquiring a company outside the United States, the U.S. lawyers need the help of local counsel. Increasingly, those transactions are handled and documented much like U.S. transactions. The business and legal concepts are, in most cases, surprisingly similar. But there are significant differences that must be identified and dealt with. In addition to differing foreign practices, international antitrust laws may be applicable, and foreign laws are generally much more protective in the area of employment law and labor relations. The tax consequences in all relevant jurisdictions must also be analyzed.

Inbound Acquisitions

Cultural Challenges   We have found that representing a foreign Buyer doing a deal in the United States can pose certain complexities resulting from cultural and experiential differences. Foreign Buyers often need to be educated on what is "market" from a U.S. perspective. This is important because any

Buyer (foreign or not) pushing for deal terms that are not market has the potential to unnecessarily cause a deal to fall apart. It would be doing such a Buyer a disservice not to at least advise it that it was taking a hard line on an issue that is not customarily accepted by a Target in U.S. deals. These issues may include:

- *Negotiation tactics.* Generally, we have found that foreign buyers have more of a propensity to revisit previously agreed upon points. It is unusual for U.S. lawyers to open up discussions of issues thought to have been already resolved. Parties in the United States will tolerate this to a point, but there can be a breaking point that will cause a party to walk away if too much is being "retraded."
- *Representations and warranties.* We have found that certain foreign deal makers favor broad, sweeping representations and warranties, while U.S.-style documents are expected to be drafted in a more precise way.
- *Indemnification.* Foreign buyers often need to be educated on what is market in terms of the customary caps and baskets applicable to indemnification provisions discussed in Chapter 5.
- *Operational oversight.* It is often an educational process for both the Buyer and management of the Target that will continue with the company after closing as to how much operational oversight will be expected from the new foreign owners. This can be an especially sensitive topic if management has significant equity tied up in the Target after the transaction and is concerned that the Target will be charged with a new layer of expenses (e.g., travel or management fees) related to oversight by the foreign owners.

Purchase Price Adjustment versus Locked Box One typical difference between U.S. and European acquisition agreements is how purchase price adjustments are dealt with. We discussed in Chapter 5 how, during the period in between signing and closing, the business may be effectively run for the account of the Target, necessitating a purchase price adjustment. A popular practice in Europe (and among U.S. private equity deal makers) is to run the business for the account of the Buyer, as if it were a "locked box." U.S. Targets may be amenable to structuring their deals this way, which gives them certainty as to the price they are receiving and limits post-closing disputes. The way it works is that the price to be paid is set prior to signing the definitive acquisition agreement, usually based on previously audited financial statements or management-prepared statements. There is no post-closing adjustment based on whether the Target delivers more, or less, value than expected in between signing and closing.

The covenants applicable to the business in between signing and closing, such as operating the business in the ordinary course and allowing distributions to shareholders, are often made more restrictive than is typical in order to protect against "leakage" of value out to the Target's owners during this period.

The representations and warranties required of the Target may also be stricter and have few carve-outs for immaterial items to ensure that the Buyer is not taking on more risk than is intended in between signing and closing. In general, the locked-box approach allows for greater certainty of price, eliminates sometimes time-consuming negotiation of purchase price adjustment provisions, and results in few post-closing disputes. However, with the certainty of price may come a price that is not based as precisely on the amount of assets and liabilities ultimately acquired, may require more due diligence on the financials of the Target if the time is available, and leaves the Buyer with the generally weaker remedy of pursuing an indemnification claim, rather than a purchase price adjustment if the Target does not deliver the expected value. In short, there are valid reasons for each approach, and the circumstances should be evaluated to determine which makes the most sense regardless of the typical experience of the Buyer and Target.

CFIUS Notices   One issue to watch for in connection with acquisitions of U.S. companies by foreign persons is the Exon-Florio Act. This statute and related regulations provide for the review of transactions that may have an effect on national security. It does not apply to passive investments; purchases by a financial entity; the acquisition of assets such as inventory, real estate, or equipment; and acquisitions of securities by underwriters. The term *national security* is not defined and is to be broadly interpreted. It could, for example, apply to technology that has military uses.

The Exon-Florio Act is a U.S. federal law implemented by the Committee on Foreign Investment in the United States (CFIUS), an inter-agency committee chaired by the Secretary of the Treasury. This statute provides CFIUS with the authority to review any foreign acquisition, merger, or takeover of a U.S. corporation that is determined to threaten the national security of the United States. Therefore, if CFIUS determines that a Buyer's acquisition of a Target poses a threat, then CFIUS may suspend or prohibit the transaction.

The statute provides for two notice alternatives. First, any member of CFIUS may submit an agency notice of a proposed or completed acquisition to CFIUS if that member has reason to believe that the acquisition may have an adverse impact on national security. Alternatively, the statute allows the transacting parties to provide CFIUS with a voluntary notice of the transaction. In the event that CFIUS submits a notice on its own, CFIUS will promptly furnish the parties with written notice of such ongoing review. CFIUS will be permitted to review or investigate the transaction for a period of three years following the conclusion of the transaction. However, if the transacting parties voluntarily provide CFIUS with notice, then any investigation must be commenced within 30 days after the notice is given and completed no later than 45 days after the expiration of such 30-day period.

CFIUS very rarely has taken action upon voluntary notice. If national security is realistically an issue, the most prudent course of action is to provide CFIUS with a voluntary notice under the statute's safe harbor provisions so that the transaction may be protected from temporary or permanent suspension. This is especially true in transactions involving defense suppliers, technology used in military applications, and where a foreign government is the direct or indirect acquirer.

Industry Specific Restrictions Congress has passed a number of laws that prohibit or restrict the acquisition of U.S. businesses in certain industries by foreign persons or by U.S. companies owned by foreign persons. Among the industries that may be affected are: aviation; broadcast; shipping; commercial fishing; mineral lands; nuclear power; other power plants on U.S. federal lands; uranium mining; real estate; banking; and farming, ranching, or timberland.

Inbound BEA Reporting Some of the major federal statutes concerned with foreign investment have less to do with restrictions and more to do with information gathering. One of these statutes is the International Investment and Trade in Services Survey Act of 1976. Under this act, the United States Department of Commerce has charged the Bureau of Economic Analysis (the BEA) with tracking foreign direct investment in the United States.

Since January 1, 2014, the BEA has required foreign direct investment in the United States to be reported on a Form BE-13.[1] Form BE-13 requires

---

[1] Each Form BE-13 is a detailed survey of a reported transaction that covers foreign and domestic ownership, the cost of the transaction and the financial and operating information of the United States business enterprise. Different Form BE-13s are tailored to cover acquisitions, operational establishments, and expansions, and each form may be downloaded by visiting http://www.bea.gov/surveys/respondent_be13.htm.

a U.S. business enterprise to report any transaction where (i) a foreign entity acquires at least a 10 percent voting interest; (ii) a new domestic business entity is established by a foreign parent with at least a 10 percent voting interest; or (iii) an existing domestic affiliate of a foreign parent with at least a 10 percent voting interest expands its operations in the United States. As long as an ultimate foreign parent controls at least a 10 percent voting interest, transactions are reportable regardless of whether the acquisition, establishment, or expansion in question was accomplished directly by a foreign parent or through a direct or indirect domestic subsidiary of such foreign parent. Such transactions are reportable only if the expected total cost to the foreign parent exceeds $3 million. Transactions that are otherwise reportable but for the $3 million threshold may instead be reported on a Form BE-13 Claim for Exemption.

In considering which domestic business enterprises have Form BE-13 reporting obligations, it is important to note that the BEA tracks foreign voting interests, not foreign beneficial interests. As a result, foreign investment in the United States without any control over the investment will not incur any Form BE-13 obligations. More specifically, the BEA has issued guidance that a general partner or manager is deemed to hold 100 percent of the voting interest in any entity unless such entity's governing documents grant limited partners or members, respectively, specific control over such entity's operations.[2] In complex transactions, this creates an added level of diligence to understand who controls the entity in question. By way of an example, suppose that an investment partnership is formed entirely by domestic limited partners, with a general partner that is a distant indirect subsidiary of a foreign parent. Because general partners are deemed to hold 100 percent of the partnership's voting control, the general partner will be required to file a Form BE-13 that reports the partnership's entire capitalization even though the general partner itself may not have contributed any money to the fund. In contrast, another investment partnership could be formed entirely by foreign limited partners but with a domestic general partner. In this case, no Form BE-13 is required even though a substantial amount of foreign money may be invested. This real-world application of Form BE-13 reporting obligations unfortunately fails to catch the very investment that the BEA was hoping to track.

All Form BE-13 reports must be filed with the BEA no later than 45 days after the acquisition, establishment, or expansion by the foreign parent is consummated. The BEA will not solicit reports, and the onus is on the U.S. business enterprise to report such transactions. The BEA may request follow-up reports from any business that indicated that a

---

[2]http://www.bea.gov/faq/index.cfm?faq_id=1062.

reported establishment or expansion was still under construction, but such obligations are only required if solicited by the BEA. In addition to the initial Form BE-13 filing there are certain additional and ongoing filing obligations with respect to foreign direct investment in the United States. The BEA may request quarterly (Form BE-605) or annual (Form BE-15) reports from entities that previously filed Form BE-13, but these forms are not required unless solicited by the BEA. Every five years, the BEA conducts a benchmark review of foreign direct investment in the United States on Form BE-12. The BEA will not solicit Form BE-12 reports, and the onus of reporting is again placed on affected U.S. business enterprises.[3]

United States business enterprises that fail to comply with the BEA's reporting obligations may be subject to a civil penalty of not less than $2,500 and not more than $32,500, in the case of Form BE-13 foreign direct investment reporting. A willful failure to report may also result in up to a $10,000 fine and up to one year of imprisonment.

BEA requirements with respect to tracking sources of American investment abroad are discussed below.

Outbound Acquisitions

Foreign Counsel and Responsibilities As noted above, local (meaning foreign) counsel will need to be obtained in connection with an outbound acquisition (or a firm's foreign offices will need to be involved). Because of the overlap of concepts and the increasing tendency to use U.S.–style documents, the U.S. lawyer generally should remain in charge of the acquisition by his or her U.S. client of a foreign business. It is essential, however, to engage local counsel early in the process. Local counsel is best equipped to do the legal due diligence, and the usual procedure is for U.S. counsel to draft the acquisition documents, other than employment agreements, which are then forwarded to foreign counsel for review and comment. The foregoing is not necessarily the paradigm for a particular foreign country, and local practices need to be identified up front.

From a practical perspective, it will make sense to get several referrals from trusted sources in order to evaluate foreign counsel's relevant expertise. Expectations as to the process and allocation of responsibilities should be determined from the outset. Expected costs should also be determined.

Assuming the transaction proceeds in a typical fashion, U.S. counsel should prepare the first draft of the acquisition document in accordance with usual practice for the Buyer's counsel in the United States, and let

---

[3]The next benchmark survey of foreign direct investment in the United States after this book is published will be due in 2018.

foreign counsel comment on the draft. Exceptions to this rule are those areas of the agreement where foreign law is the critical consideration (e.g., the representation on taxes should be prepared by foreign counsel, as well as representations in the employment and benefits areas). A typical area of contention is choice of law and dispute resolution. Foreign entities are loath to submit to U.S. jurisdiction, and frequently a compromise is struck for a mutually convenient (or inconvenient) venue for arbitration.

Entity Formation   In many acquisitions a new entity is formed in the jurisdiction of the Target to act as the Buyer or entity to be merged into the Target. In the United States, a Delaware corporation or limited liability company can be established as the acquisition vehicle in a single day and is sometimes one of the last items to be accomplished before signing. It is important to bear in mind that in foreign jurisdictions, the process of entity formation can be a lot more involved and time consuming. Getting started late could be an unnecessary impediment to closing the deal.

Some countries require much more significant disclosure requirements than in the United States in order to form an entity and may have limits on foreign board members and officers. Some jurisdictions essentially require that an investment by U.S. persons be structured as a joint venture with locals having an equity interest.

Tax Planning   Careful planning will be required in order to structure an international acquisition in the most tax-efficient manner. In this regard, it may be more tax efficient to set up the acquisition vehicle, or an intermediary acquisition vehicle, in a separate jurisdiction to take advantage of certain tax treaties. The considerations can be complex and a detailed review would be outside the scope of this book, but they may include foreign income tax exposure, foreign currency implications from foreign operations, the U.S. income tax implications of creating foreign entities and other cross-border transactions, transfer pricing policy and compliance requirements, and other issues related to the repatriation of cash.

Other Jurisdictional Issues

- *Restrictions on foreign investment.* As in the United States, there are similar laws in foreign countries restricting acquisitions in certain industries.
- *Labor laws.* Buyers should be particularly aware of foreign labor laws, which can be much more employee favorable than what is typical in the United States.
- *Noncompete agreements.* Similarly, structuring enforceable noncompete agreements for key employees may be difficult or impossible under circumstances in other countries.

■ *Data protection laws.* Data protection and privacy requirements in Europe and other countries can generally be more restrictive than U.S. practices. Careful due diligence on the Target's compliance in this regard should be conducted, as well as a determination as to whether the Buyer's U.S. operations will be impacted by expanding its business into other countries.

Outbound BEA Reporting   The Department of Commerce has also charged the BEA with tracking sources of American investment abroad. Every five years, the BEA requires any American company with foreign affiliates to report such relationship on a Form BE-10.[4] This reporting obligation is broken into two parts. First, the consolidated American parent must file a Form BE-10A if it had direct or indirect ownership or control of at least 10 percent of any foreign subsidiary at any time during the fiscal year prior to the date of the report. This form requires a very detailed reporting of the domestic parent company's operations. Second, the American parent company must also file an additional Form BE-10 for each of its directly and indirectly owned foreign subsidiaries where such parent company holds at least a 10 percent ownership interest. Unlike the Form BE-13 for direct investment in the United States, there is no minimum investment threshold that would exempt American parents or their foreign subsidiaries from these filing requirements. A foreign affiliate may, however, file an abbreviated subsidiary form depending on (i) whether such foreign subsidiary is majority or minority owned by the American parent and (ii) the amount of such subsidiary's total assets, sales/gross operating revenues, and net income.[5] Foreign affiliate forms must be filed by both direct and indirect subsidiaries of the American parent.

---

[4]Each Form BE-10 may be downloaded by visiting http://www.bea.gov/surveys/respondent_be10.htm.

[5](i) A Form BE-10B must be filed by majority-owned foreign affiliates with total assets, sales/gross operating revenues or net income after provision for foreign income taxes of at least $80 million; (ii) a Form BE-10C must be filed by (x) majority-owned foreign affiliates with total assets, sales/gross operating revenues or net income after provision for foreign income taxes of at least $25 million but less than $80 million, (y) minority-owned foreign affiliates with total assets, sales/gross operating revenues, or net income after provision for foreign income taxes of at least $25 million, and (z) each foreign affiliate that does not have total assets, sales/gross operating revenues, or net income after provision for foreign income taxes of at least $25 million but is the parent of another subsidiary that must file a Form BE-10B or BE-10C; and (iii) a Form BE-10D must be filed for each foreign affiliate that does not have total assets, sales/gross operating revenues, or net income after provision for foreign income taxes of at least $25 million and that is not the parent of another subsidiary that must file a Form BE-10.

U.S. companies that are subject to Form BE-10 reporting obligations must file all reports by the end of May following the fiscal year that is the subject of the report. U.S. companies who are required to file 50 or more forms are granted an automatic extension through the end of June. The BEA will not solicit Form BE-10 reports for the five-year benchmark survey, and a response is required from persons subject to the reporting requirements whether or not they are contacted by BEA.[6] If a U.S. business enterprise is contacted by the BEA with respect to Form BE-10 reporting obligations and such entity has no 10 percent ownership interest in any foreign subsidiary, such enterprise may file a Form BE-10 Claim for Not Filing. Otherwise, U.S. business enterprises with no foreign subsidiaries have no Form BE-10 obligations. In addition to the five-year benchmark Form BE-10 filing there are also certain periodic filing obligations. The BEA may request quarterly (Form BE-577) or annual (Form BE-11) reporting of U.S. direct investment abroad, but these forms are not required to be filed unless they are solicited by the BEA.

U.S. business enterprises that fail to comply with the BEA's reporting obligations may be subject to a civil penalty of not more than $25,000 in the case of Form BE-10 U.S. investment abroad reporting. As with Form BE-13 reporting, a willful failure to comply may result in up to a $10,000 fine and up to one year of imprisonment.

Extraterritorial Application of U.S. Laws

Certain U.S. laws that are of general application may have specific application to an acquisition of a foreign business by a U.S. person, or the acquisition of a U.S. business by a foreign person.

Securities Laws   One example of such laws is the federal securities laws. Offers and sales of securities to persons who are in the United States (and sometimes to "U.S. Persons" whether or not in the United States) must be registered with the SEC or be exempt from registration. Similarly, offers and sales by U.S. companies of securities to foreign investors must be registered or exempt. The principal exemption for the latter transaction is Regulation S under the Securities Act of 1933. The essence of Regulation S is to require U.S. companies to use certain specified procedures to ensure that the sales are in fact outside the United States to non–U.S. persons and that those securities do not immediately flow back to the United States. Certifications of non–U.S.

---

[6]The next benchmark survey of American investment abroad after this book is published will be due in 2020.

status are required, and the securities are treated as restricted securities for resale purposes.

There are also complicated rules in the case of a tender or exchange offer, rights offering, or business combination where there are both U.S. and foreign persons who hold the securities of a foreign issuer. In the past, U.S. investors were frequently excluded from participating in these transactions. The SEC has adopted rules that attempt to strike a balance between protecting U.S. investors and depriving them of the opportunity to take advantage of the tender or exchange offers. Exemptions are generally applicable where U.S. persons hold only a small percentage of the securities of the foreign issuer.

Antitrust Laws The antitrust laws present two different issues from the U.S. perspective: When does U.S. law apply to anticompetitive foreign acquisitions where there is some impact on U.S. commerce? And when do U.S. laws apply when an acquisition of a U.S. company affects foreign markets? Guidelines are issued by the DOJ and the FTC with regard to acquisitions with international ramifications and should be examined in connection with any such proposed transaction. In addition, acquisitions with an impact on the European Union (EU) are subject to antitrust review by the European Commission as well.

Foreign Corrupt Practice Act The Foreign Corrupt Practices Act of 1977 (FCPA) was enacted for the purpose of making it unlawful for certain types of individuals and companies to make payments or give other items of value in order to influence foreign officials in their official capacity, induce the foreign official to commit a violation of his or her lawful duty, or secure any improper advantage in obtaining or retaining business for or with, or directing business to, any person.

Since 1977, the anti-bribery provisions of the FCPA have applied to all U.S. persons and certain foreign public companies. With the enactment of certain amendments in 1998, the anti-bribery provisions of the FCPA now also apply to foreign companies and individuals who cause a bribe to take place within the United States. Careful due diligence should be done on the Target to ensure that it is in compliance with all provisions of the FCPA as well as any analogous foreign laws applicable to the Target.

CHAPTER 9

Joint Ventures

REASONS FOR JOINT VENTURES

Joint ventures are business arrangements entered into by two or more parties in order to further their business objectives through a collaboration, usually intended to be long lasting, assuming the venture accomplishes its objectives. The joint venture (JV) could be set up to develop technology, commercialize a product, acquire assets, or conduct joint marketing efforts, or do all of these things in order to maximize value for the parties' respective shareholders. The joint venture in this regard is a combination of components of the parties with an end goal that may be similar to what a merger or acquisition is intended to accomplish but usually without as much risk, since there is no change in the ultimate control of one of the parties. A seller could argue that a joint venture may be more attractive than a sale for cash, since it has the potential to deliver shareholder value on an ongoing basis, rather than through a single M&A event.

Joint ventures can be akin to a merger of equals, where each party contributes significant assets in order to develop a single business. Some examples of well-known joint ventures include Dow Corning, Sony-Ericsson, and the former MillerCoors joint venture (now wholly owned). The public may not generally think of these as joint ventures given the familiarity of the names, although they are obvious combinations. Some well-known joint ventures are not so transparent, such as Hulu, whose partners include Comcast, Disney, and NewsCorp.

Often joint ventures are not a merger of equals, but allow a smaller party to access the benefits that come with a partnership with a larger party. Such a joint venture can help the smaller party solidify its relationship with an important (or maybe its only) customer or help it gain access to much needed capital. These deals can look a lot like the acquisition of the smaller

292

party by the larger party, and it is important for the smaller party to structure its joint venture agreement in a way that it can maintain its independence and exit the deal if needed. We'll point out some of the pressure points in this regard throughout the chapter.

TYPES OF JOINT VENTURES

There are generally two types of joint ventures. On the one hand, the parties may structure the deal by becoming joint owners of a new entity (or group of entities, depending on how complex the structure may be), and it is the new entity that conducts the business of the joint venture. On the other hand, the parties may enter into an agreement (i.e., a contractual joint venture) outlining their rights and obligations in connection with the business partnership to be conducted by the respective parties through their respective separately owned entities.

Entity JVs

Entity JVs are generally formed by requiring the parties to contribute assets, such as cash, equipment, facilities, and/or personnel to an entity in exchange for equity in the entity. The entity could be a limited liability company, corporation, or another type of entity.

As with any acquisition, careful attention should be paid to the tax and accounting implications of choosing one type of entity over another, or using a contractual JV. In an entity JV, the rights and obligations of the parties will usually be governed by the organizational documents associated with the entity (such as the limited liability company operating agreement or certificate of incorporation) and potentially additional agreements governing operations.

LLCs are often utilized for tax purposes due to their flexibility and pass-through nature. Furthermore, in some states fiduciary duties to the respective partners arising under state law can be disclaimed in the LLC operating agreement.

Exhibit 9.1 depicts a typical entity JV structure.

Contractual JVs

Here, the terms of the joint venture will be included solely within written agreements between the parties, rather than a jointly owned entity's

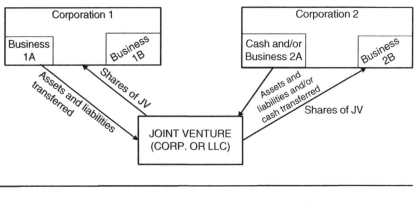

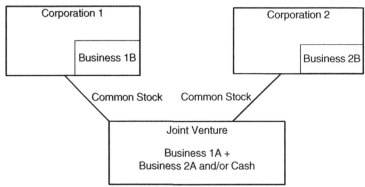

EXHIBIT 9.1   Joint Venture Subsidiary

governing documents, and each partner's "contributed" assets or personnel will continue to be held by that partner or, if cash, paid over to the other
partner. Since there are no inherent governance mechanisms in a contractual
JV, the rights and obligations of the parties and manner of operations often
will need to be set forth in great detail in the contract. With an entity JV,
some of the governance features at least can default to the law of the jurisdiction governing the entity without the need for spelling this out in detail
if acceptable to the parties. Again, tax considerations are key. Even if the
parties do not intend to form an entity for state law purposes, a partnership

for tax purposes could be the result under the tax code, which may or may not be the intention of the parties. Tax advisers should be consulted prior to structuring either type of joint venture.

TYPICAL JOINT VENTURE TERMS

To say there are typical joint venture terms is somewhat misleading. Like every M&A deal, and perhaps even more so, each joint venture has its own peculiarities and nuances. But once the parties determine that moving forward with a business arrangement like a joint venture makes sense, then at that point it usually is a good idea to memorialize the parties' understanding in a term sheet. As with other complex deals, we would recommend that the lawyers get involved at this early stage or sooner to ensure that material terms do not get overlooked, which could lead to a party (usually the smaller party) giving up leverage as the deal moves forward. The terms set forth below are the types of items that would typically be found in a term sheet, while the deal itself will dictate how the parties approach these items. A checklist of matters to be considered in forming a JV also appears in the appendix to this chapter.

Scope/Business Plan

It will be important from the outset to clearly define the scope of the joint venture to avoid any arguments later as to what is expected. One party may think the joint venture will gradually take on responsibility for the associated business function, while another may think that its entire business is being devoted to the joint venture, and consequently the other partner should be doing the same. In short, it will be insufficient for the parties to state that they simply intend to enter into a joint venture. A detailed understanding must be reached as to what activities will be conducted under the joint venture.

Often it will make sense for the parties to develop a detailed business plan in order to set expectations as to what it will take for the business to achieve success, who will undertake what responsibilities, what contributions will be required, and when the foregoing can reasonably be expected. Funding requirements, employee hires, office space, contractual commitments, milestones for the development of products, and sales and marketing efforts may all be covered in great detail from the outset or very little. Of course, the level of detail contained in the plans will be a matter of personal preference among the parties involved.

Capitalization/Contributions

In an entity JV, capitalization is the initial contributions to be made by the parties in exchange for their equity. Usually, this takes the form of some combination of cash and assets. Cash may be contributed all at once, at specified intervals based on time, or in stages subject to milestones. Loans, which may be convertible into equity of the JV, can also be made to the joint venture. A common capital structure involves the contribution of cash by one party and the contribution of intellectual property by the other party with an equivalent valuation, in order to get to a 50/50 equity split. In a contractual JV, the parties may commit similar resources to the business venture's operations, with the expectation of receiving cash payments or other consideration in return.

Due Diligence

Due diligence is an important part of the M&A process, given that one party will need to justify its valuation of the target or its assets and may be assuming, or susceptible to, the liabilities of the target. In a joint venture, due diligence should be conducted by each party on the other, in order to confirm that the other party's asset contribution will be as advertised and that the other party will have the capability to perform as expected. For example, the parties will want to confirm whether any contracts or licenses with third parties necessary for operations can be assigned or used by the joint venture without the need for obtaining a third party's consent.

Also similar to the M&A context, the parties will also be expected to make representations and warranties regarding the assets and any liabilities that they are contributing to the joint venture, with the potential for indemnification in the event of a breach.

Management/Voting

In an equity JV, traditional officer and employee roles will need to be filled. The parties may choose a CEO, CFO, and the like from among their own ranks, or, less typically, hire from the outside. Prior to the JV entity hiring its own employees, the partners may choose to second their employees to the entity. In a contractual JV, each party will need to ensure that its own employees are assigned the requisite roles in order to meet the party's obligations under the JV agreement. Each party should also be required to maintain appropriate levels of insurance, including workers' compensation and general liability, depending on the nature of the joint venture.

Representatives from each party should be designated to meet, review the operations of the JV and the performance of its officers, and make important decisions. This body could be the board of directors in an entity JV, or act much like one in a contractual JV. The number of representatives could be evenly split in a 50/50 joint venture, although a partner contributing all or most of the cash may be able to argue for greater decision-making authority. The frequency of the meetings should also be determined.

If the balance of power is not equal, it will be important for the minority partner to have some say over material decisions in the form of veto rights (or conversely, requiring unanimous approval for such decisions), rather than run the risk of being outvoted at every juncture. The list of potential decision points is often heavily negotiated and will be influenced by the business, but it will often look like the list of consent rights that a venture capital investor will require in connection with a substantial minority investment. The following is a list of potential items (some of which may not apply to contractual JVs) that may be subject to veto rights and the reasons why:

- *Selling new equity.* Generally, if new cash is required to fund the business, the original partners should have the first option to fund the business or have some consent rights on suffering dilution in the event the JV needs to raise new equity from outside parties.
- *Borrowing in excess of a specified amount.* Taking on material amounts of debt may not be palatable to one of the parties, especially if the assets of JV will be used as security.
- *Guaranteeing obligations of third parties or the owners themselves.* This is similar to the bullet point just above.
- *Purchasing assets in excess of a specified amount.* Significant investment decisions that are outside of the original business plan may be fairly left for both parties to determine.
- *Forming or acquiring a subsidiary, or doing a material acquisition.* Each party should be comfortable with any material changes to the organizational structure or expanding the business through acquisitions.
- *Redeeming equity from any investor.* Cashing out one of the partners to any extent should be the subject of a preexisting agreement.
- *Amending an entity JV's organizational documents.* This is a basic protection for the benefit of each party.

- *Setting budgets.* The process for approving budgets, and any material deviations, should be covered.
- *Entering into C-level employment contracts or committing to a salary in excess of a specified amount.* Each party should be comfortable with senior level management and material compensation arrangements.
- *Making significant changes to a line of business.* Any material changes to the business purpose of the JV should be mutually agreed upon.
- *Entering into other joint ventures or contracts valued in excess of a specified amount.* If these items are outside the initial business plan of the JV, it may make sense to require the consent of both parties.
- *Conducting a public offering or selling the JV entity.* An exit event will usually require the consent of both parties, even if the JV is not owned 50/50.
- *Dissolving the company.* This is an important point. A minority partner may contribute all of its intellectual property and other assets to the joint venture. If the majority partner is unhappy with how the business is performing, it could force a dissolution and avoid any obligations it or the JV may have to the minority partner, while the minority partner risks losing its intellectual property that it could have monetized on its own or with another partner.

Exclusivity/Noncompetition

Whether the partners will work exclusively with each in a contractual JV or only through an entity JV can be a difficult topic in negotiations. Where one party is smaller than the other, it may wish to maintain the flexibility to deal with other partners in similar fields, unless it has a significant financial incentive to remain exclusive to the JV partner. It could maintain this flexibility by licensing its intellectual property to the JV or by otherwise retaining rights (e.g., a license back) to use the IP in other arrangements. This will allow a party with little funding some recourse in the event that its larger partner fails to perform its obligations.

For its part, a larger strategic partner in the JV with other business lines may wish to block its competitors from gaining access to the JV's technology by locking its partner into an exclusive arrangement. While neither party will want to give up on this point easily, creative compromises on exclusivity tied to geography, length of time, milestones, and other areas are likely to be found.

Similar to exclusivity, to ensure commitment to the JV's business, the parties may require exclusivity during the term of the JV and for a specified period, usually two to five years, thereafter. Whether or not the parties are willing to bind themselves to a noncompete, they will want key executives and employees of the JV to be subject to noncompetition agreements similar to many operating businesses. Noncompetition agreements for individuals were further discussed in Chapter 3.

Intellectual Property

Background IP   Each party to a JV must be concerned with protecting its existing intellectual property. First, the JV agreement needs to clearly set forth exactly what background IP is being contributed for use in the joint venture. This could be all, some, or none of a party's intellectual property. The contribution could be a contribution of the IP to an entity joint venture, or a limited license to the other party with the requirement that the IP be used exclusively for the purposes of a contractual JV.

Generally, a startup that is party to a JV will want to limit its contributed or licensed background IP to that which it feels is necessary to the JV and chooses to make available to the joint effort. On the other hand, a larger strategic partner typically will seek access to all of the startup's background IP, subsequently acquired IP, and any improvements to either created by the startup, although the larger party will want to limit its own disclosures, especially if it has multiple business lines. For example, a gas and oil company partnering with a biofuel startup will not want to make available intellectual property unrelated to a biofuel-driven JV, which could be the result if the provisions are not carefully drafted.

Resulting IP   The rights to the resulting IP, that which is derived from the development efforts under the JV, may be allocated in a number of ways. In an entity JV, resulting IP generally should vest with the JV entity because it or its employees have conducted the development efforts. Where a contractual JV is in place, a startup's position may be that jointly developed IP should be jointly owned by the parties, although exclusively used toward the contractual JV effort while its operations are continuing and then freely exploited, or exploited with restrictions when operations cease. The case for joint ownership may also be made in an entity JV to preserve rights in the IP should the venture be dissolved. Maintaining joint ownership can be easier said than done, however. It raises a number of issues with respect to which party bears the responsibility for patent prosecution, as well as maintenance, defense, and enforcement of intellectual property—all points to be negotiated. A larger party with financial wherewithal may insist that it is the owner of resulting IP, since it will have the resources to keep the IP portfolio intact, with the requirement that it grant appropriate licenses to the JV and JV partner. Depending on the circumstances, it may make sense to allocate ownership of resulting IP in other ways, such as based on different fields of use (e.g., the biofuels startup may take ownership of developed materials, while its chemicals manufacturer partner takes ownership of any manufacturing process technology).

A common JV structure involves an IP development phase, with commercial agreements benefiting the partners in the JV to be negotiated at a later stage. If the parties succeed in their goals and create resulting IP that is able to be commercialized, usually the parties stipulate that they will enter into agreements relating to the manufacture, supply, and/or distribution of the technology-based products, so ownership of resulting IP is less of an issue while this commercial arrangement is in effect. One caveat is that if the terms of the agreements to commercialize resulting IP are not fleshed out enough at the IP development phase, the parties may be left with an agreement to agree on a future agreement, which may not be enforceable in many jurisdictions if the parties cannot come to terms at this later stage.

Reversion of IP Rights

Once an asset is contributed to an entity JV by one of the parties, it becomes the property of the JV. Ordinarily, a dissolution of the entity JV means that its assets will be sold if possible and the resulting cash, after payment of liabilities, is distributed to the members. A concern of a smaller party to the JV may be what happens to the IP if its partner does not put forth the time, effort, or additional capital required to successfully commercialize the IP. Will the project "die on the vine" by virtue of the JV becoming less of a priority for the bigger joint venture partner on which the smaller party is relying?

For this reason, the smaller party contributing IP may wish to structure its contribution as a revocable license, which would terminate upon the dissolution or extended inactivity of the JV. Failing agreement to this type of arrangement by the larger JV partner, the smaller party may request the right to receive distribution in kind of its contributed IP upon dissolution of the JV entity, if there are sufficient assets to pay creditors. The theory here is that it would be unfair if the smaller party were to put all of its eggs in one basket with no chance to capitalize on the IP it has developed with another partner should the JV fail for reasons unrelated to its own performance.

Distributions

The parties to the JV will ordinarily want written parameters around how and when cash will be distributed. An operational plan or the governing board of the JV may require reserves to be established for corporate needs, such as debt service or capital expenditures. Absent agreement to the contrary, cash available for distribution may be distributed on an annual basis, or sometimes in shorter periodic increments. What is available for distribution is usually a component of net profit or free cash flow, with various adjustments to be negotiated and documented. Usually, provisions are made to distribute cash in order to pay taxes on income attributable to a joint venture that is a tax "flow-through" entity, such as an LLC.

Financial Reporting

The parties will want to ensure they are receiving adequate financial reports and information. Once operations warrant it, the parties will want the JV to pay for an audit of its financial statements on an annual basis. Quarterly and sometimes monthly financial statements may be produced by management for distribution as well. This type of visibility will be crucial for more passive parties that are not heavily involved with the management of the JV, as well as smaller parties in order to ensure they are being dealt with fairly by a larger partner. Record-keeping requirements and rights to inspect or audit records may also be added.

Exit—Restrictions on Transfer; Tag-Along, ROFR, Put Right, Drag-Along

Once a party gets into a joint venture, how easy is it to get out? JVs are collaborations between two are more parties presumably entered into based on a relationship, experience, or other intangible considerations in addition to the assets being contributed. Typically no party can be easily replaced by another party. For these reasons it is usually made difficult to exit a joint venture by selling one's interest to a third party.

Transfers of JV interests may be prohibited for a period of time or allowed only upon the consent of the other parties to the JV. Exceptions usually exist for transfers to affiliated entities, so long as the transferring entity remains "on the hook" for its obligations. It should also be specified that the transfer to an affiliate is only permitted for so long as the transferee is an affiliate. A poorly drafted agreement could permit a transfer of a JV interest to an affiliate followed by a sale of the affiliate, allowing for a de facto sale to a third party without the consent of the partner to the JV.

The parties will also need to determine whether a party will be able to pledge its JV interest to a bank in support of the party's credit obligations. If the answer is no, the party may need to get permission from its lenders.

If sales of JV interests to third parties are permitted, each party and the JV should have a right of first refusal with respect to the sale. This will allow the nontransferring party the ability to take ownership of its partner's interest without having to partner with a third party with which it has no relationship, or perhaps a poor relationship. If the JV or the nontransferring party does not exercise the right of first refusal, the nontransferring party may have the right to sell a proportionate interest in the JV, along with the transferring party. This is commonly referred to as a *tag-along* or *co-sale* right. Rights of first refusal and tag-along rights are sometimes resisted by a party more likely to sell its interest because these restrictions can make the interest less marketable, but they are commonly accepted protections for parties to a JV.

In order to assure liquidity, a party may negotiate the right to sell or "put" its interest to the JV entity or its JV partner after a period of time under certain circumstances. The price to be paid could be based on an independent appraisal or a formula utilized by the JV's particular industry in valuing similar companies. Similarly, the JV entity or a party may have a right to buy out its partner or "call" the interest of the other JV partner after a period of time or in certain circumstances, such as a material breach of an agreement with the JV. Such a buyout may be made at a discount or over an extended period to discourage a party from seeking a buyout by virtue of breaching its agreements with the JV. Sometimes a provision is included for one party to defer the transaction in order to protect it against calculations that may be based on atypical financial results during a measurement period.

Put and call arrangements may also be put in place if the parties are deadlocked on fundamental issues of governance or operational direction and are not able to resolve their differences.

A *drag-along provision* allows one party to force the other party to agree to the sale of the entire joint venture to a third party. This may be an appropriate right of a majority owner if it finds an offer for the joint venture that delivers a suitable return for all parties. A drag-along may also be a remedy in the event of a breach of one party, or otherwise appropriate in connection with a dissolution of the joint venture for other specified reasons. If the parties' economic interests differ on dissolution, the potentially disadvantaged party may require protective provisions such as an outside fairness opinion.

Termination/Dissolution

The parties will usually want to specify certain triggering events for a dissolution or termination of the joint venture. These events may include:

- The failure to meet certain objectives of the joint venture within a specified period of time.
- The elapse of a period of time without regard to whether milestones have been met. This will give either party the opportunity to walk away absent mutual agreement to continue the joint venture.
- A material breach by one of the parties that has not been cured or is not susceptible to cure.
- A deadlock on fundamental decisions that the parties or the joint venture's governing board is unable to resolve.
- The sale or other change of control of one of the joint venture partners. This may be exercisable by the party changing control, the other party, or both.

Other Considerations

Dispute Resolution Dispute resolution mechanisms can be very elaborate or nonexistent. If there are issues that cannot be resolved by operational employees, or at the joint venture board level, sometimes these issues will get escalated up to higher-level decision makers at the respective joint venture parties in an attempt to resolve differences. Failing resolution by the parties, mediation or arbitration provisions can be inserted instead of resorting to litigation.

Antitrust Compliance Joint ventures must be reviewed for any Hart-Scott-Rodino Act compliance requirements, similar to those discussed for M&A transactions in Chapter 3. Ordinarily, investments of cash in a joint venture will be exempt from HSR requirements, but contributions of assets could trigger these provisions. Additionally, the Federal Trade Commission and U.S. Department of Justice issued the "Antitrust Guidelines for Collaborations Among Competitors" in April of 2000. These are useful guidelines for competitors that enter into joint ventures as to how these agencies will analyze joint ventures and why certain activities may be challenged as anti-competitive behavior.

International Issues Of course, if a joint venture is operating internationally, or one of the parties is not a U.S. entity, compliance with international requirements will need to be reviewed. This may include international antitrust filings or other regulatory requirements, issues related to international tax structuring and accounting, and employment-related concerns.

APPENDIX

The following appendix is located on the website that accompanies this book. For information on the website, see the "About the Website" section at the back of this book.

Appendix 9, Joint Venture Checklist

About the Website

As a purchaser of this book, you have access to the supporting website: www.wiley.com/go/acquisitions2e

The website contains files for the appendixes that are mentioned in this book:

Appendix 2A, Investment Bank Engagement Letter with Target's Comments

Appendix 2B, Confidentiality Agreement

Appendix 2C, Letter of Intent

Appendix 2D, Stay Bonus Plan

Appendix 2E, Business Due Diligence Checklist

Appendix 2F, Legal Due Diligence Checklist

Appendix 2G, IP Due Diligence Checklist

Appendix 2H, Merger Closing Agenda

Appendix 3A, Convertible Preferred Stock Term Sheet

Appendix 3B, Stock Option and Incentive Plan

Appendix 3C, Employment Agreement

Appendix 5A, Annotated Long-Form Merger Agreement

Appendix 5B, Annotated Long-Form Asset Purchase Agreement (economic sections only)

Appendix 6A, Sample Memorandum to Board of Directors on Fiduciary Duties in Connection with an Acquisition

Appendix 9, Joint Venture Checklist

The appendixes are provided in Word format.
The password to enter this site is: millersegall2

Index

Printed and bound by CPI Group (UK) Ltd, Croydon, CR0 4YY

23/04/2025

14661008-0002